*Love Flows
Like A River*

Also by
Dadisi Mwende Netifnet
aka Marvin Leroy Alston

Poetry for Today's Young Black
Revolutionary Minds

Need I Say More?

Love Flows Like A River

Dadisi Mwende Netifnet aka
Marvin Leroy Alston

AuthorHouse™
1663 Liberty Drive
Bloomington, IN 47403
www.authorhouse.com
Phone: 1-800-839-8640

© 2011 by Dadisi Mwende Netifnet aka Marvin Leroy Alston. All rights reserved.

No part of this book may be reproduced, stored in a retrieval system, or transmitted by any means without the written permission of the author.

First published by AuthorHouse   07/19/2011

ISBN: 978-1-4634-1652-2 (sc)
ISBN: 978-1-4634-1651-5 (hc)
ISBN: 978-1-4634-1650-8 (ebk)

Library of Congress Control Number: 2011909588

Printed in the United States of America

Any people depicted in stock imagery provided by Thinkstock are models, and such images are being used for illustrative purposes only.
Certain stock imagery © Thinkstock.

This book is printed on acid-free paper.

Because of the dynamic nature of the Internet, any web addresses or links contained in this book may have changed since publication and may no longer be valid. The views expressed in this work are solely those of the author and do not necessarily reflect the views of the publisher, and the publisher hereby disclaims any responsibility for them.

CONTENTS

Acknowledgement xvii
Baby Let Me Rap To You xix
Love Is The Greatest 1
Alpha 2
That Old River 3
My Angel 4
Welcome Welcome 5
It's So Good 6
Let Them Know 7
Stop 8
Condition 9
No Certification 10
Always 11
No Matter 12
Sensitive 13
Enhancement 14
Log On 15
Particularly 16
Observed 17
Divided Love 18
I Am Confident 19
Dearest Friend 20
Your Choice 21
Build Trust 22

Instruction	*23*
Faceless	*24*
Goodwill	*25*
To All Vistors	*26*
Color	*27*
Peace	*28*
Nutrition	*29*
Your Burden	*30*
Warning:	*31*
I Got It	*32*
Acknowledge It	*33*
LoVe Is Nice	*34*
Six Feet	*35*
Wonder	*36*
Magic	*37*
Reach	*38*
Lead By Example	*39*
You'll Be Surprised	*40*
Time	*41*
Like None Other	*42*
For Real?	*43*
Let's Look At It	*44*
Go With The Flow	*45*
Reality	*46*
Fallin In Love	*47*
How High	*48*
Heaven Knows	*49*
Triumph	*50*
You Go Boy	*51*
Culitivate Love	*52*

Please	53
Recommended	54
Tell Me	55
Do You Hear Me?	56
People	57
Be Prepared	58
Too Soon	59
Whatever It Is	60
Vulgarity	61
Smooth Talker	62
Admission	63
Wake Up	64
Soliciting	65
Acceptance	66
Internet Covers	67
I'm Sorry	68
Fugitive	69
Where	70
Final	71
Just A Hint	72
Illness	73
Reverence	74
Attention	75
Volunteer	76
Warehouse	77
Caution You	78
Platinum	79
You Need To Understand	80
Nothing	81
I Am Honored	82

I Discover	83
Jealousy	84
Worth Pondering	85
The Dance	86
My Friend	87
I Don't Care	88
He/She Was Not A Kisser	89
Back Stabber	90
I'm Out Of Here	91
Important	92
Mercy, Mercy	93
Think About It	94
Do Good Things	95
You Should	96
Submit	97
Mistake	98
Watch Yourself	99
If You Believe	100
Request	101
Smile In	102
Love Heals	103
Greetings	104
You Got It	105
Inseparable	106
Burn, Baby Burn	107
You Are Crazy	108
On This Day	109
Whisper	110
Forever	111
We Gonna Make It	112

Moments Alone	113
Reassuring	114
Fantasy	115
The Joy Of Life	116
Be Lovable	117
Legend Says	118
We're Going To Grow	119
Be Smart	120
Come On In	121
Why Love More?	122
Self Love	123
Fearminded	124
Remember	125
Excitement	126
Program	127
Wait A Minute	128
Visualize It	129
Accommodate	130
Heat	131
Quest	132
I Say	133
Don't Shy Away	134
Listen	135
Really	136
Conflict	137
More Times Within	138
Admit	139
True To Thyself	140
Don't Forget	141
Love Policy	142

You Group	143
Best Friends	144
The Human Soul	145
Extingusish	146
My Opinion	147
You Know	148
Empathize	149
Wait	150
Conely One	151
No Secord Guest	152
Confronting	153
Prescribe	154
Radiance Of The Soul	155
It's Good To Know	156
Disaster	157
Breathe Easy	158
Never Forget To	159
Fulfillment	160
Passport	161
Sacred Love	162
Heavy Case	163
Take Into Consideration	164
Prove It To Me	165
Chocolate	166
It's Up To You	167
Lovingness	168
Done Deal	169
Unconditionally	170
Truth About Love	171
Permit	172

Meditation	173
For The Record	174
Kiss And Make Up	175
Surrender	176
Personal	177
Represent	178
Let's Talk	179
My Perspective	180
Roses	181
Book Smart	182
Mystery	183
Animal Covers	184
Image That	185
Bountiful	186
Jazzy Love	187
Recognition	188
Release Yourself	189
No Problems	190
Yes	191
Kiss	192
Player, Player	193
Sleeping Beauty	194
The Glow Of Love	195
Looking Back	196
Gentle	197
I Feel For You	198
I Repeat	199
A Cry For Love	200
AppalliNg	201
Danger	202

Inspect Yourself	203
L-O-V-E	204
Fairground	205
Honesty	206
There Were Problems	207
Question	208
My God	209
I Am Serious	210
Song Bird	211
You Can Be All That	212
The Great Conquerer	213
Unwind	214
Warm Love	215
Refine	216
Someone Like You	217
Foster Child	218
Transfusion	219
Likelihood	220
The Principle	221
Untangles	222
Answer	223
Stop Thinking About Love	224
Dream	225
Income	226
Evil	227
Gentlemen's Club	228
Let It Go	229
The Solution	230
Clock	231
Experience The Moment	232

Friendship	*233*
Speak Love	*234*
Baby It Is Good	*235*
Making A Wish	*236*
Face It	*237*
A Piece Of My Heart	*238*
The Law Of Marriage	*239*
To My Wife, Ramona	*240*
A Mother's Love	*241*
Mothers And Daughters	*242*
Father & Son	*243*
Relatives	*244*
In-Laws	*245*
People Come Together	*246*
Rites Of Passage	*247*
Cry	*248*
Dig It	*249*
Give More	*250*
Be The First	*251*
A Waste Of Time	*252*
People Watching	*253*
Are You Really Sure?	*254*
Practitioner Cover	*255*
First Date	*256*
I Am A GQ Man	*257*
Perfume	*258*
Sensuous	*259*
Spices	*260*
Music To My Ear	*261*
Blend With Me	*262*

Merry Christmas	263
Emerald	264
No Bull	265
Human Resources	266
Secret Cover	267
Ride Baby	268
That Day	269
Stop By	270
It's True	271
Ice Cream	272
Nobody Told Me	273
Security	274
My Precious Blood	275
Money	276
Wow	277
Top Of The List	278
Be The Light	279
Do Something	280
Praise God	281
Touch	282
Love Your Mind	283
What's Up	284
Appreciation	285
Against Evil	286
Terrific	287
Passion	288
Goodbye My Sweet Angel	289
About The Author	291

Dedication

This book is dedicated to my loving parents

Elijah & Anna Mae Alston.

My parents loved each other through the good and bad times of their lives for 52 years.

My father departed from my mother to return to the ancestors on January 2, 1999.

My parents loved their nine children unconditionally, and we, Wonnie, Clifford, Miriam, Clarissa, Annette, Mamie, Edward, Izetta and I in return love them unconditionally with complete devotion.

ACKNOWLEDGEMENT

This book was truly a labor of love. As this book evolved so has my love for my family, friends, and strangers. This is a book I wanted to write for a long time. Thanks to my wife Ramona for giving me time and space to write. I love you. To my step daughters Monique, and Andrea, and my grandson Anthony. My love for you grows by the day. Stay blessed. Much love goes to my two editors Ms. Rita (Fd.Fabu) Houston and Ms. Jackie Aguilera. Without your finishing touches, this book would still be locked up in my bedroom closet. Thanks two million! Special thanks to Mr. Bracy Johnson, Ms. Jimmie Green and the entire staff at Eastside University Village Community Learning Center in Houston, Texas. They all have lent a helping hand with this book. May the love of God bless you. I would like to thank Wanda

(Mawiyah) Griffith and Ed (Asante) Boutte for their technical support. May God bless you two for bringing love and generous support to others. Special thanks to Dr. Naomi Long Madgett Poet Laureate City of Detroit, Michigan. Her encouragement and insights always comes at the right time. I love you. I wish to express my deepest gratitude to Leroy Wes, Crystal Tuara and the entire staff of Author House Publishing Company. Thanks you for bringing my dream book into reality.

A shout out goes to the members with whom I fellowship in Christ at the Shrine of the Black Madonna Christian Church in Houston, TX, Detroit, MI, Atlanta, GA and Calhoun Falls, SC. I love each and every one of you. There are a lot of people I would like to thank; however, this book is too small to mention them all. I love you all.

BABY LET ME RAP TO YOU

The date was Wednesday October 26, 2005. The Houston Astros were playing in their first World Series Baseball game against the Chicago White Sox. This was Chicago's first World Series since 1919. I was working for the Houston Astros Customer Service Department as an usher. The excitement that night at the game was electrifying.

My co-worker Donna Rosette Cortez came up to me and said, "Dadisi, you know what, my 11 year old daughter Pamela out of the blue asked me? Mama, how come I never see Mr. Dadisi with a woman? He is always by himself". I said, "Maybe he likes being by himself." I was tickled to death when Donna told me this. I wanted to see Pamela and give her a big hug for touching my heart. She inspired me to write this book. In the past Donna and Pamela have supported me by attending my poetry readings and book signings.

To answer my little friend Pamela's question I've been in love with many women over the years. Many of them are still good friends of mine. My parents taught me at a very early age not to rush and get married once I became an adult. They told me I will know when the right woman comes along. I have listened, and on August 9, 2008 I married my wife Ramona. In the past I tried to live my life in peace and love. When I was not in love with a woman I was still at peace with myself, and with God, family, friends and neighbors.

Each day I try to love to the fullest as if I will not be here tomorrow. Therefore, I pray, Pamela, that as you grow into life you will find that being alone with yourself is not being alone at all—if you have a heart full of love. Here are some of my experiences and imaginations of the power of love. Dadisi

Love Flows Like A River

LOVE IS THE GREATEST

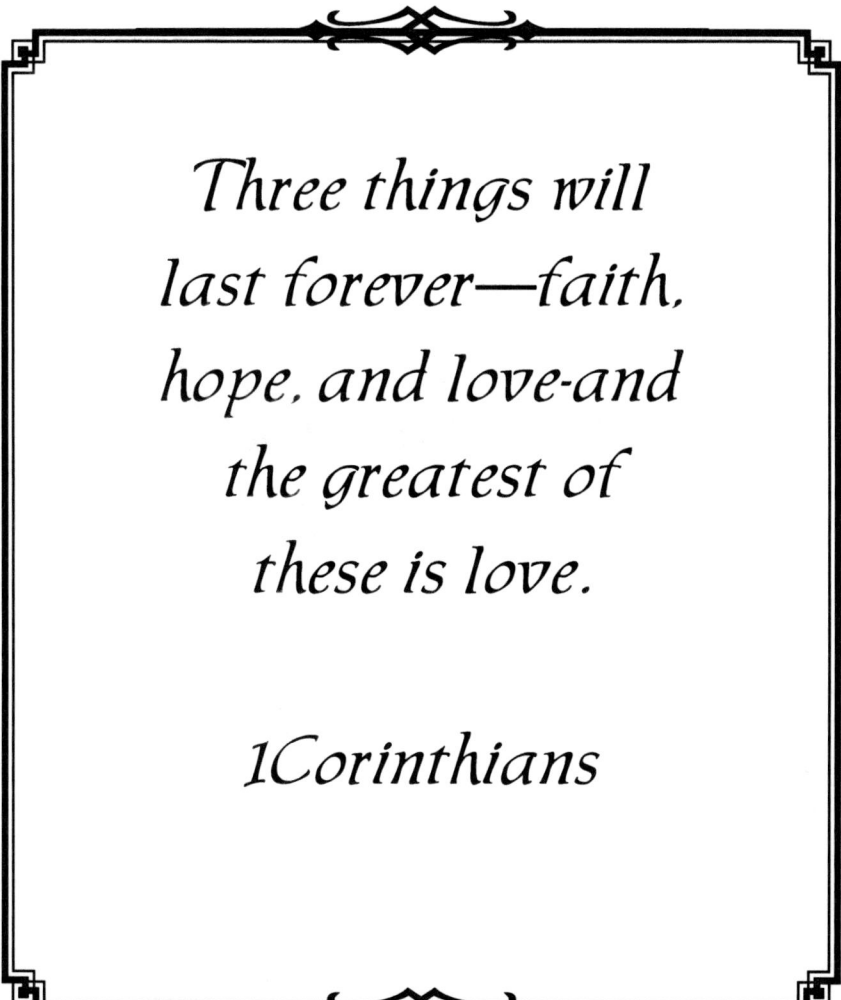

Three things will last forever—faith, hope, and love-and the greatest of these is love.

1Corinthians

ALPHA

Love gave birth to the world.

THAT OLD RIVER

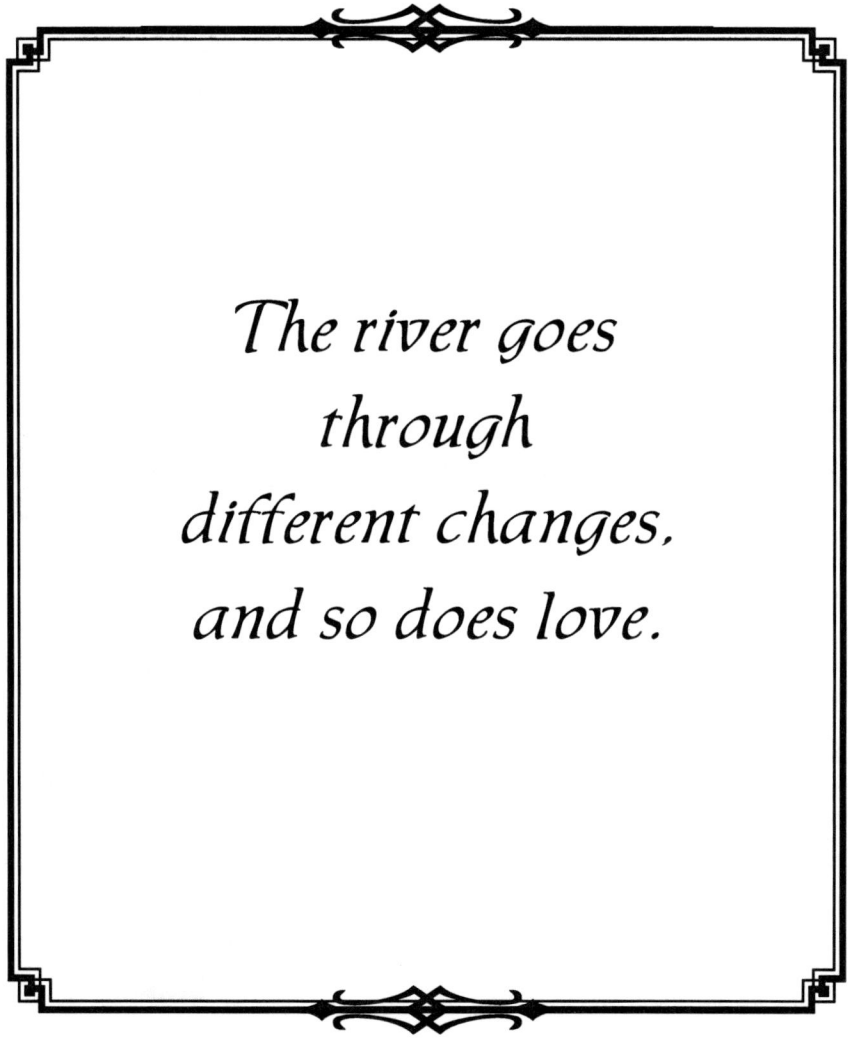

The river goes through different changes, and so does love.

MY ANGEL

An angel from above came and taught me the meaning of love.

Love Flows Like A River

WELCOME WELCOME

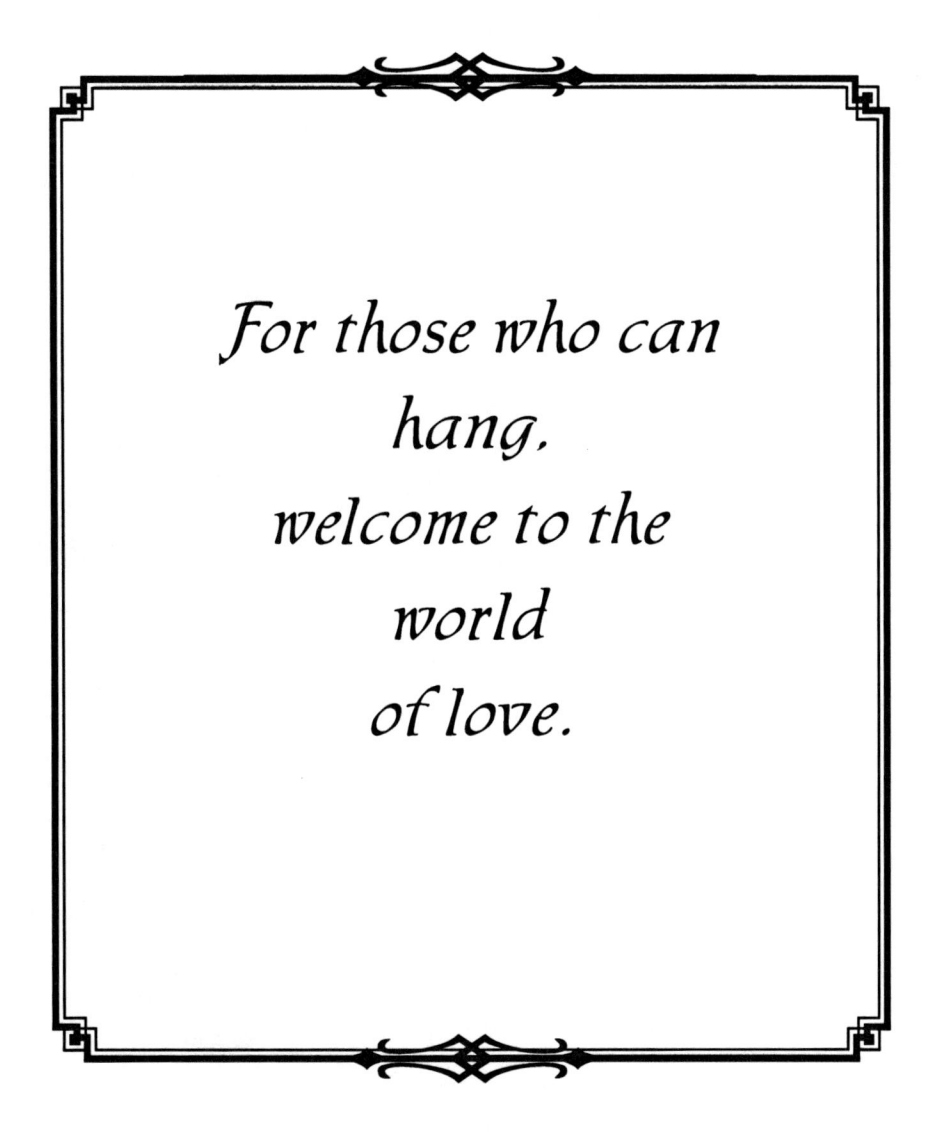

For those who can hang, welcome to the world of love.

IT'S SO GOOD

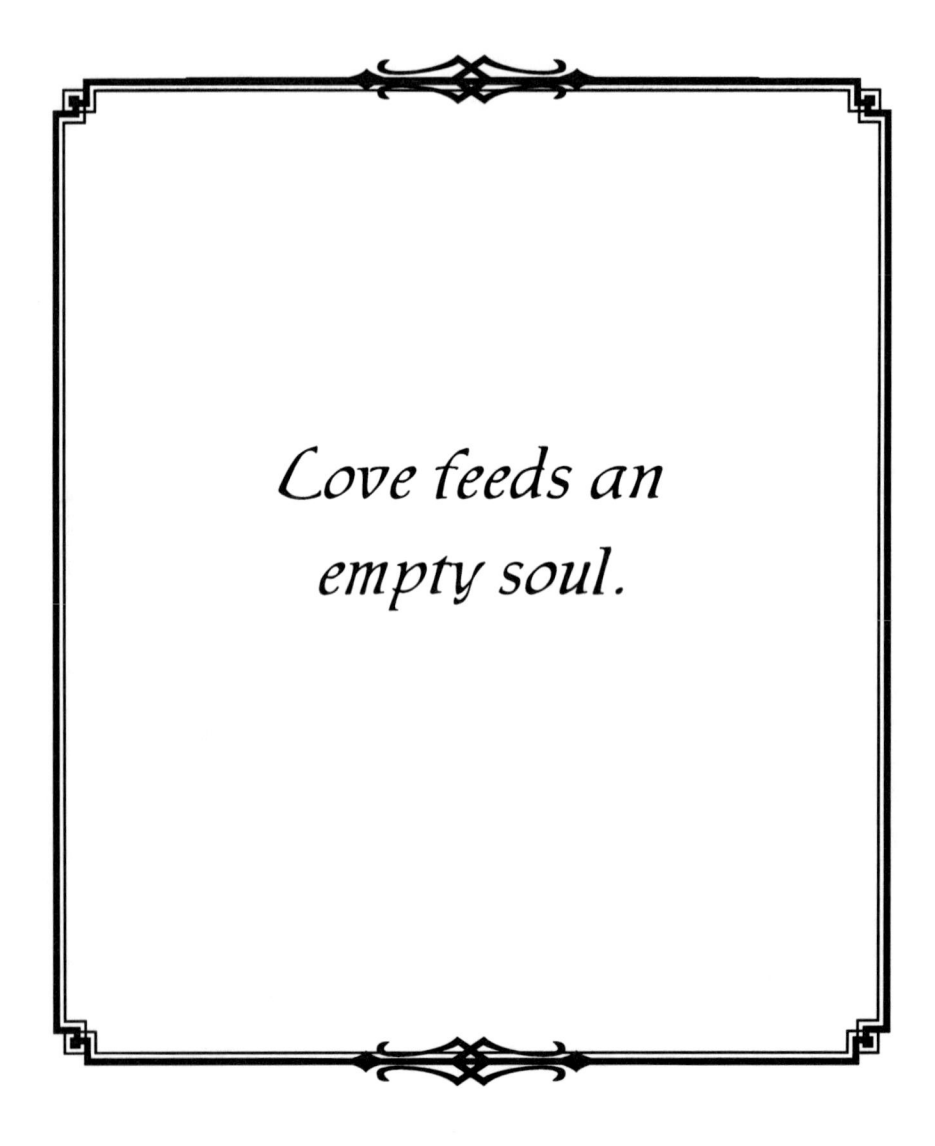

Love feeds an empty soul.

LET THEM KNOW

Love has never been this much fun!

STOP

Please do not leave your love at home.

CONDITION

Listen and respond to love.

NO CERTIFICATION

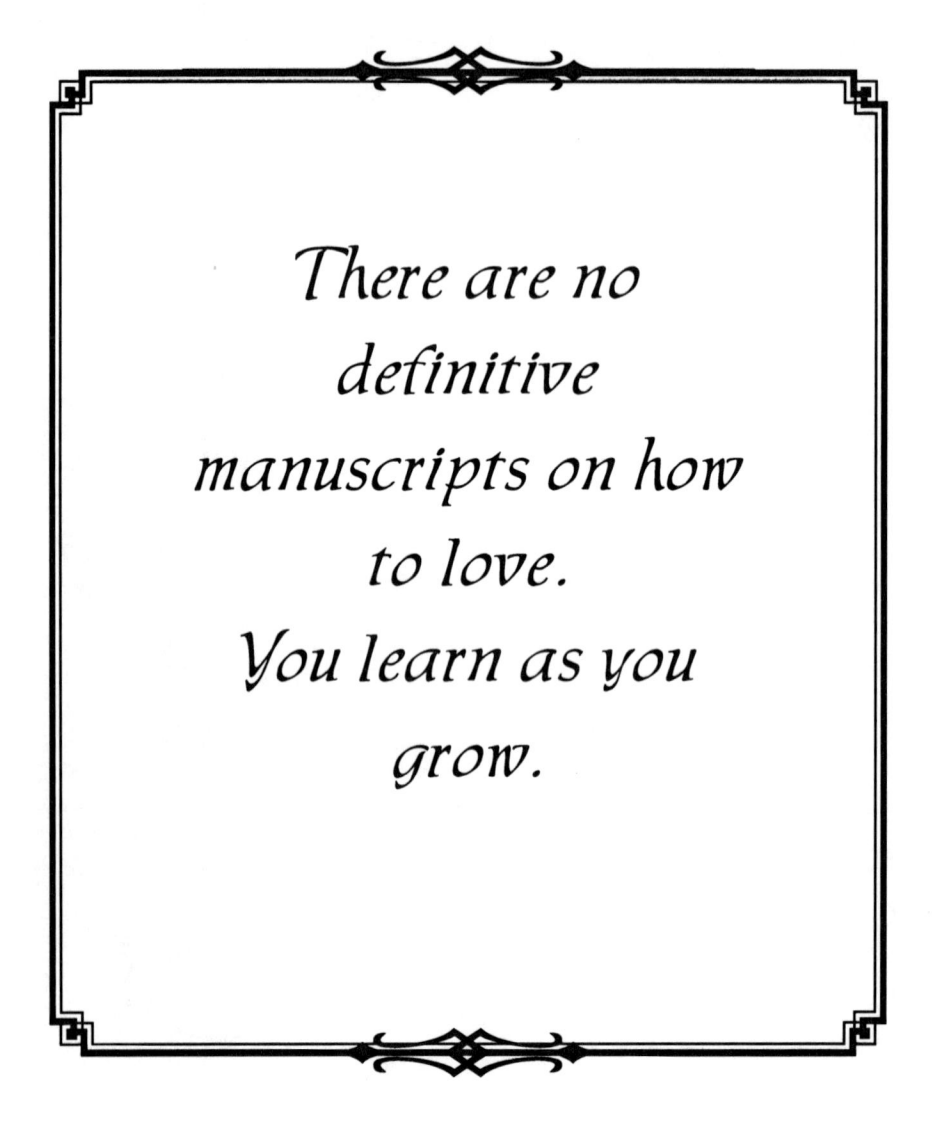

*There are no definitive manuscripts on how to love.
You learn as you grow.*

ALWAYS

Remain calm when someone is madly in love with you.

Dadisi Mwende Netifnet

NO MATTER

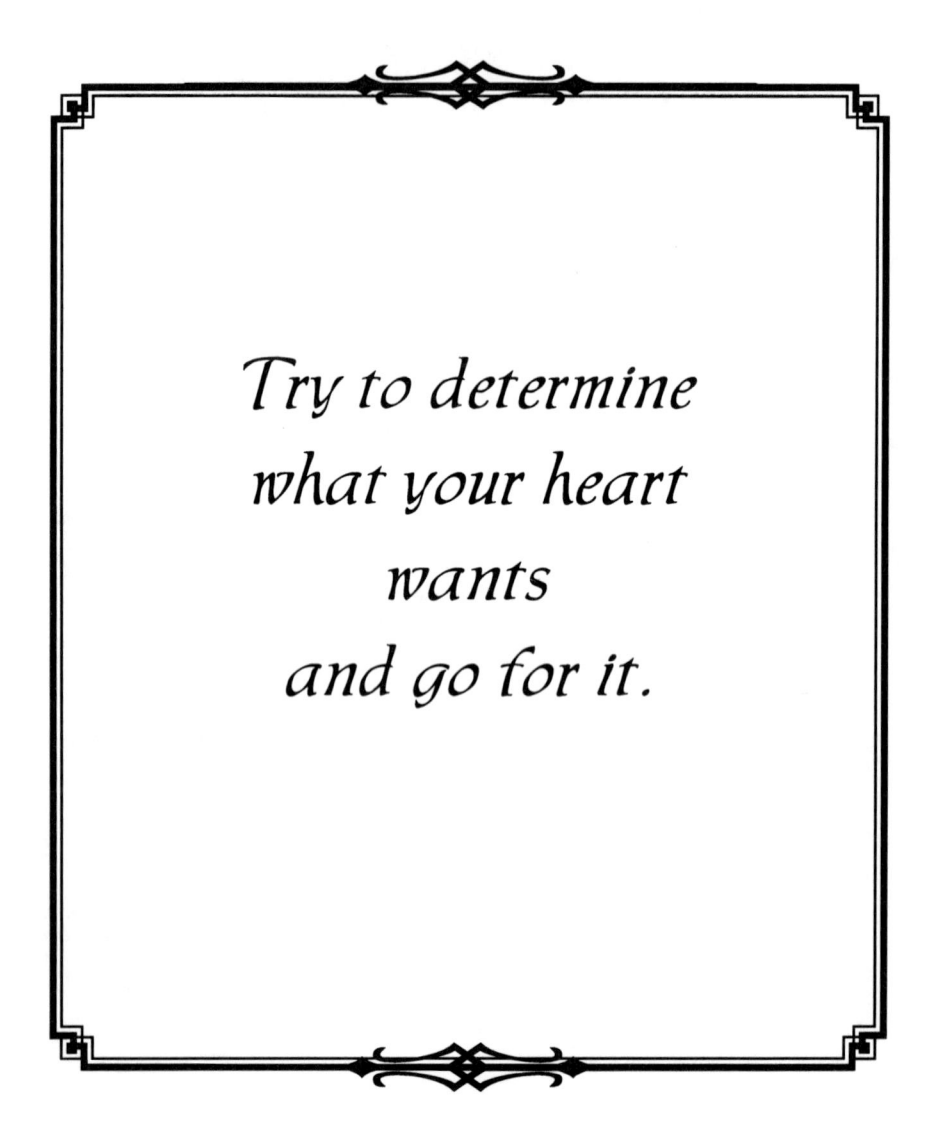

*Try to determine
what your heart
wants
and go for it.*

SENSITIVE

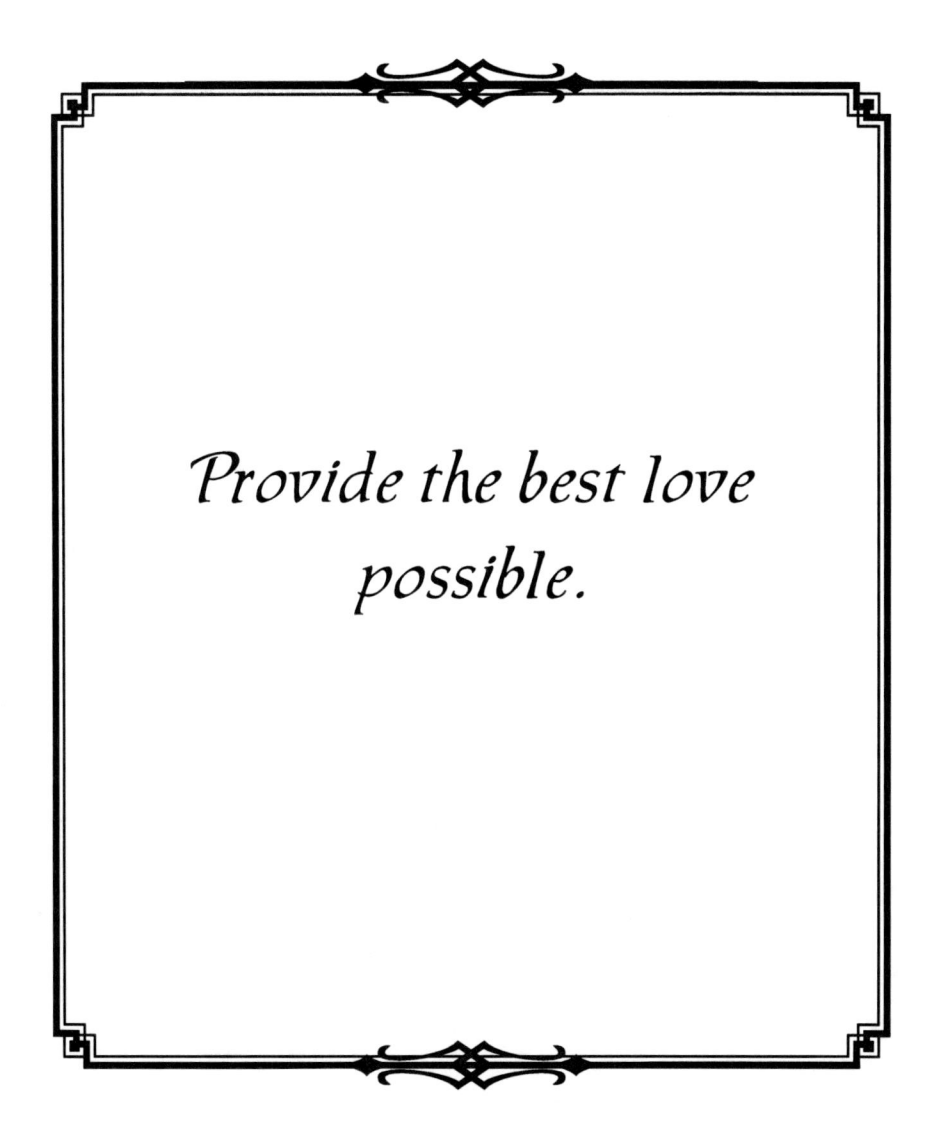

Provide the best love possible.

ENHANCEMENT

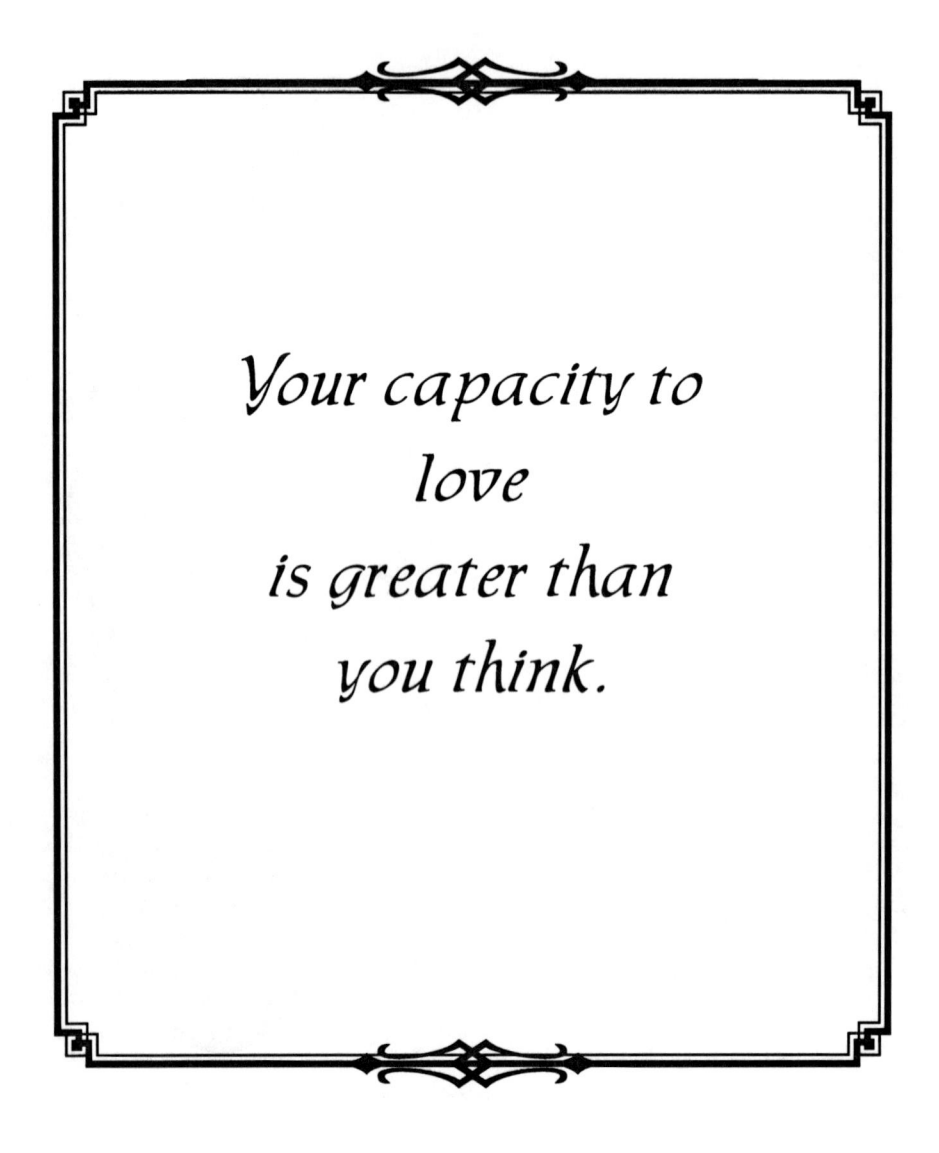

*Your capacity to
love
is greater than
you think.*

LOG ON

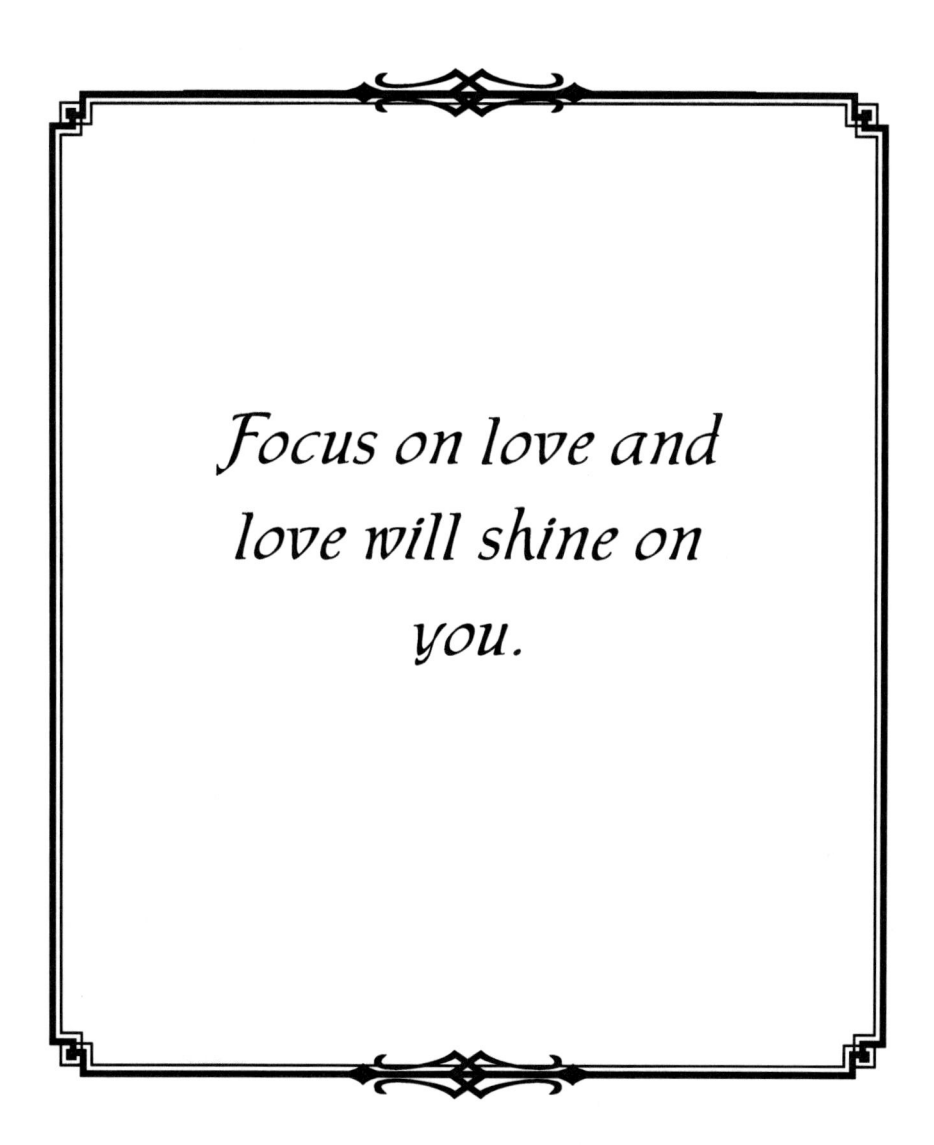

Focus on love and love will shine on you.

PARTICULARLY

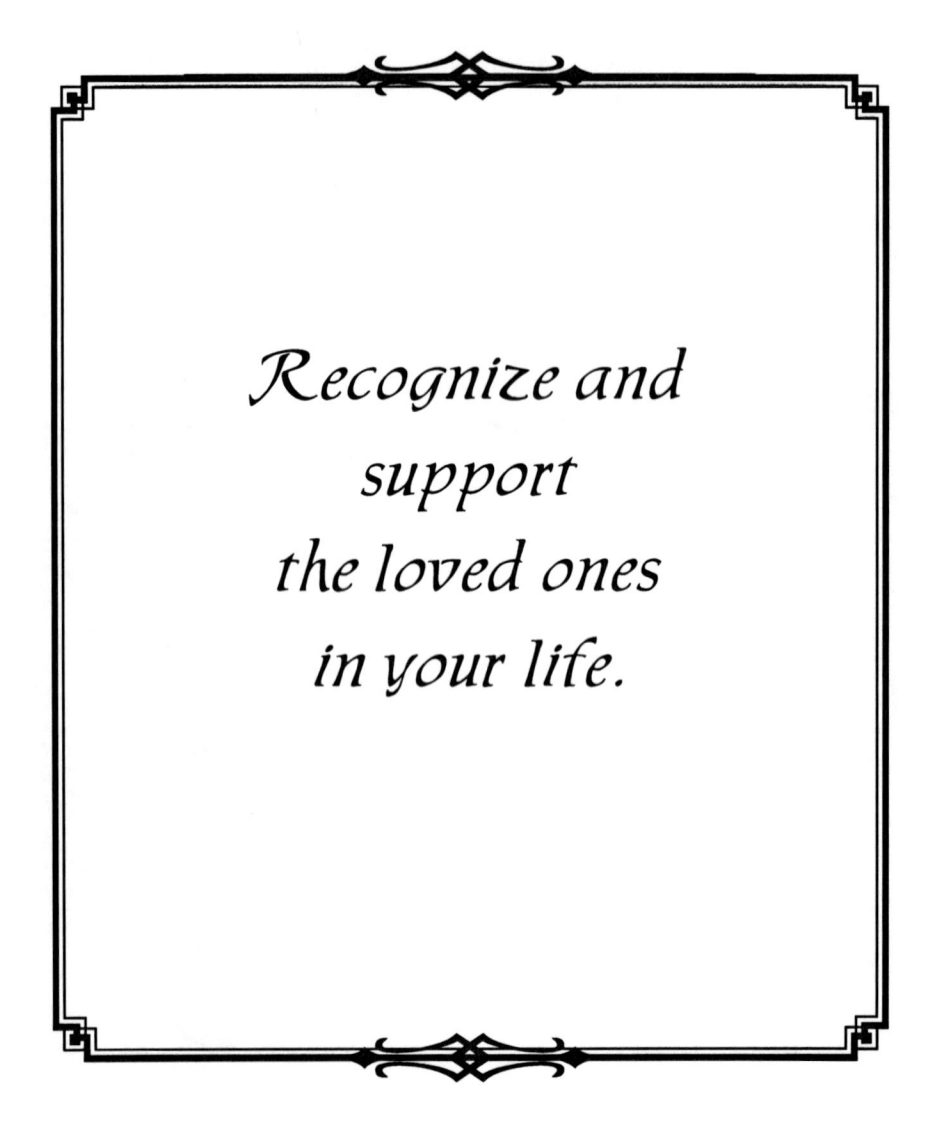

Recognize and support the loved ones in your life.

OBSERVED

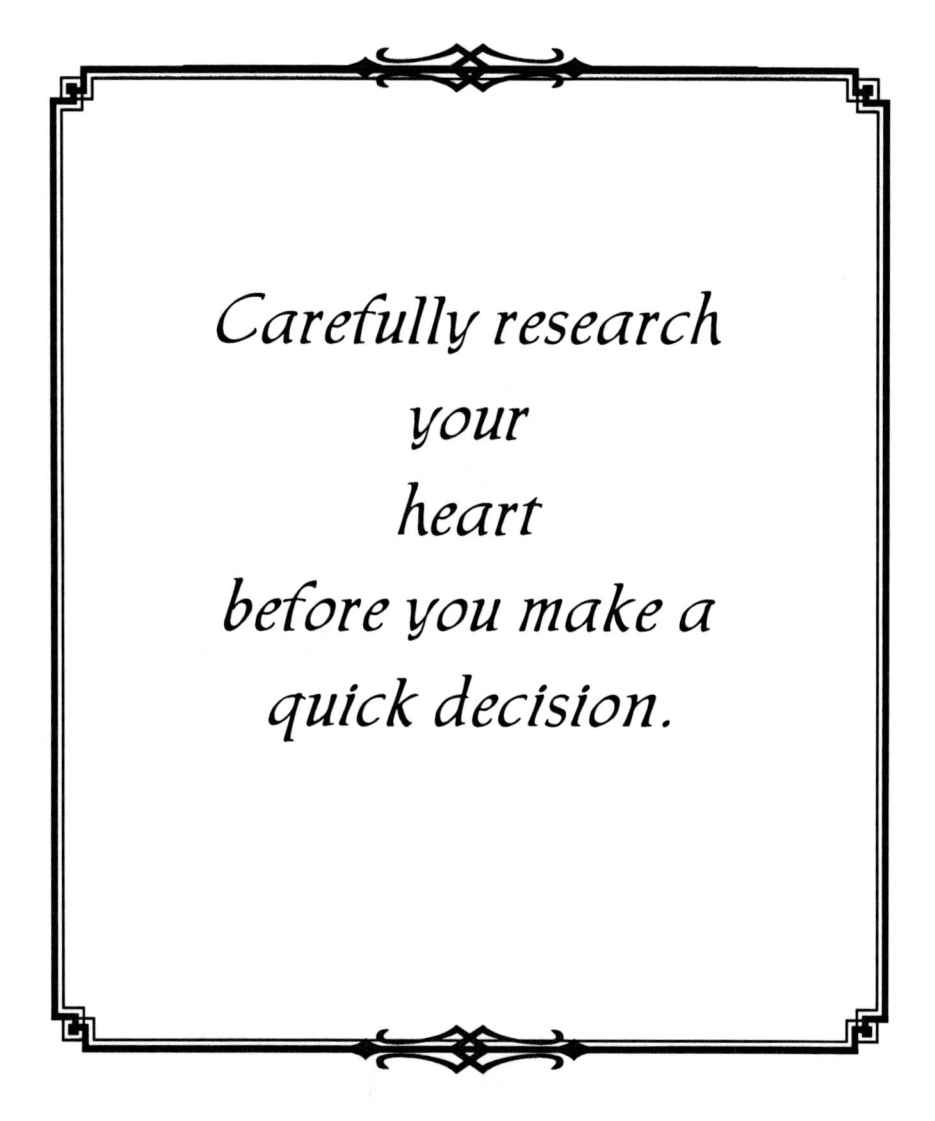

*Carefully research
your
heart
before you make a
quick decision.*

DIVIDED LOVE

*Our love has become
like two birds
in the sky.
One flying low
and the other flying
high.*

I AM CONFIDENT

Love will find me soon.

DEAREST FRIEND

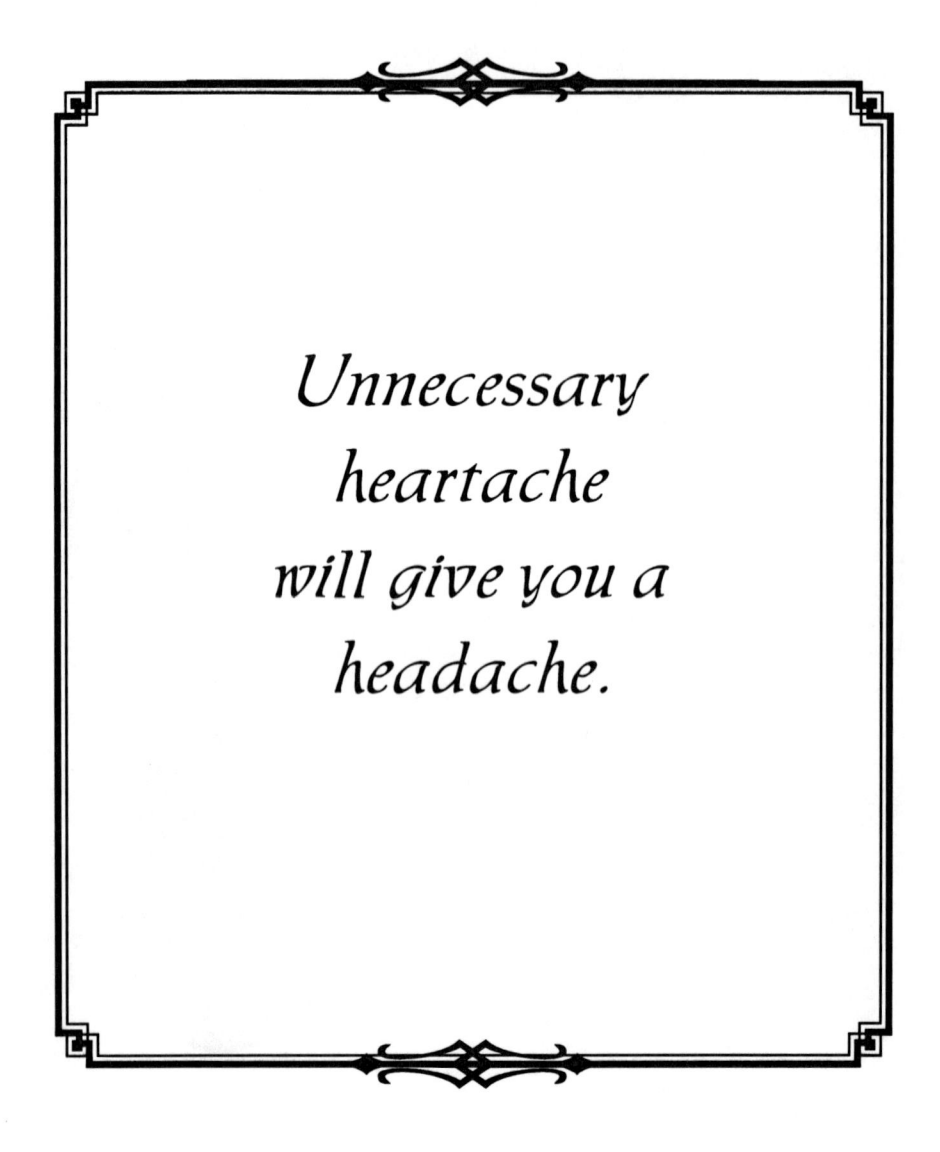

Unnecessary heartache will give you a headache.

YOUR CHOICE

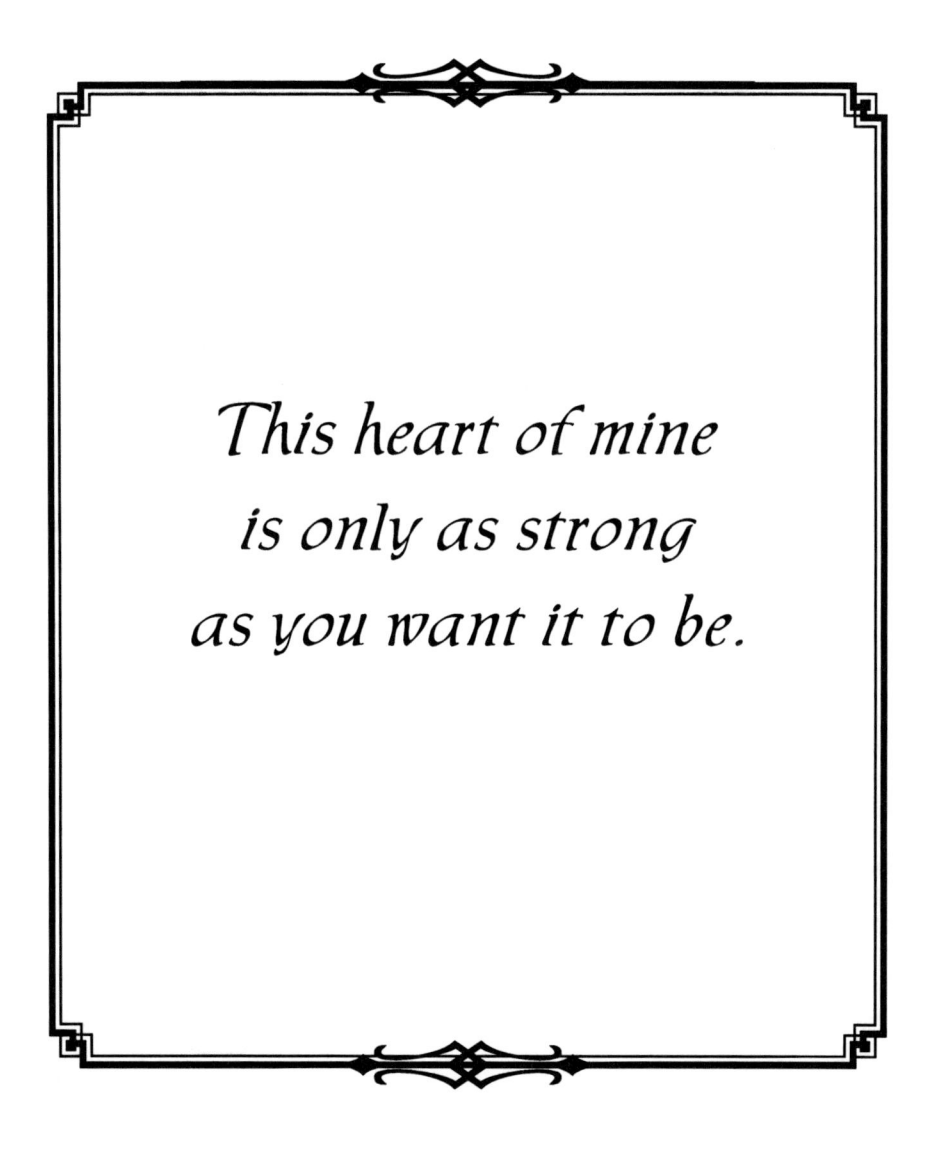

*This heart of mine
is only as strong
as you want it to be.*

BUILD TRUST

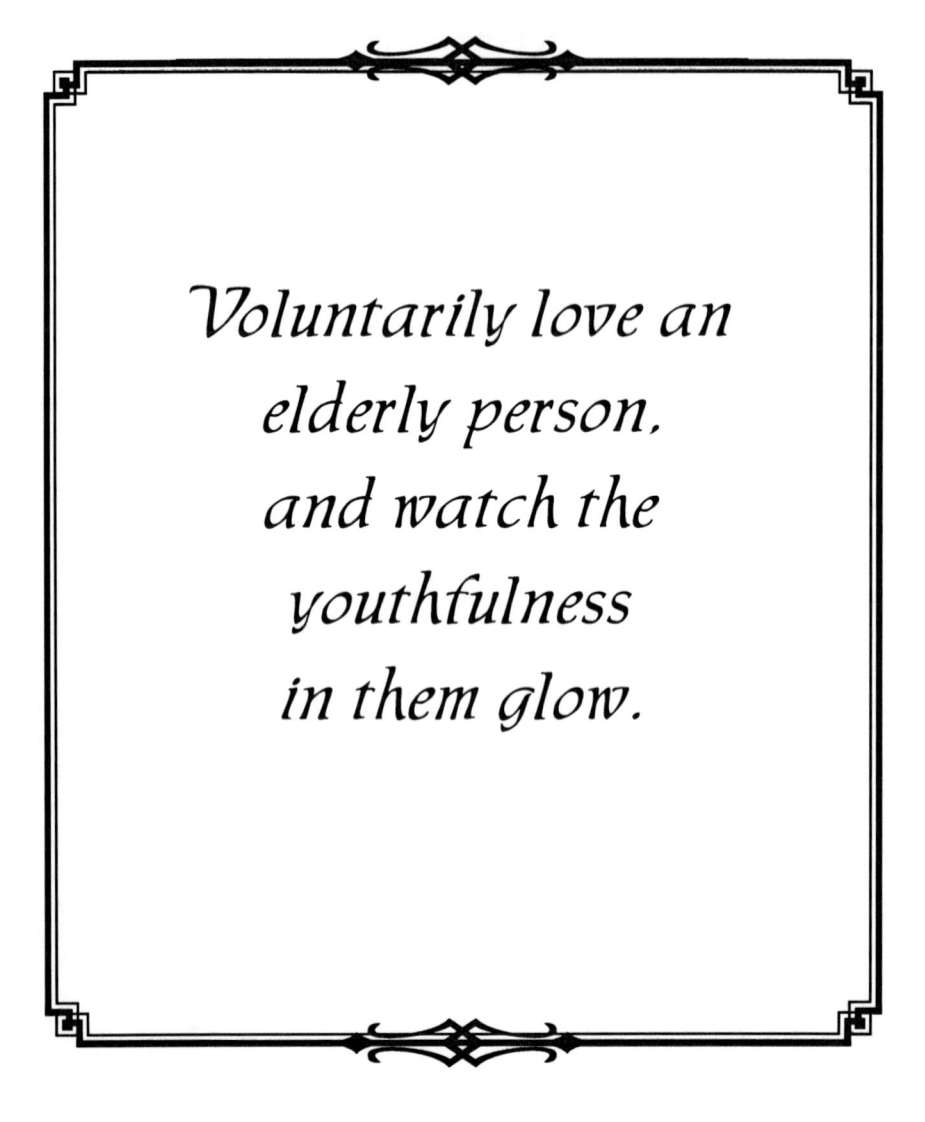

Voluntarily love an elderly person, and watch the youthfulness in them glow.

INSTRUCTION

Look beyond color for love.

FACELESS

*Love has many faces.
Love is not races.*

GOODWILL

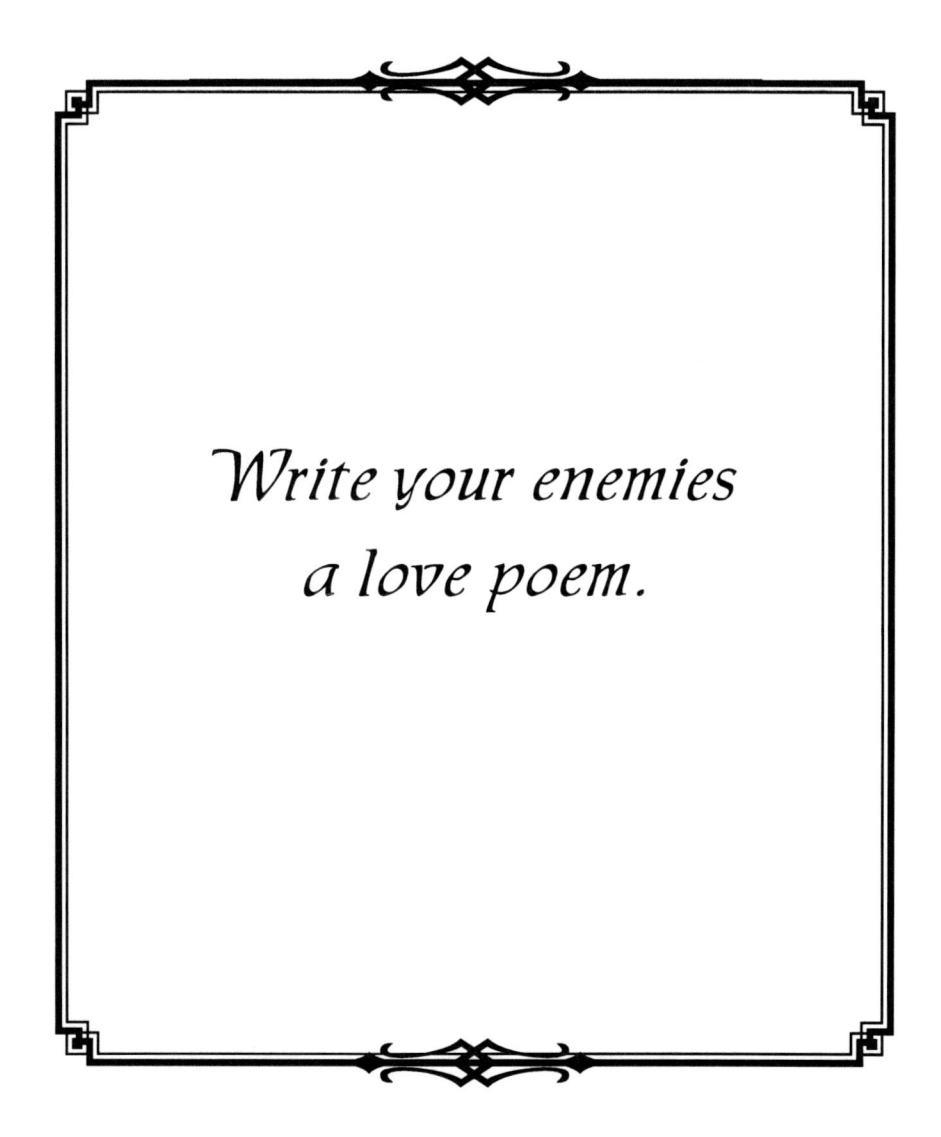

Write your enemies a love poem.

TO ALL VISTORS

*Come and feel the
love
that I have for each
one of you.*

COLOR

Love the skin you are in. You won't get anymore.

PEACE

*Love with kind
words
and a forgiving
heart.*

NUTRITION

Give your body the best of love.

YOUR BURDEN

*Love can carry
a heavy load.*

WARNING:

*Love tolerates
a lot
of behaviors.*

I GOT IT

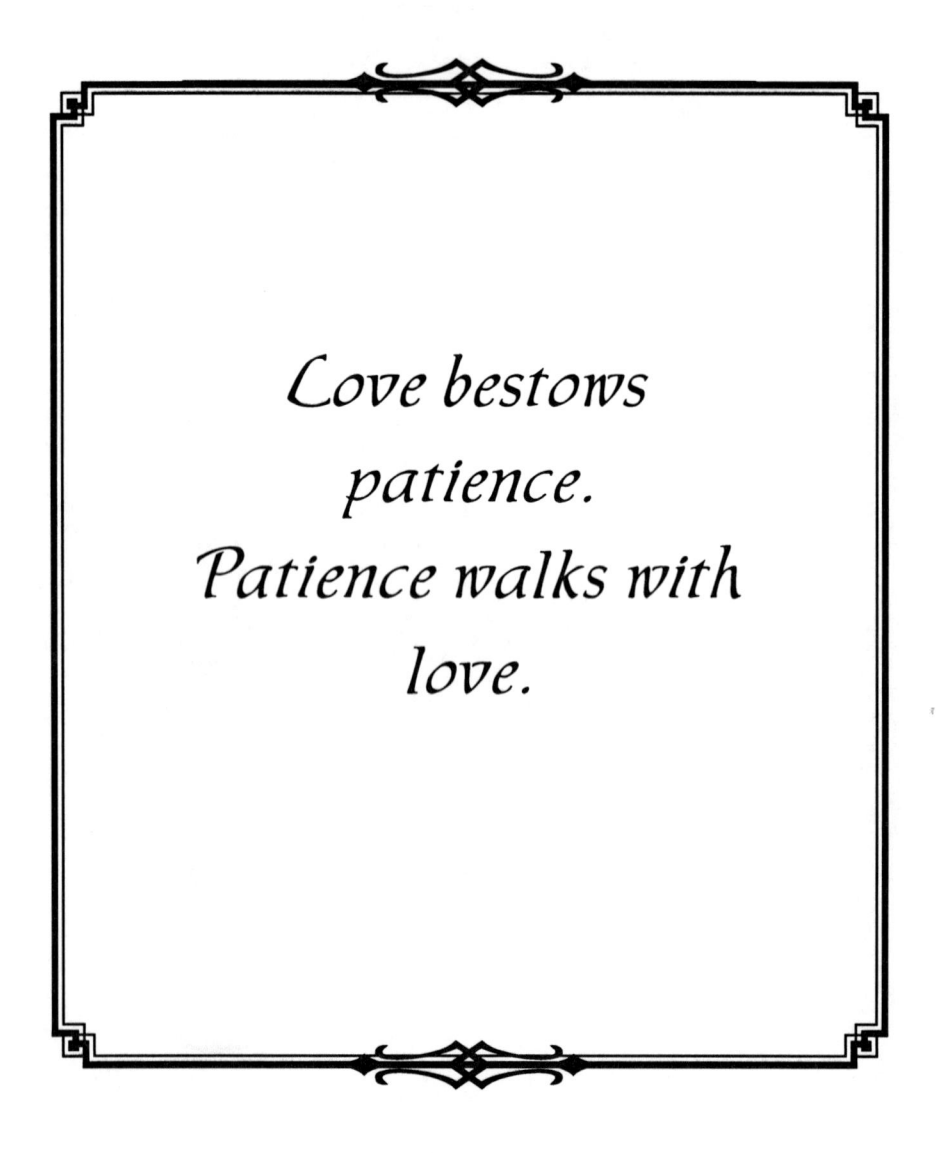

*Love bestows patience.
Patience walks with love.*

ACKNOWLEDGE IT

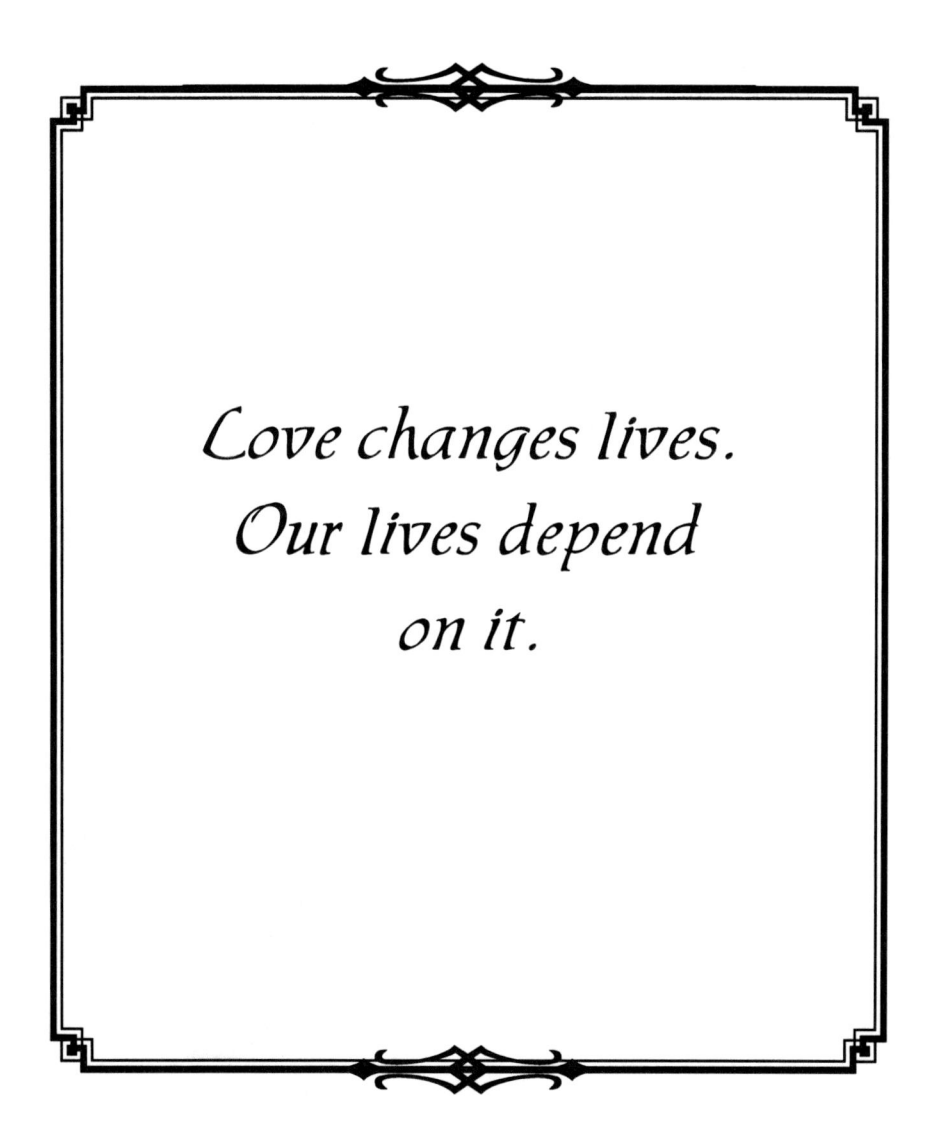

Love changes lives. Our lives depend on it.

LOVE IS NICE

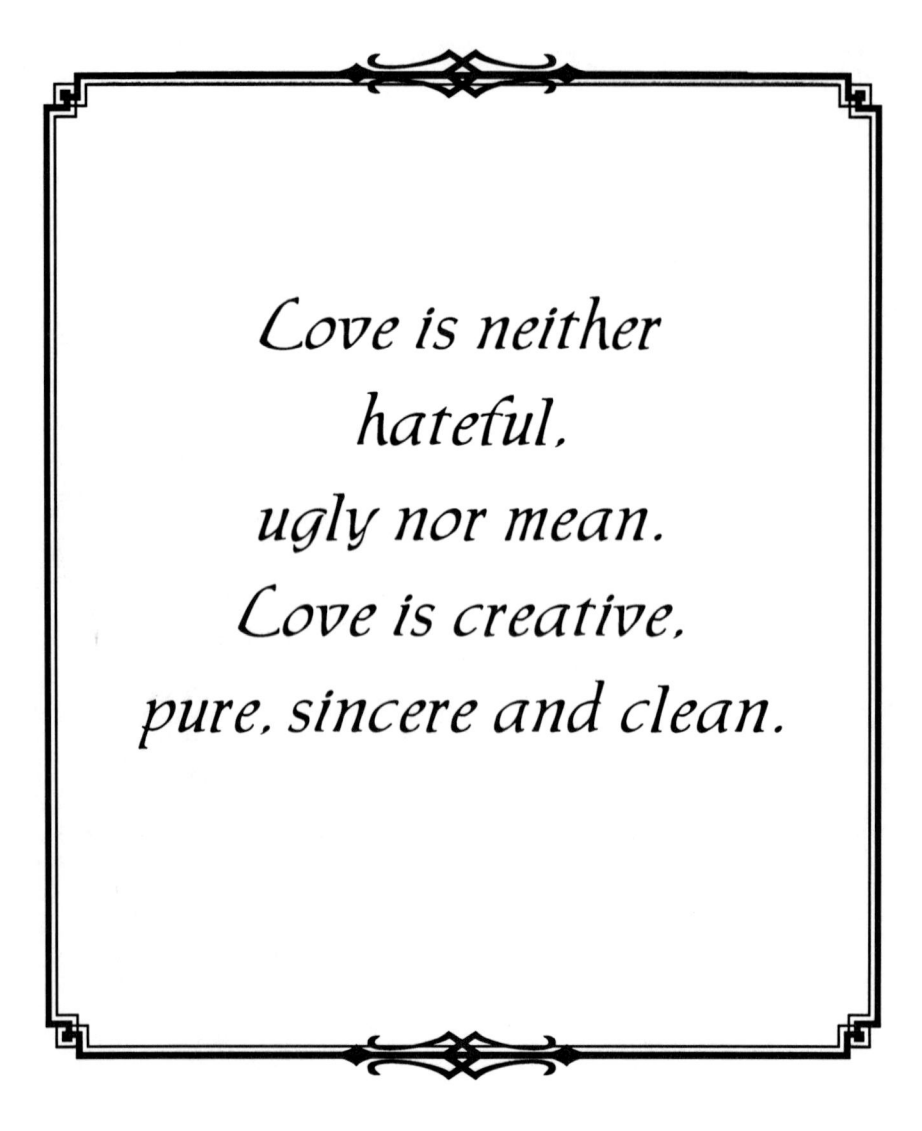

*Love is neither
hateful,
ugly nor mean.
Love is creative,
pure, sincere and clean.*

SIX FEET

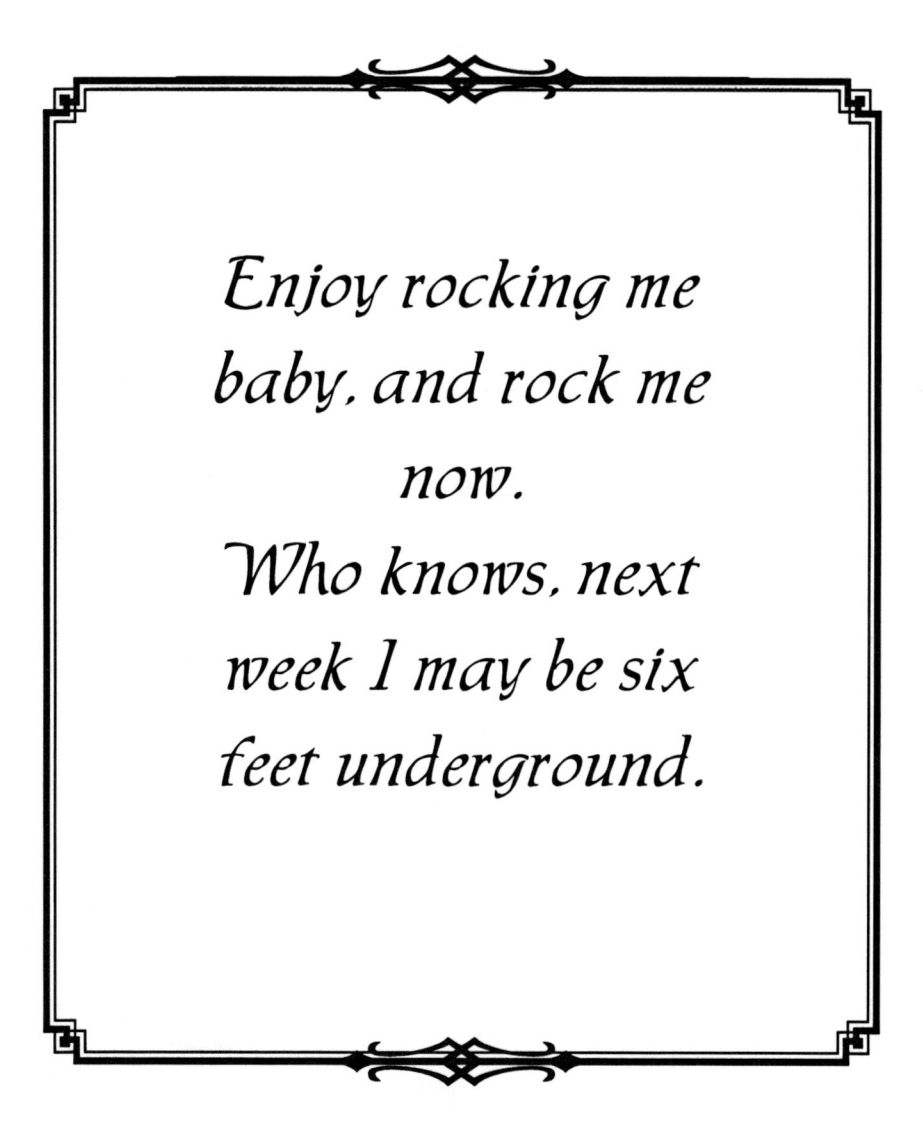

Enjoy rocking me baby, and rock me now.
Who knows, next week I may be six feet underground.

WONDER

I am excited to have you as my new love.

MAGIC

*Love is magical.
Sometimes you feel it.
Sometimes you don't.*

REACH

I reach out for love, and love reaches back.

LEAD BY EXAMPLE

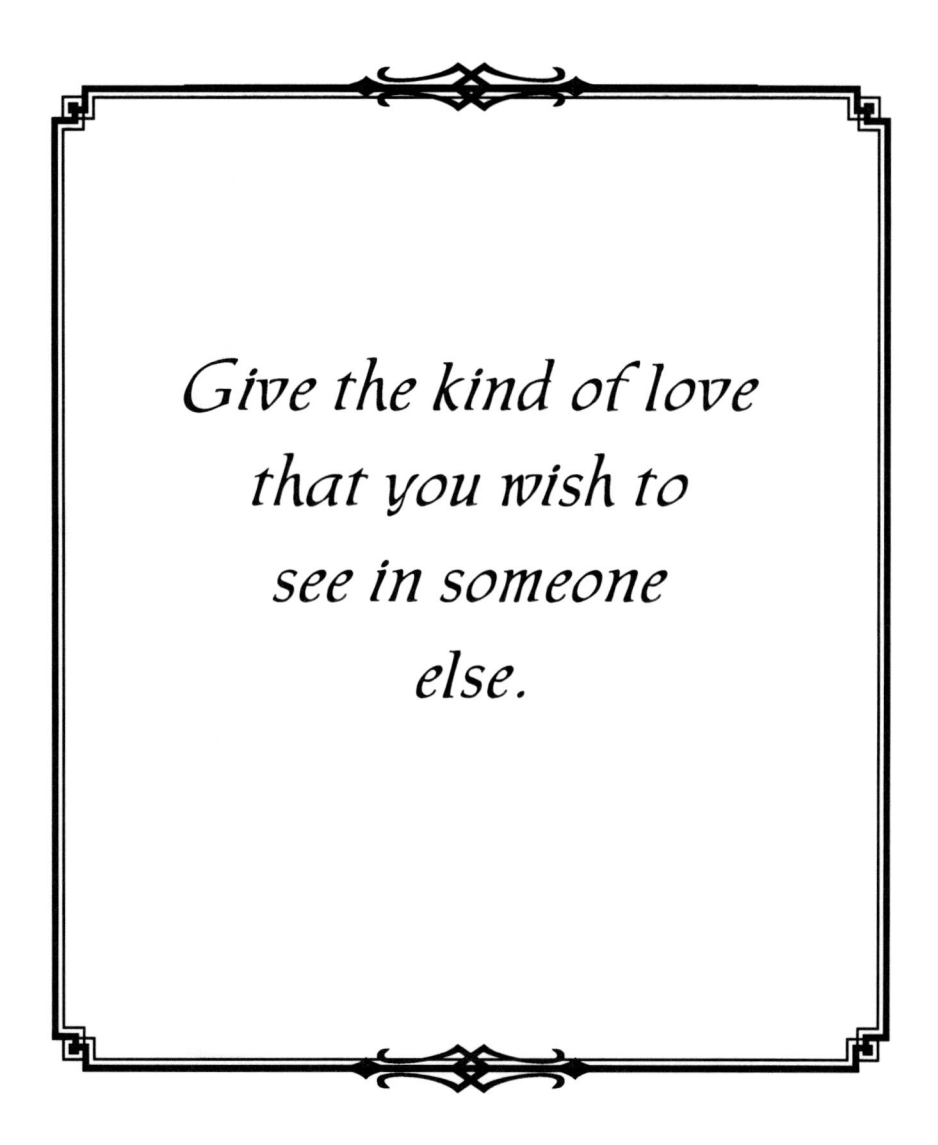

Give the kind of love that you wish to see in someone else.

YOU'LL BE SURPRISED

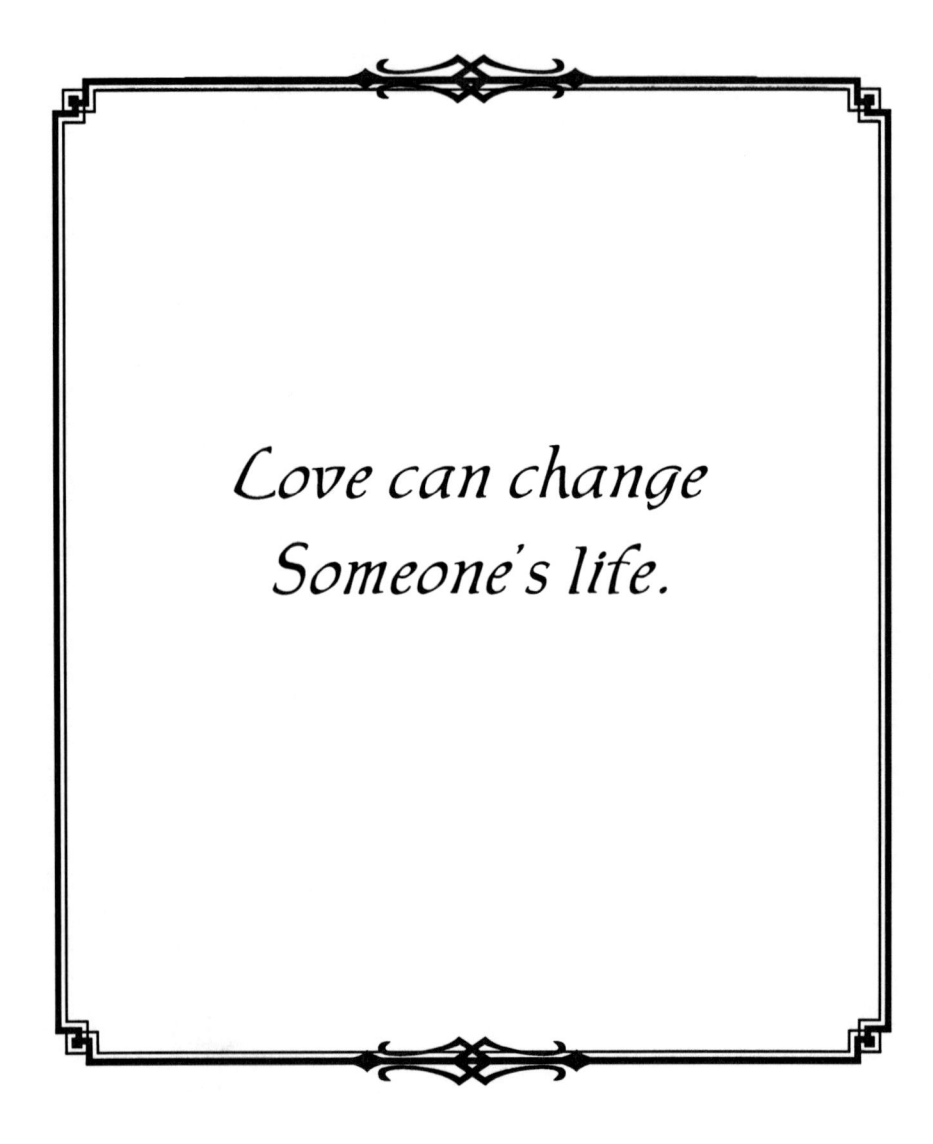

*Love can change
Someone's life.*

TIME

Time is love.
Love takes time.

LIKE NONE OTHER

Love is God.
God is
the divine lover.

FOR REAL?

The first time I made love, I made it with you.

LET'S LOOK AT IT

*You think love is
what
you can see,
taste, and feel. But
honey
there is much more
to the deal.*

GO WITH THE FLOW

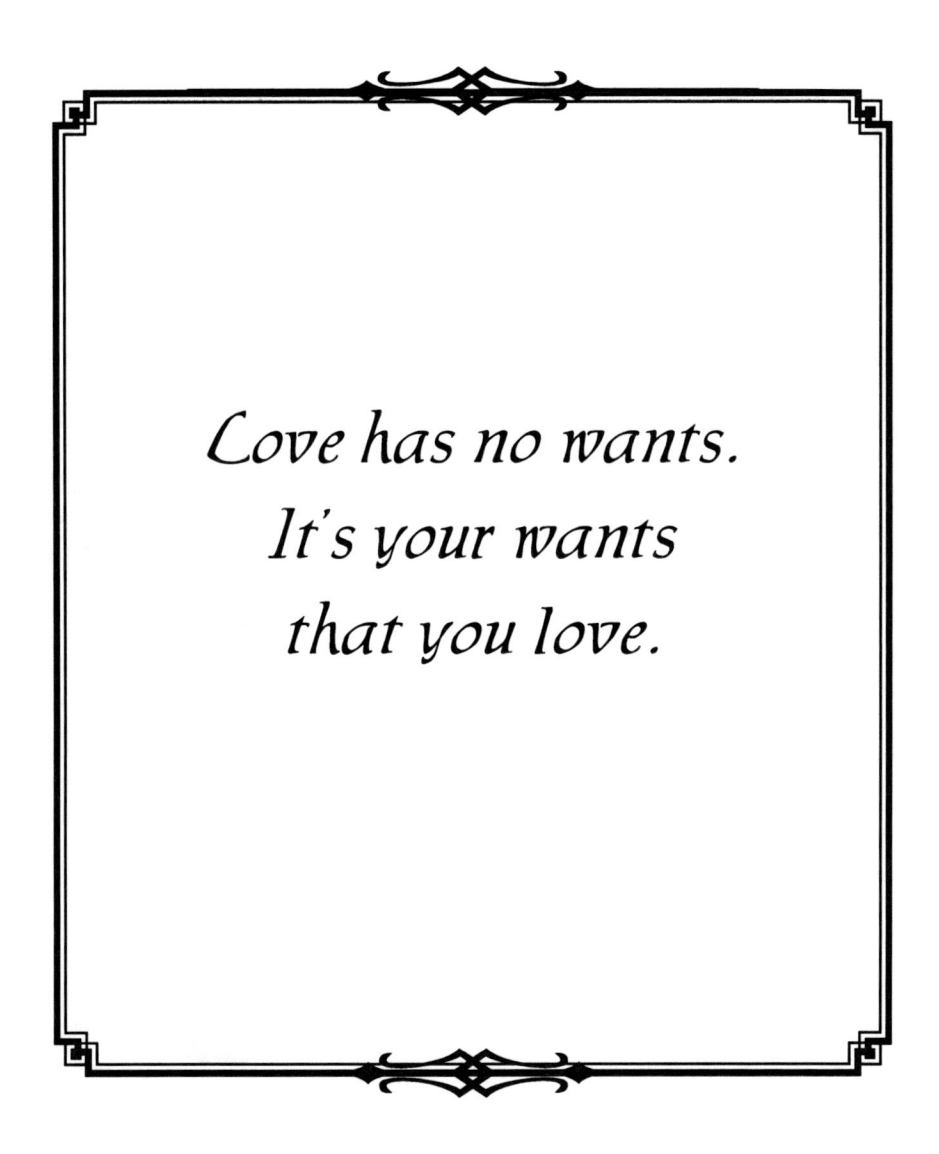

*Love has no wants.
It's your wants
that you love.*

REALITY

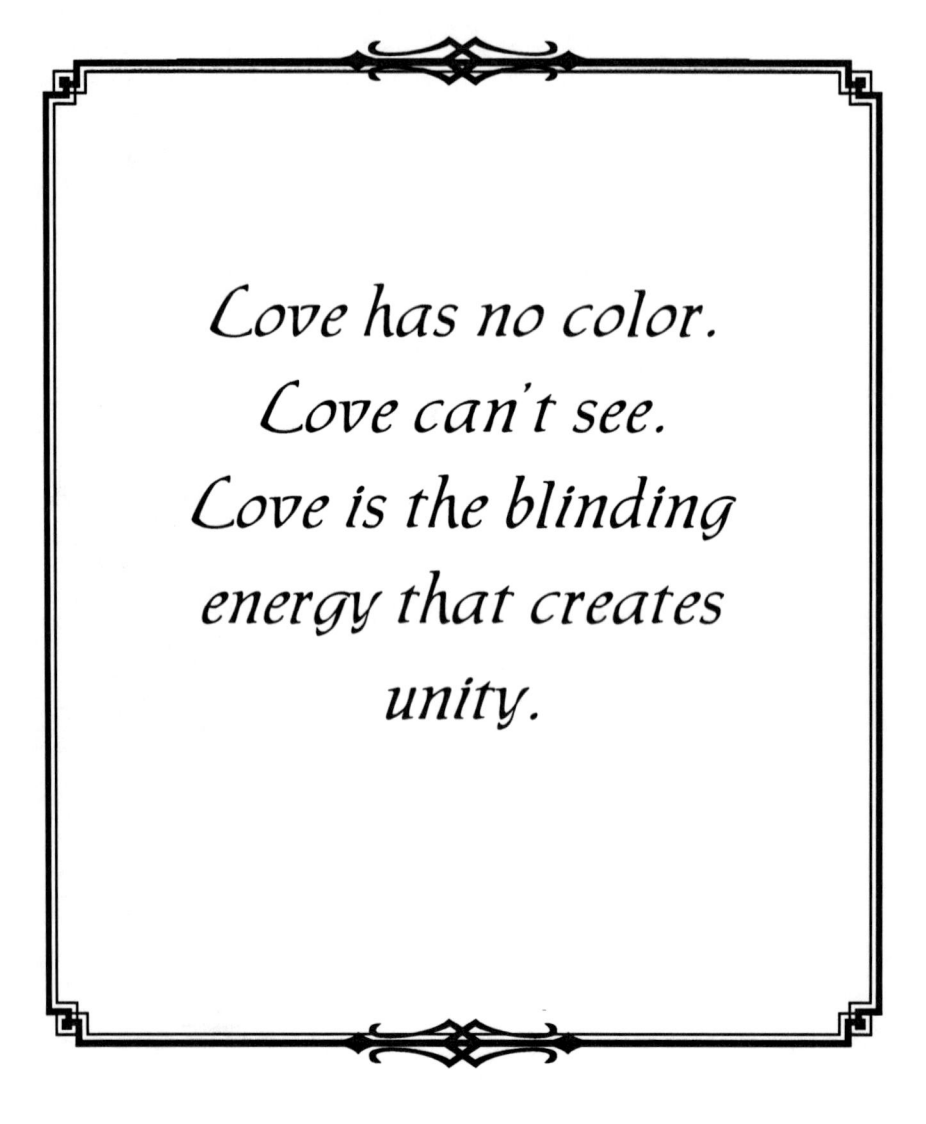

*Love has no color.
Love can't see.
Love is the blinding energy that creates unity.*

FALLING IN LOVE

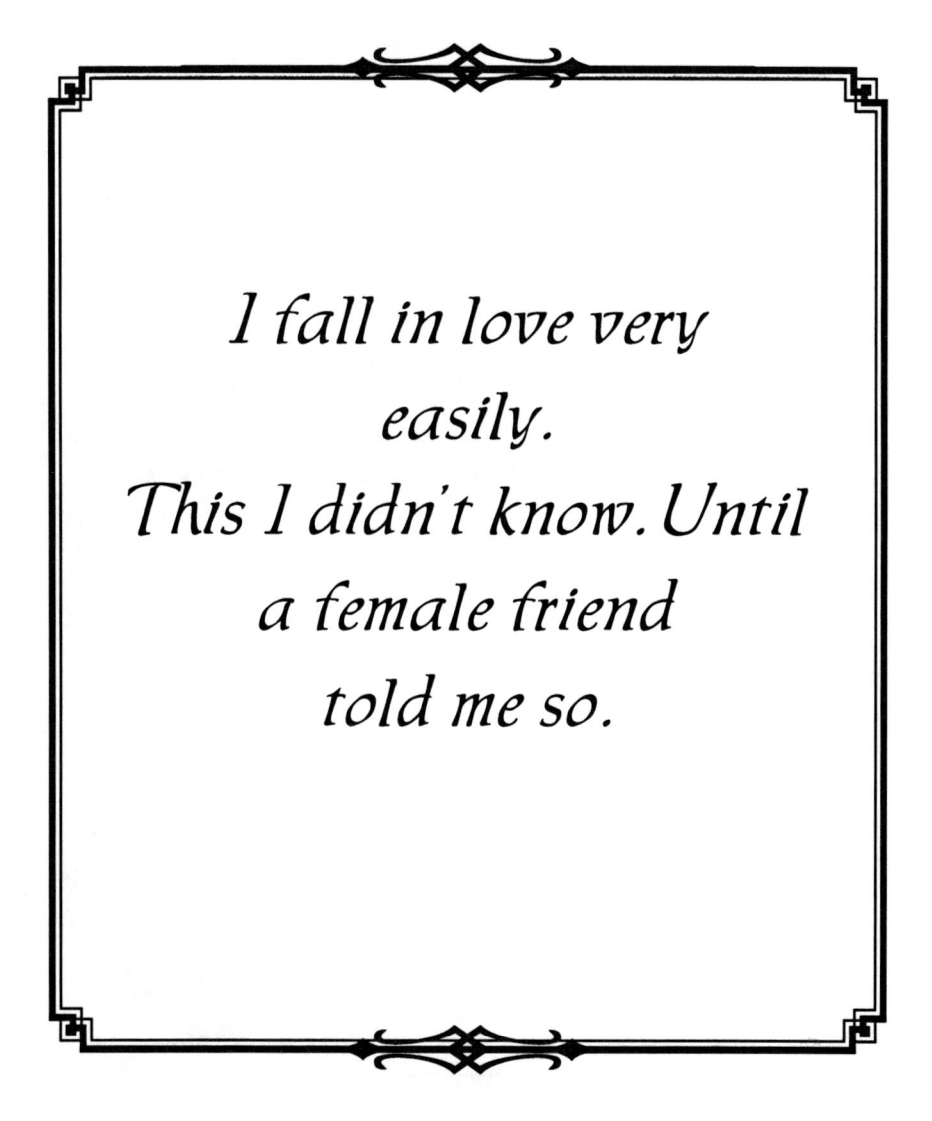

*I fall in love very easily.
This I didn't know. Until
a female friend
told me so.*

HOW HIGH

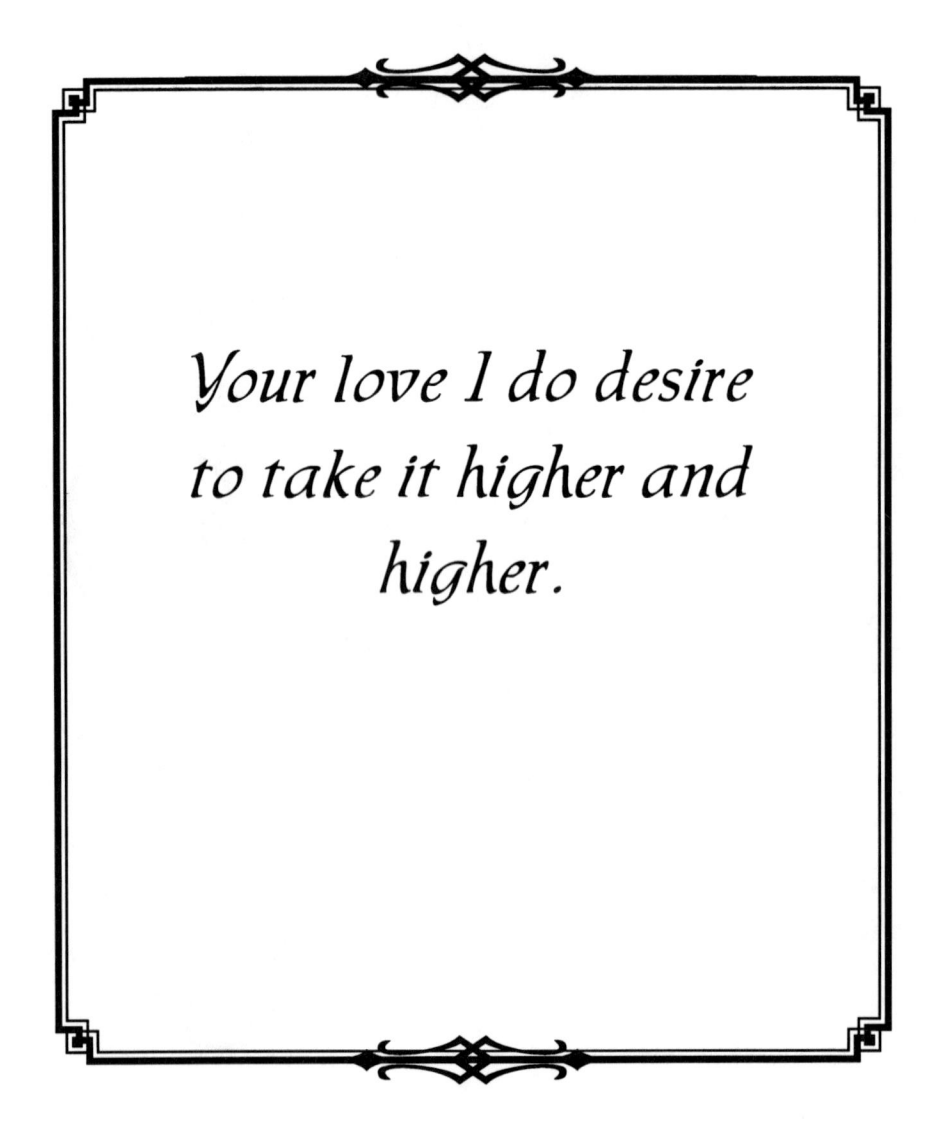

Your love I do desire to take it higher and higher.

HEAVEN KNOWS

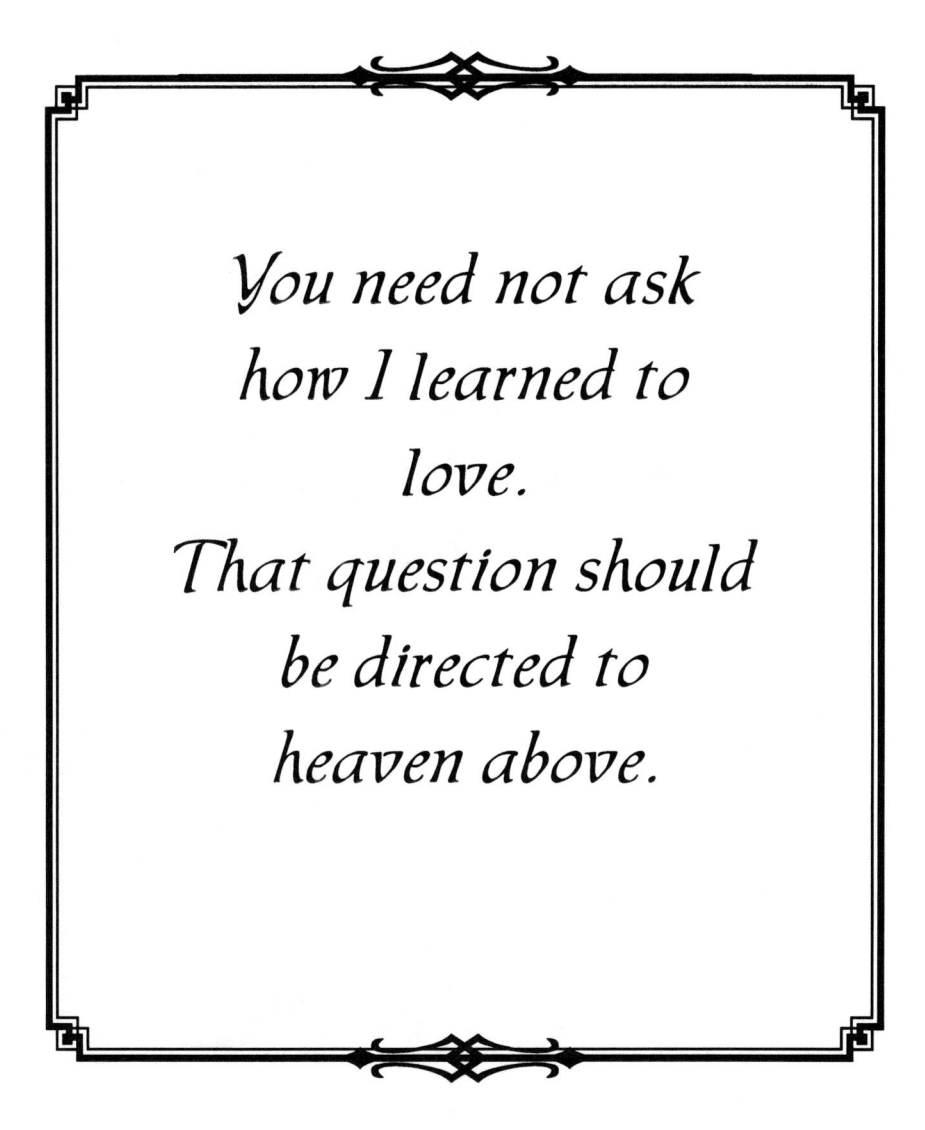

*You need not ask how I learned to love.
That question should be directed to heaven above.*

TRIUMPH

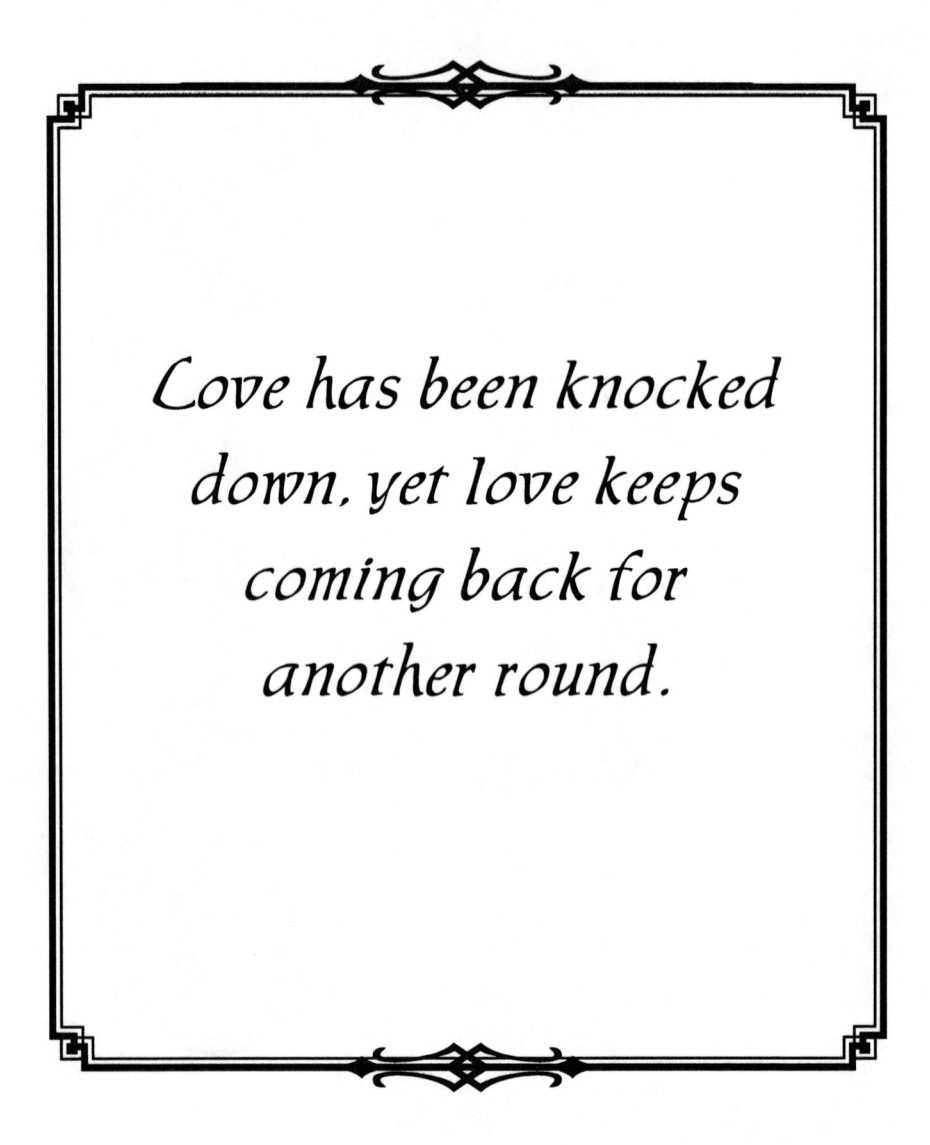

Love has been knocked down, yet love keeps coming back for another round.

YOU GO BOY

*She said my love is as good as whipped cream.
I do it so good it makes her wanna scream.*

CULITIVATE LOVE

Quality love guarantees satisfaction.

PLEASE

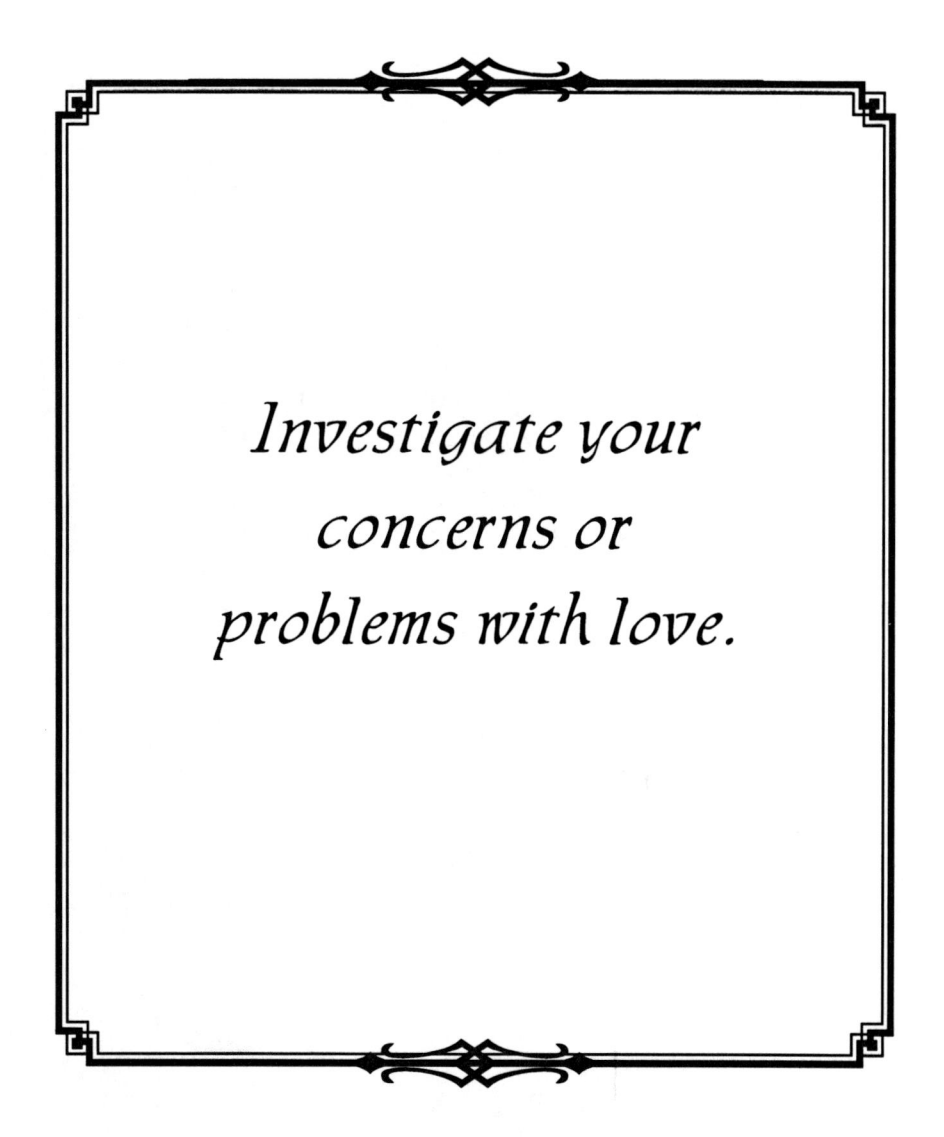

Investigate your concerns or problems with love.

RECOMMENDED

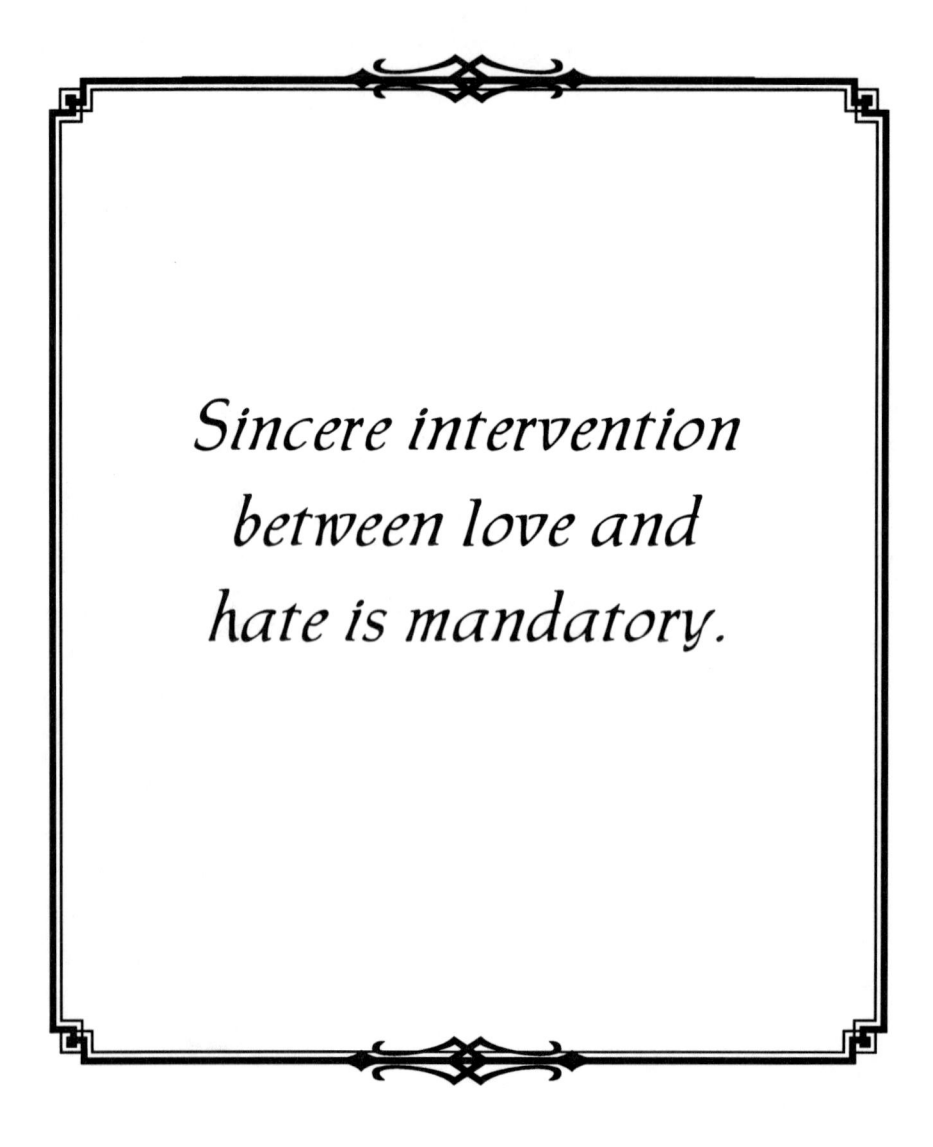

Sincere intervention between love and hate is mandatory.

TELL ME

*How much is
too much love?*

DO YOU HEAR ME?

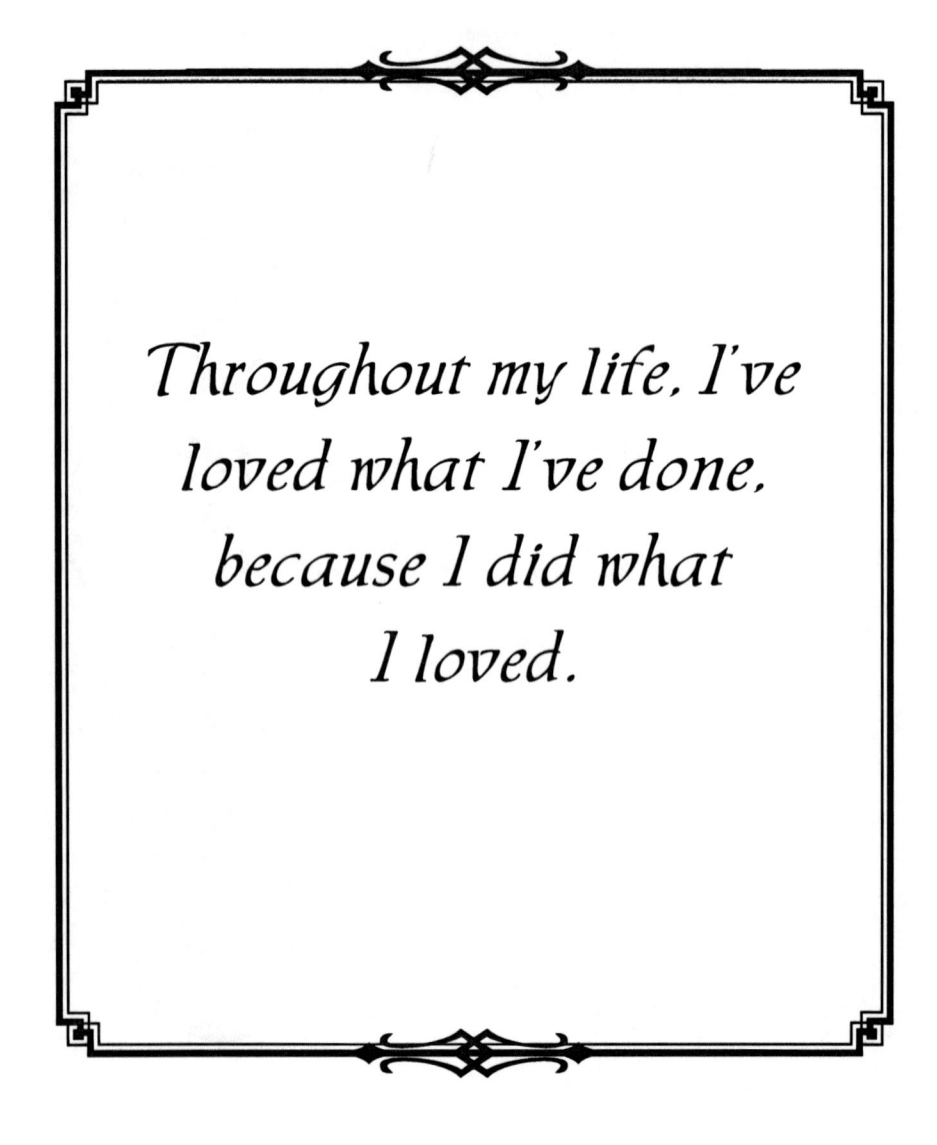

Throughout my life, I've loved what I've done, because I did what I loved.

PEOPLE

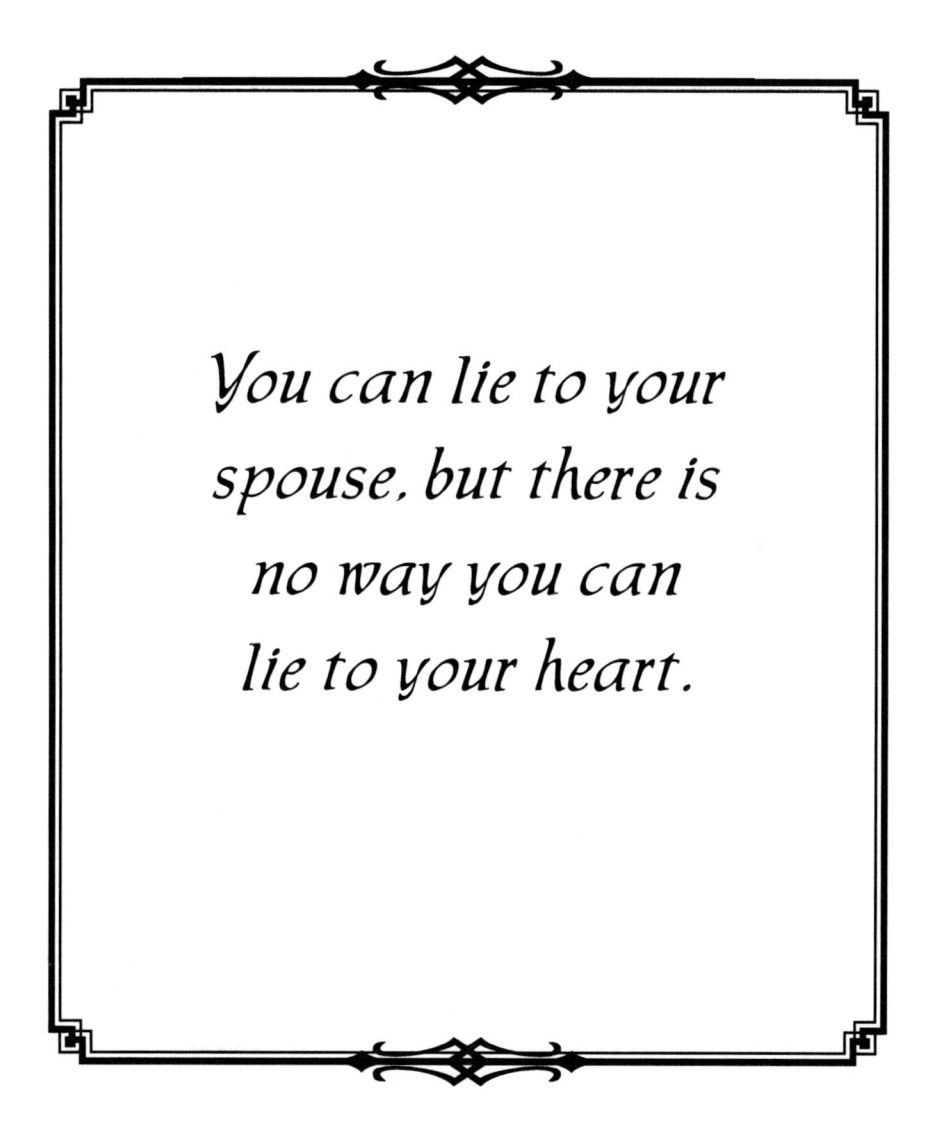

You can lie to your spouse, but there is no way you can lie to your heart.

BE PREPARED

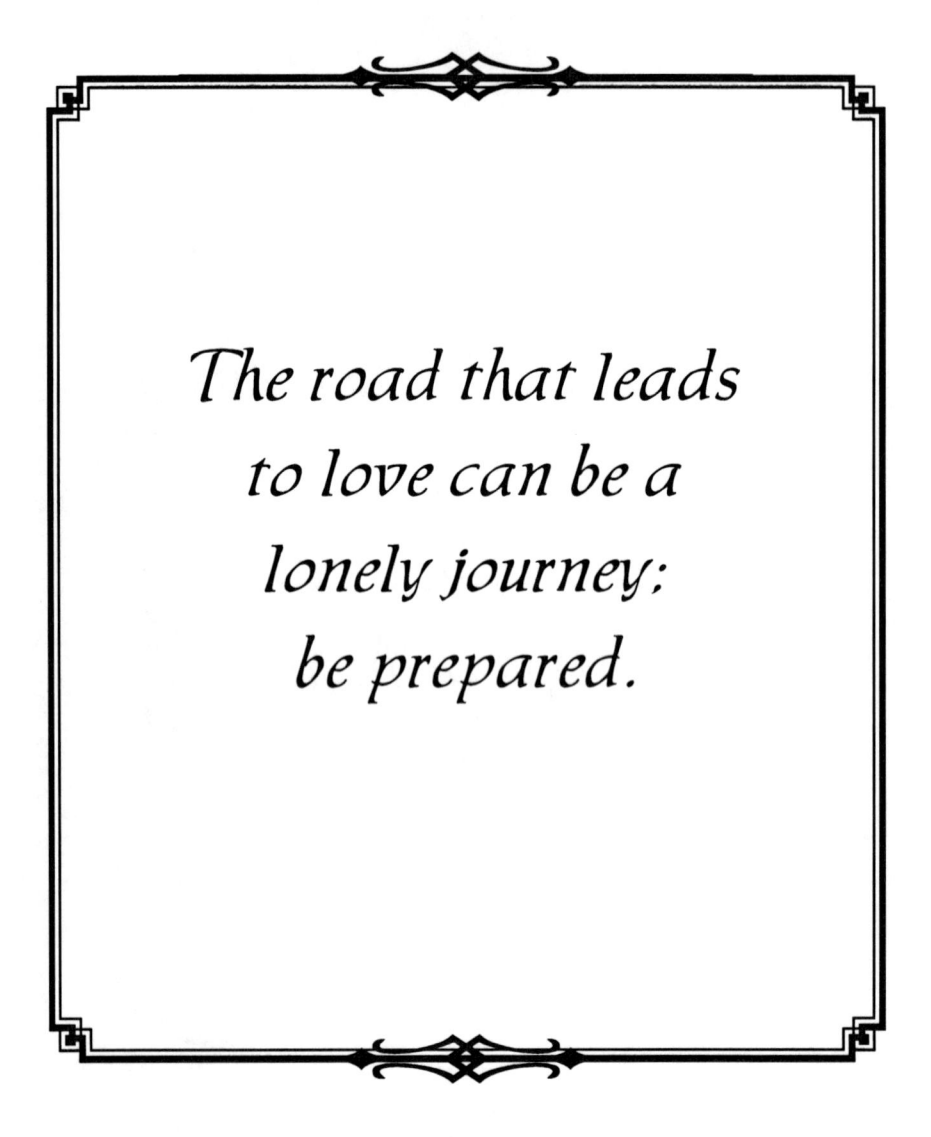

The road that leads to love can be a lonely journey; be prepared.

TOO SOON

Don't claim someone as your soul mate, if you've only gone out on one blind date!

WHATEVER IT IS

Where you see no love, don't even go there.

VULGARITY

Profanity hurts the heart.

SMOOTH TALKER

Girl you look so fine you're blowing my mind. If you were in love with me I'd be making love to you all the time.

ADMISSION

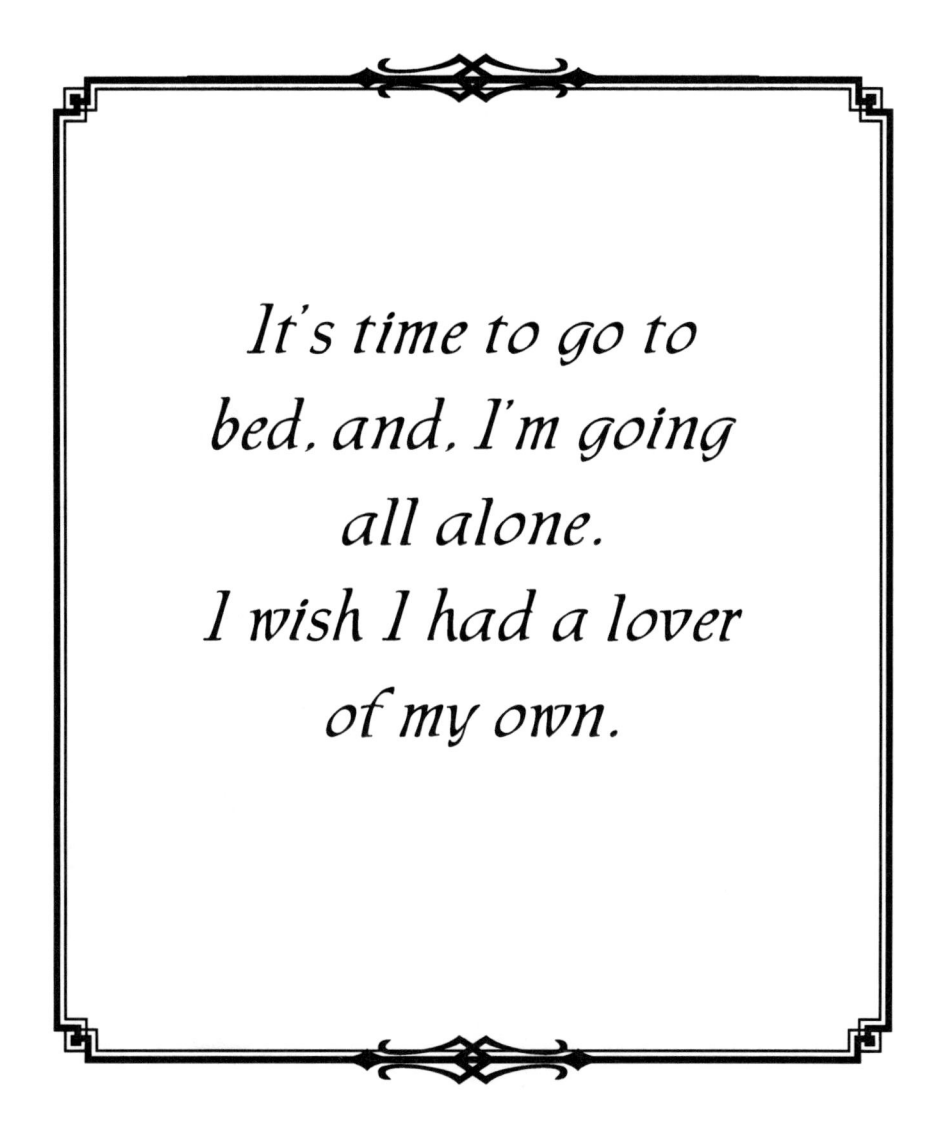

*It's time to go to bed, and, I'm going all alone.
I wish I had a lover of my own.*

WAKE UP

*Wake up
to the
spirit
of love.*

SOLICITING

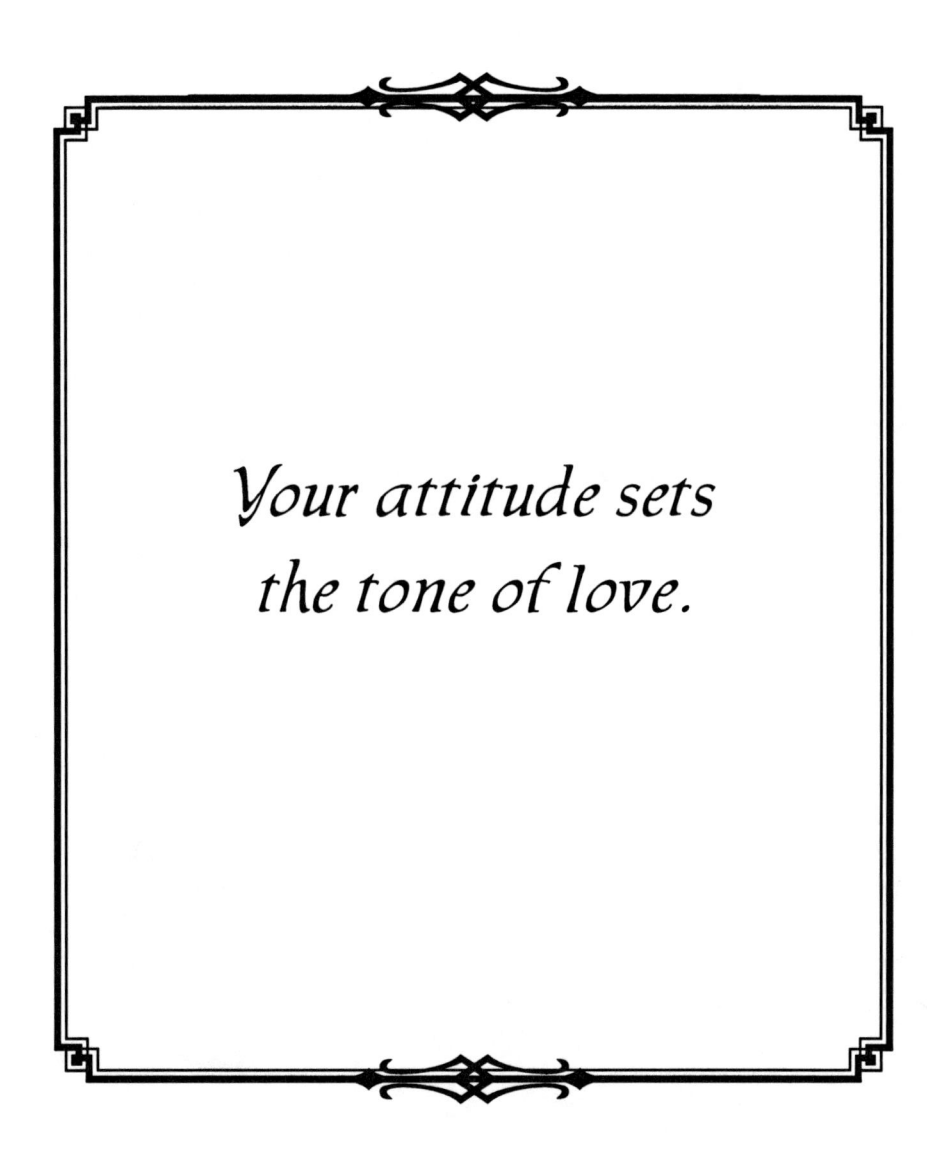

Your attitude sets the tone of love.

ACCEPTANCE

Wow, she stole my heart.

INTERNET LOVERS

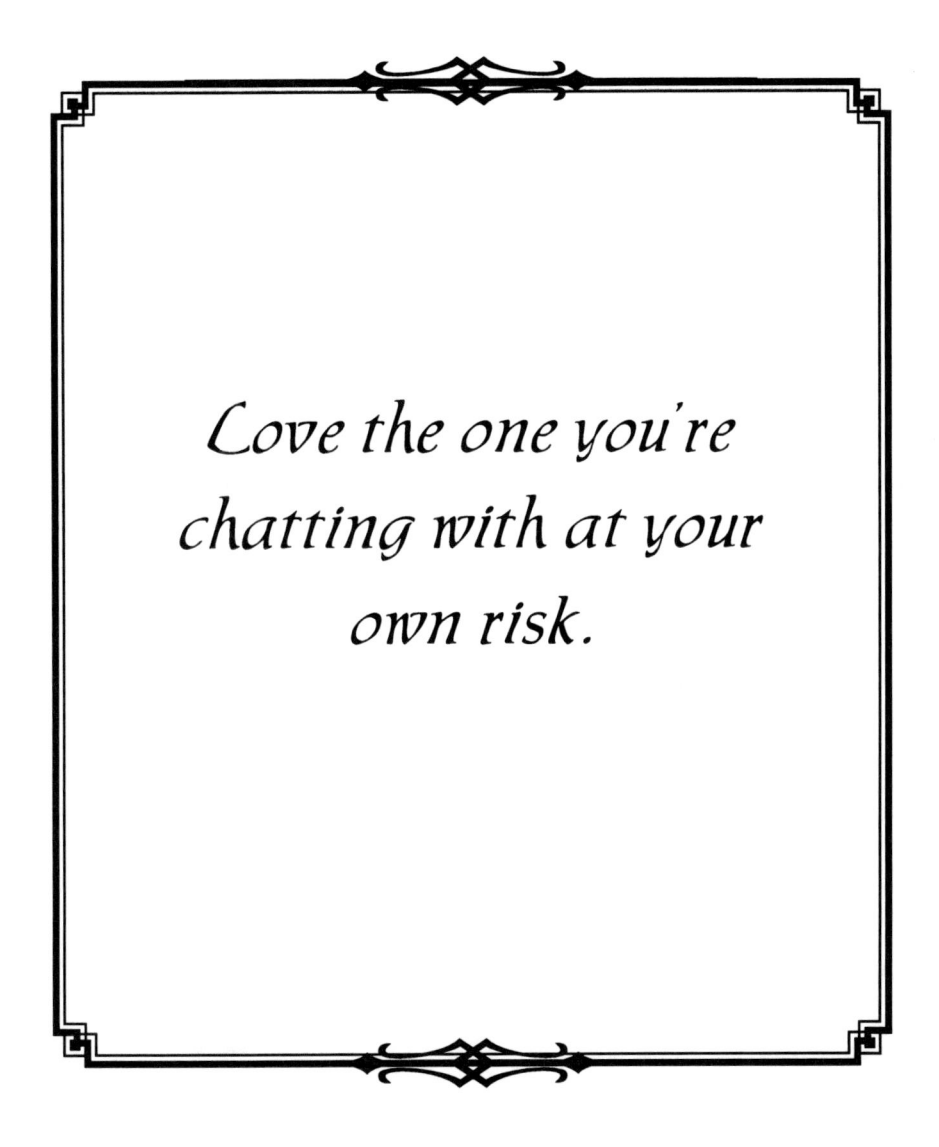

Love the one you're chatting with at your own risk.

I'M SORRY

Long distance love has no guarantee.

FUGITIVE

Just because I told you I love you right away doesn't mean I'm here to stay.

WHERE

*If love doesn't live
here anymore,
where does love live now?*

FINAL

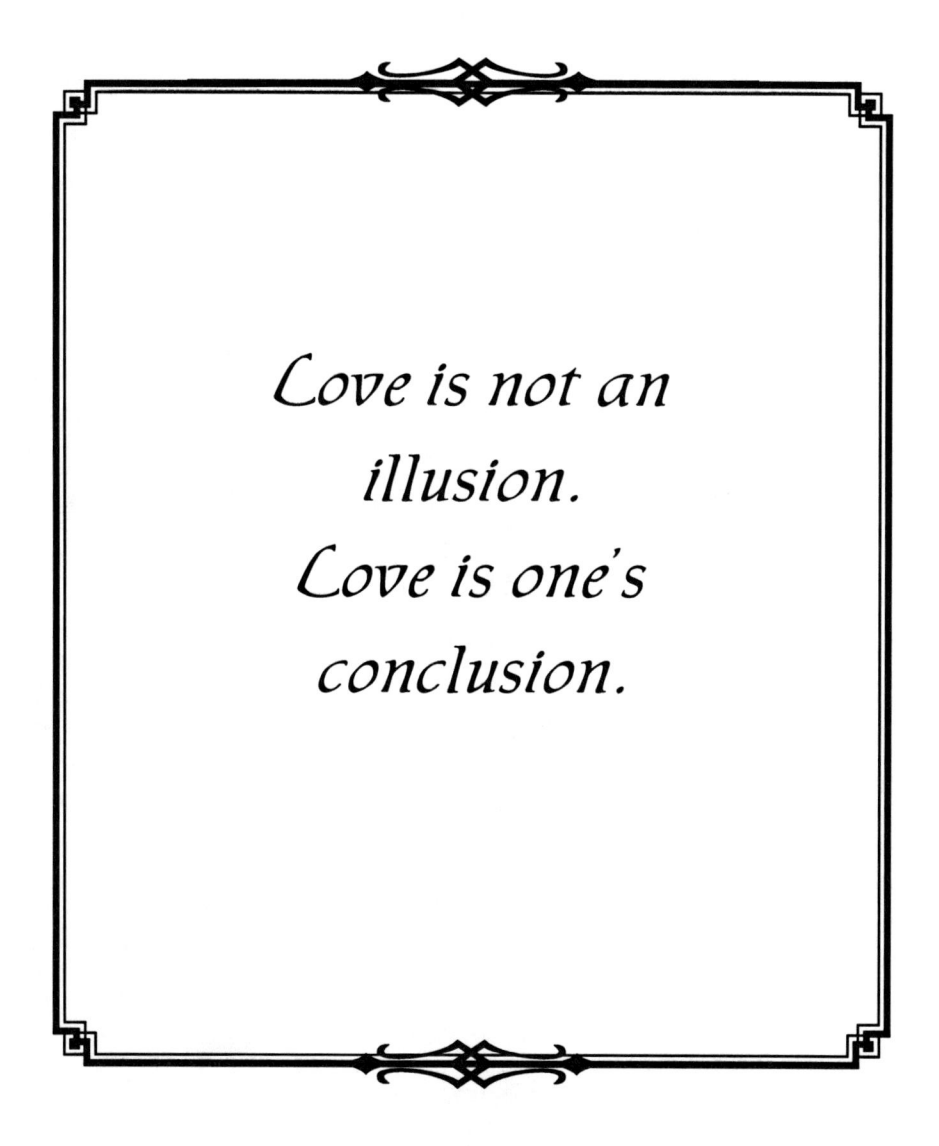

*Love is not an illusion.
Love is one's conclusion.*

JUST A HINT

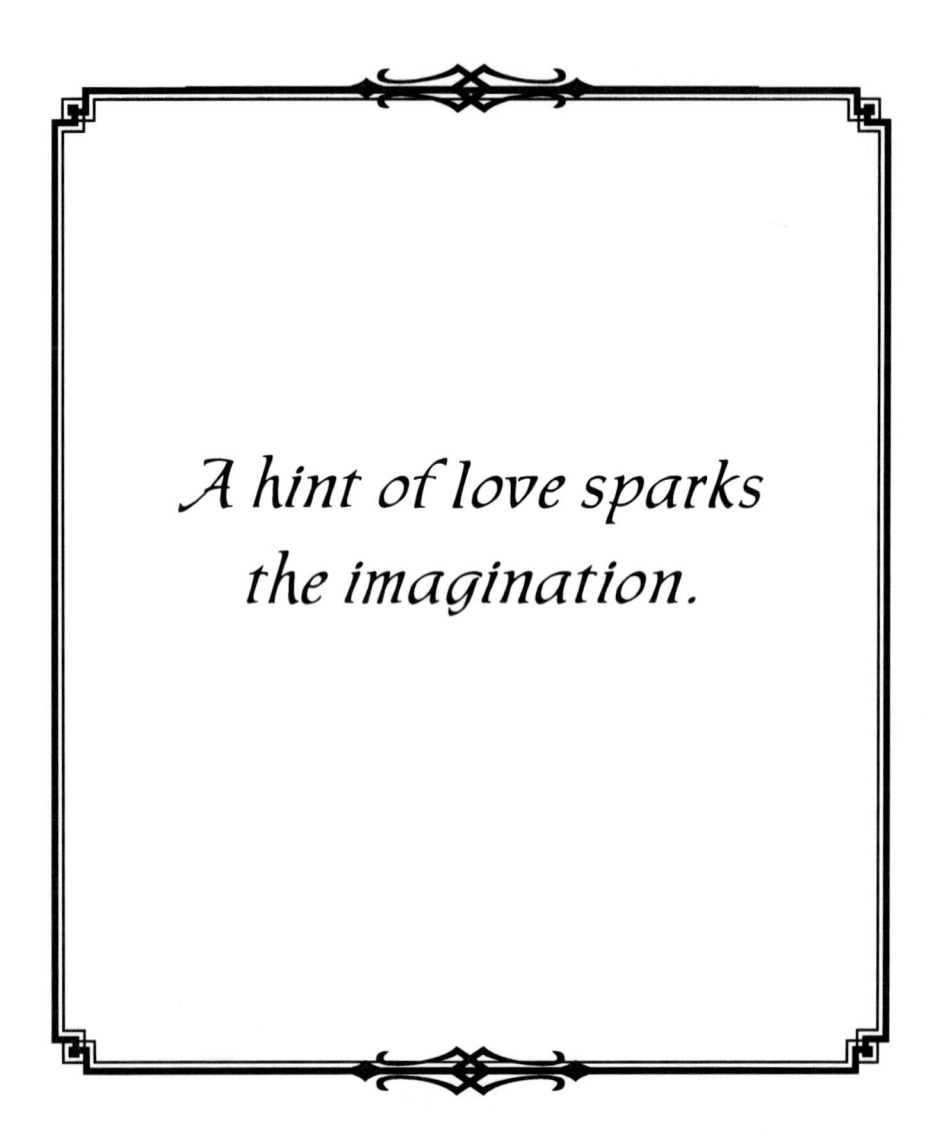

A hint of love sparks the imagination.

ILLNESS

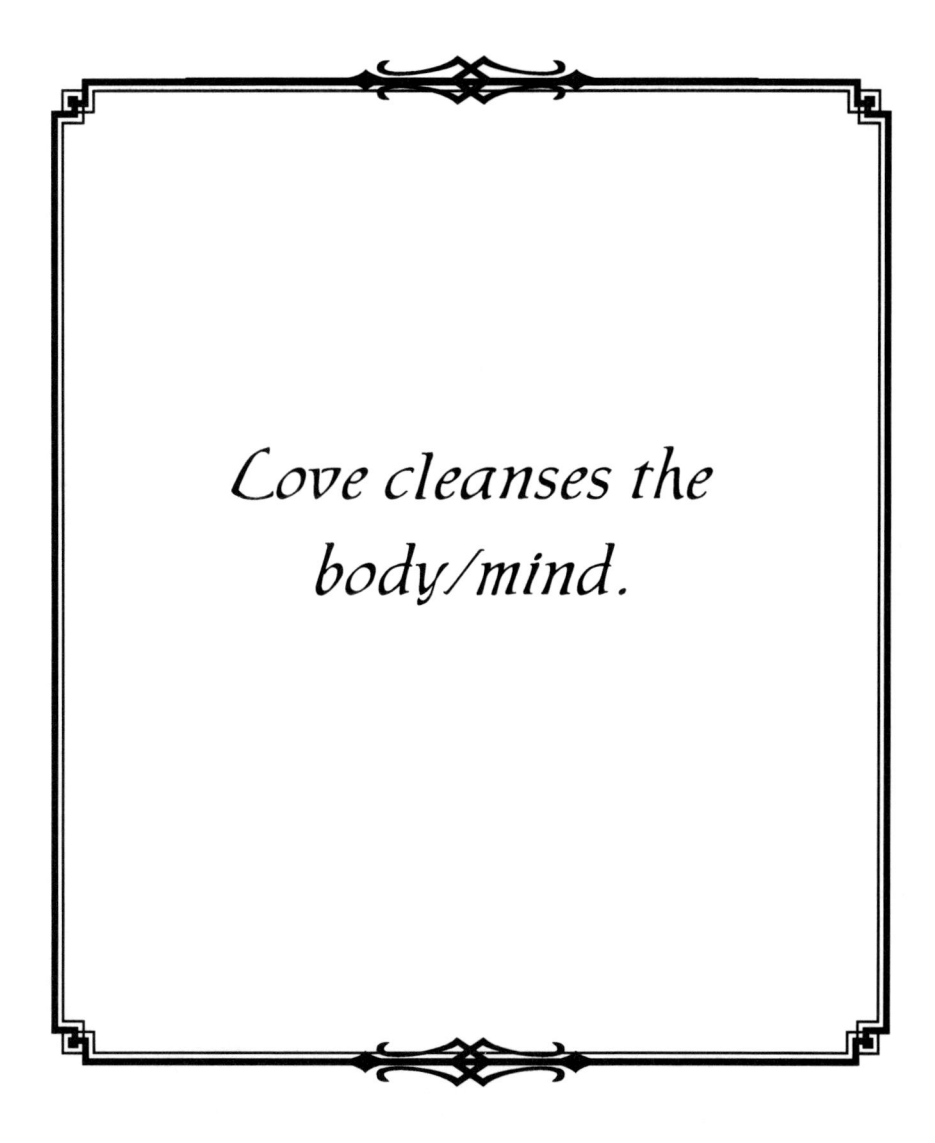

Love cleanses the body/mind.

REVERENCE

Love is God's way of giving.

ATTENTION

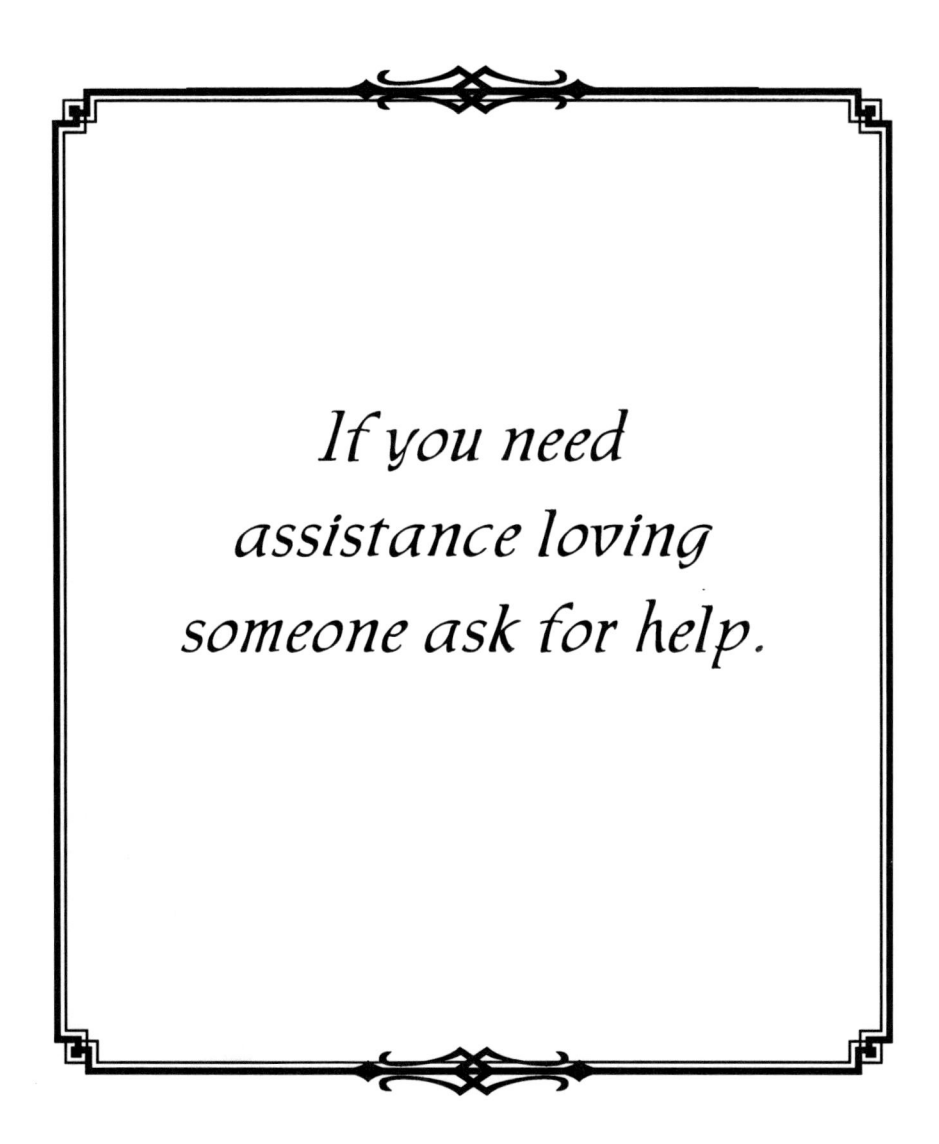

If you need assistance loving someone ask for help.

VOLUNTEER

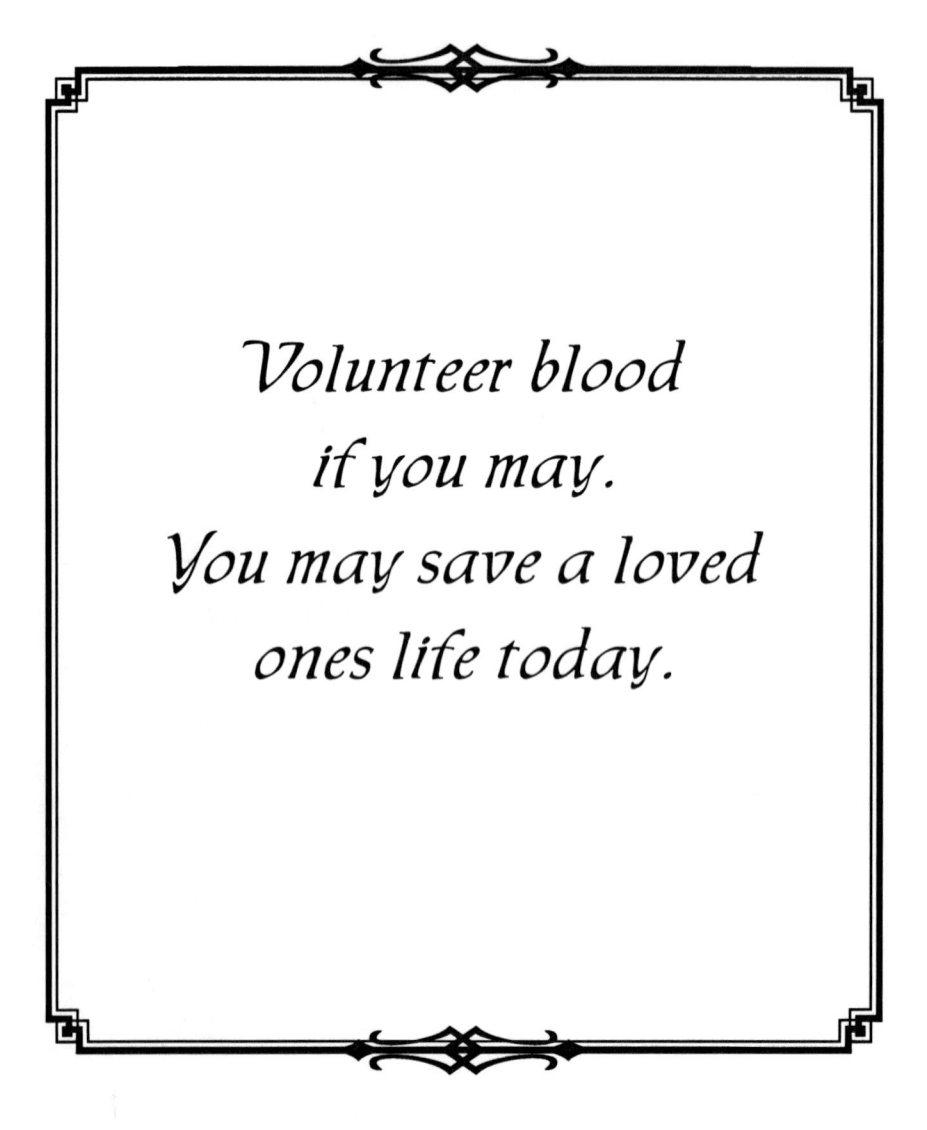

*Volunteer blood
if you may.
You may save a loved
ones life today.*

WAREHOUSE

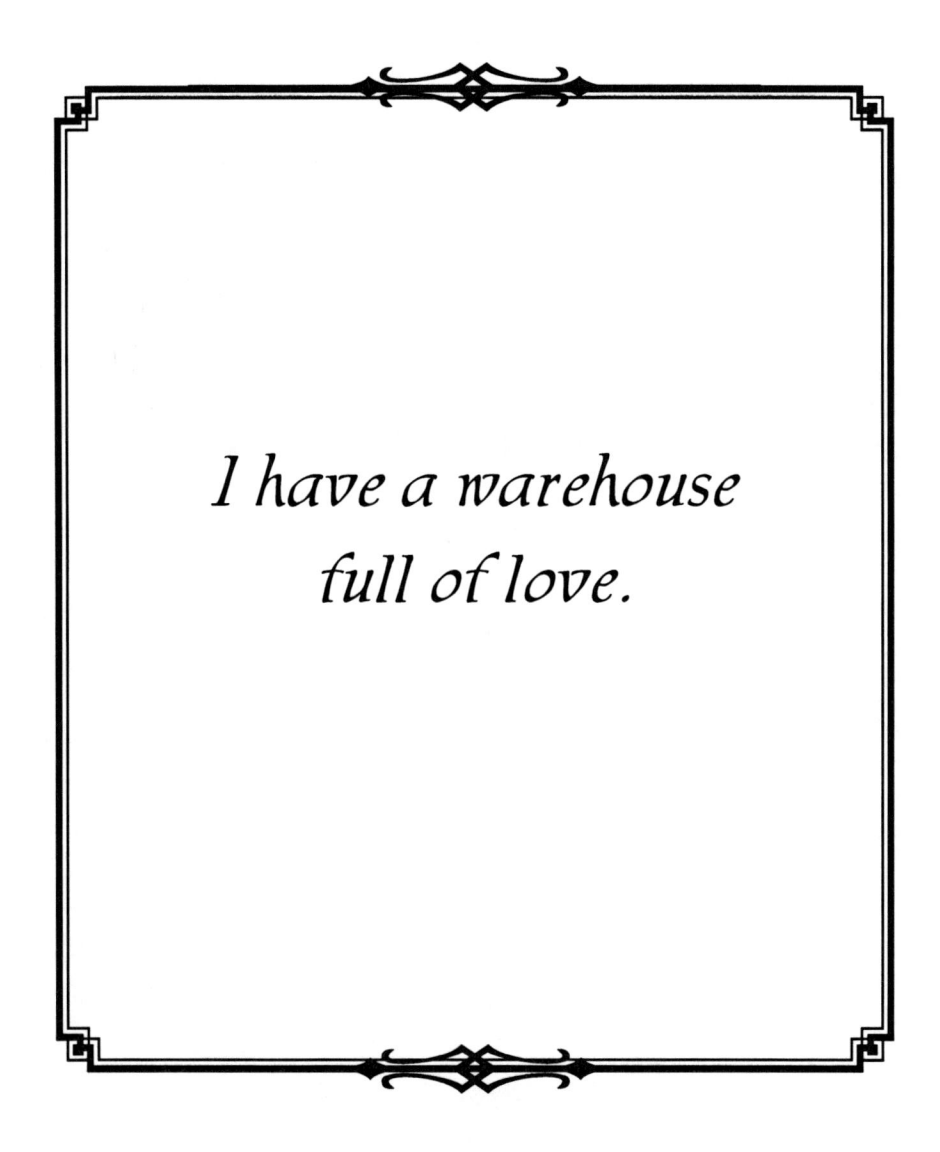

I have a warehouse full of love.

CAUTION YOU

*Caution!
If you can't love you
don't belong here.*

PLATINUM

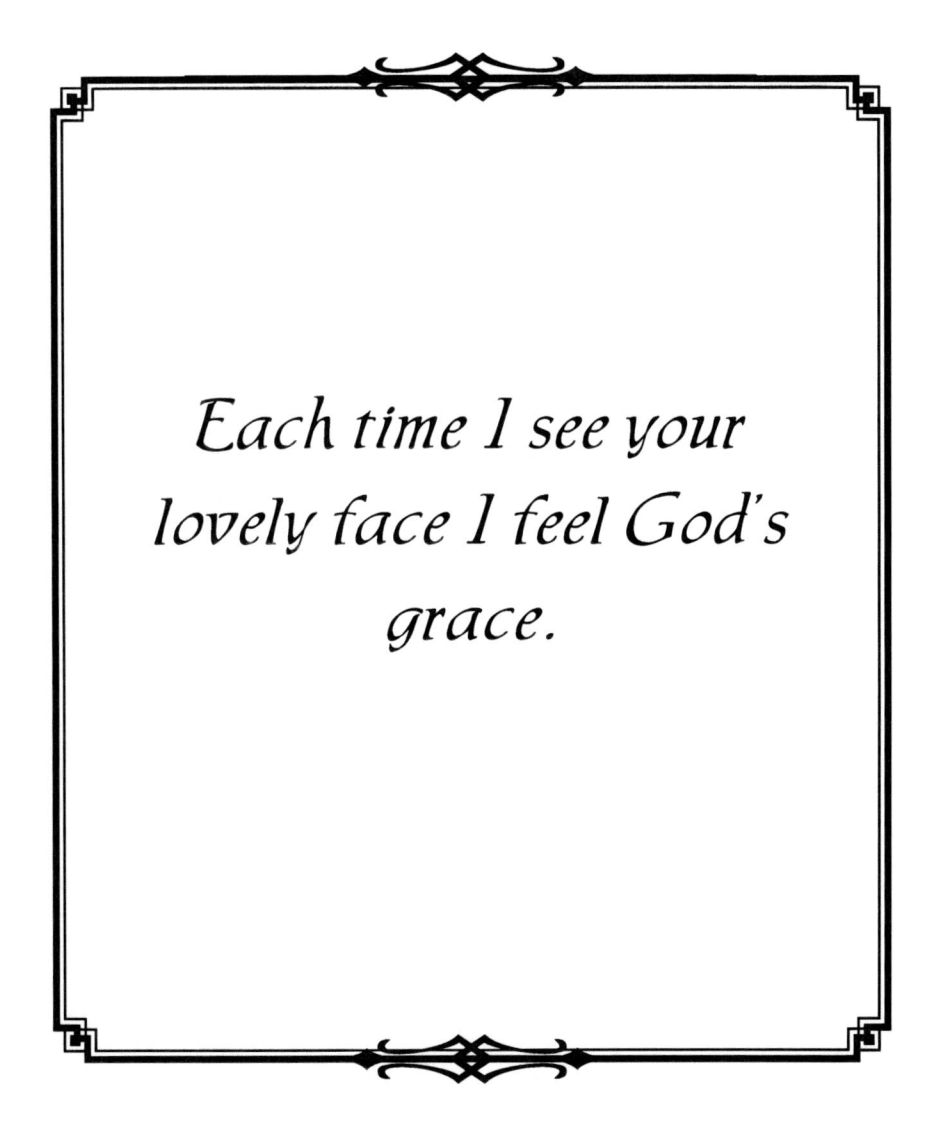

Each time I see your lovely face I feel God's grace.

YOU NEED TO UNDERSTAND

*When I found love,
I found joy.*

NOTHING

Nothing beats being in love.

I AM HONORED

*My angel said,
"I am her most
famous love poet".*

I DISCOVER

Love inspires when it touches your heart and sets it on fire.

JEALOUSY

A jealous heart knows no love.

WORTH PONDERING

*You said you love
me many times
when I was
financially strong.
Now I'm merely
broke,
and python you can't
hold on?*

THE DANCE

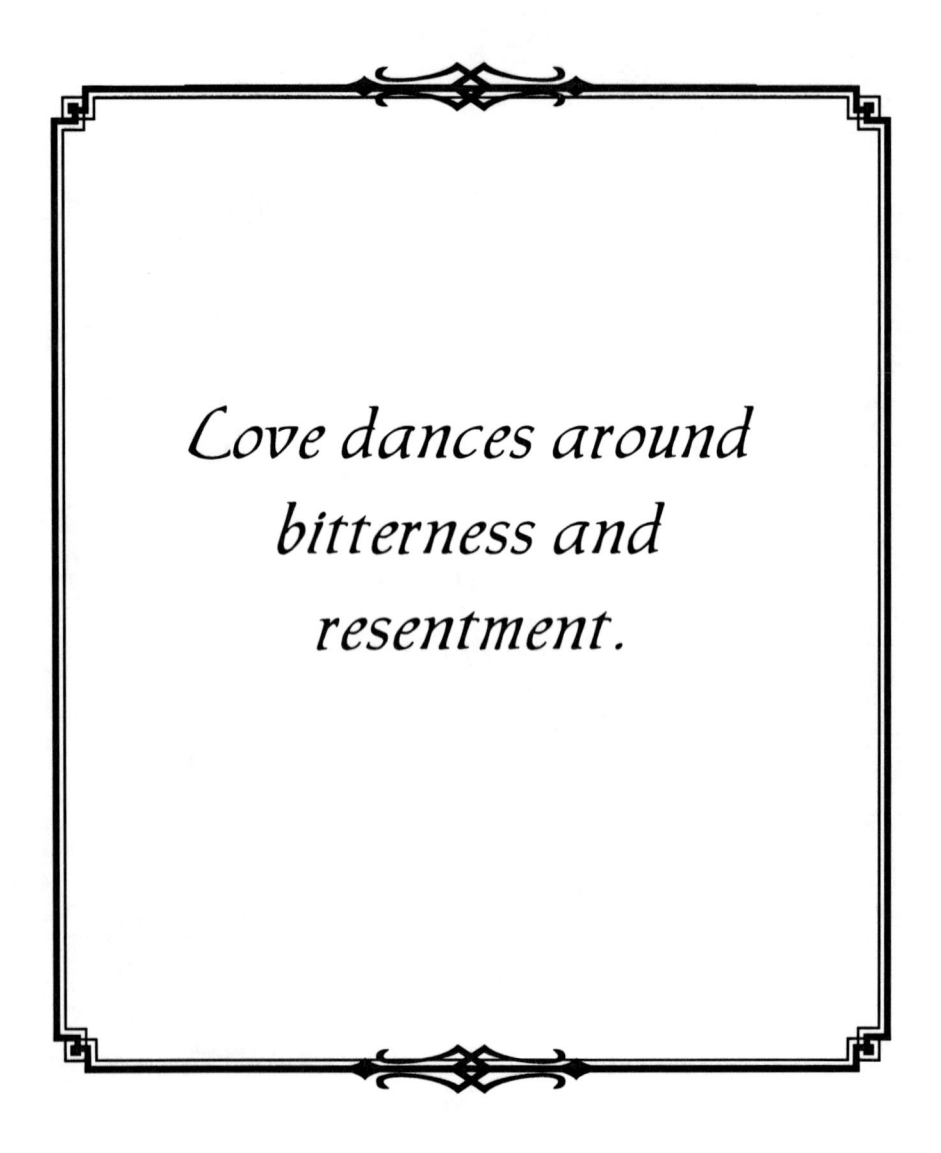

Love dances around bitterness and resentment.

MY FRIEND

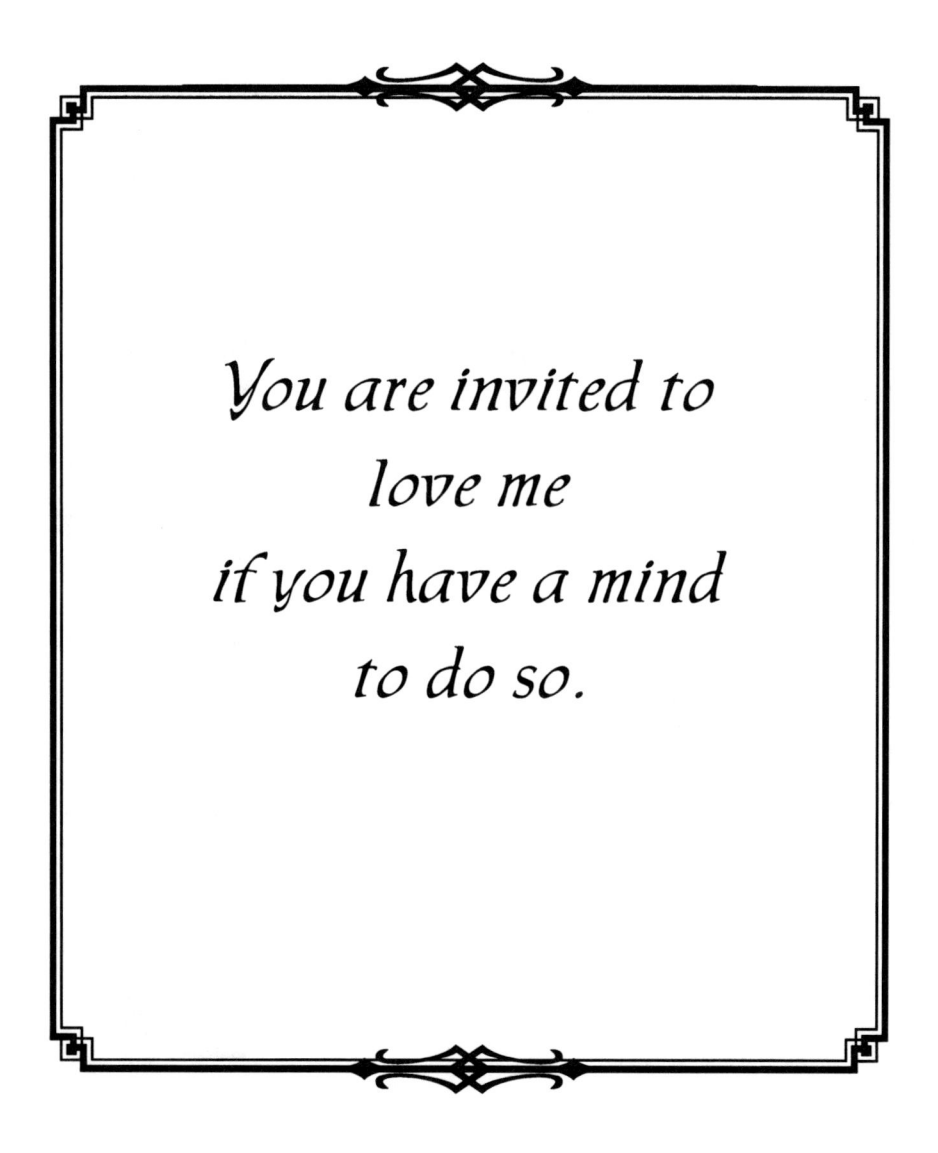

*You are invited to
love me
if you have a mind
to do so.*

I DON'T CARE

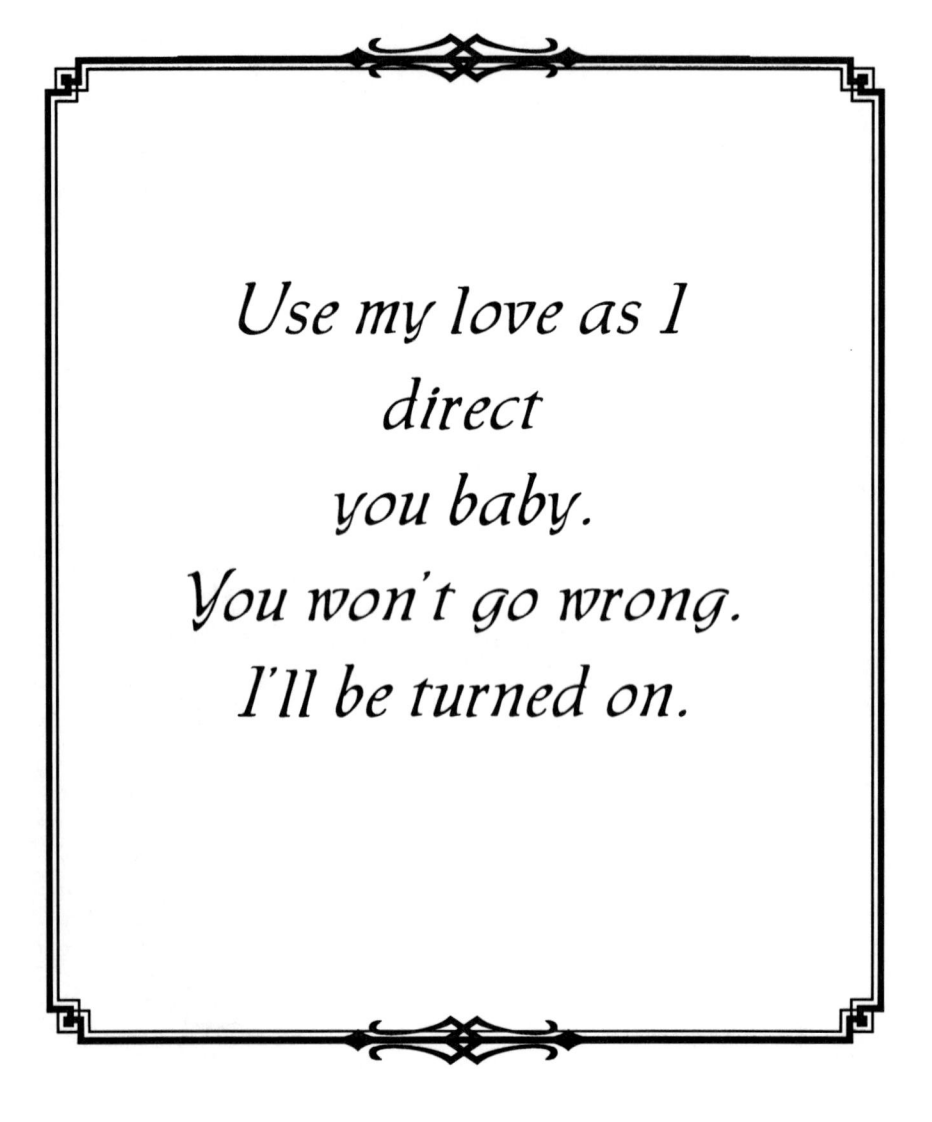

*Use my love as I
direct
you baby.
You won't go wrong.
I'll be turned on.*

HE/SHE WAS NOT A KISSER

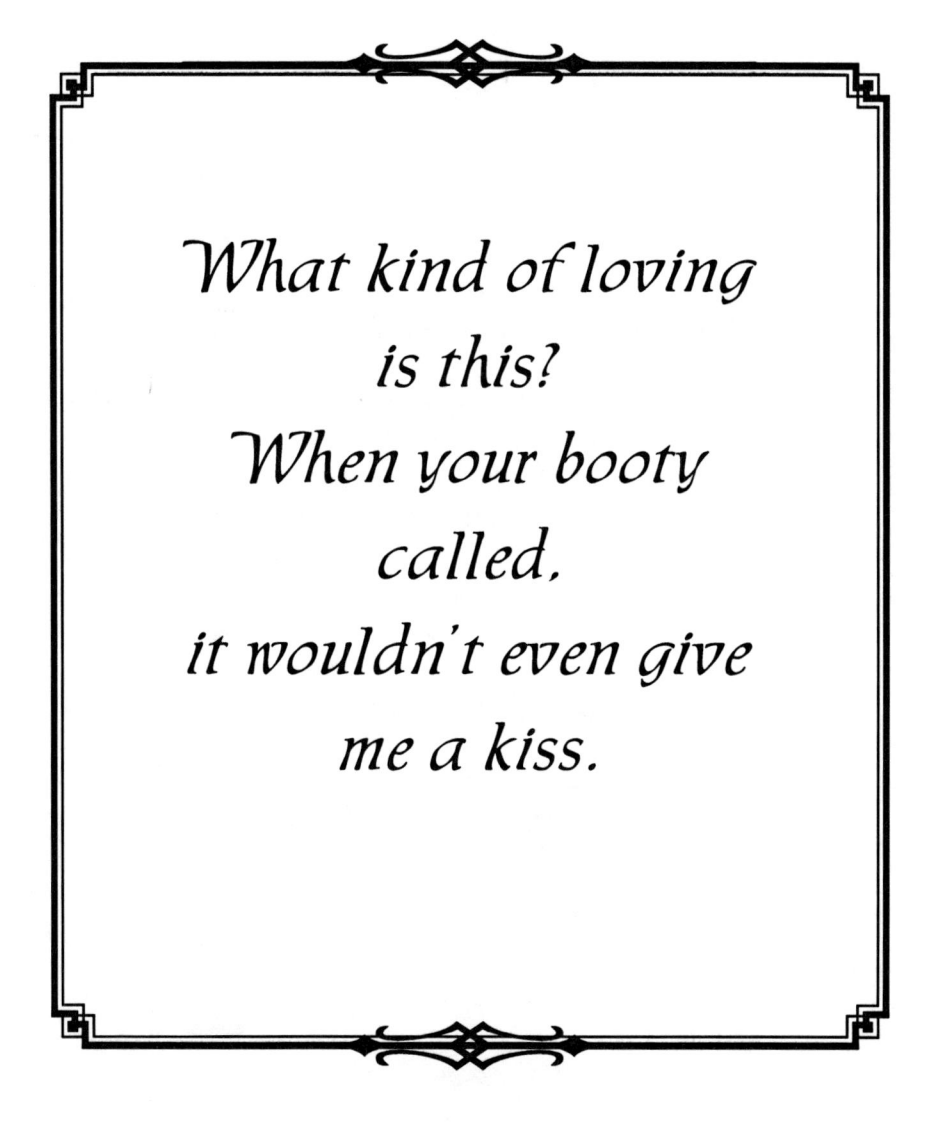

What kind of loving is this?
When your booty called,
it wouldn't even give me a kiss.

BACK STABBER

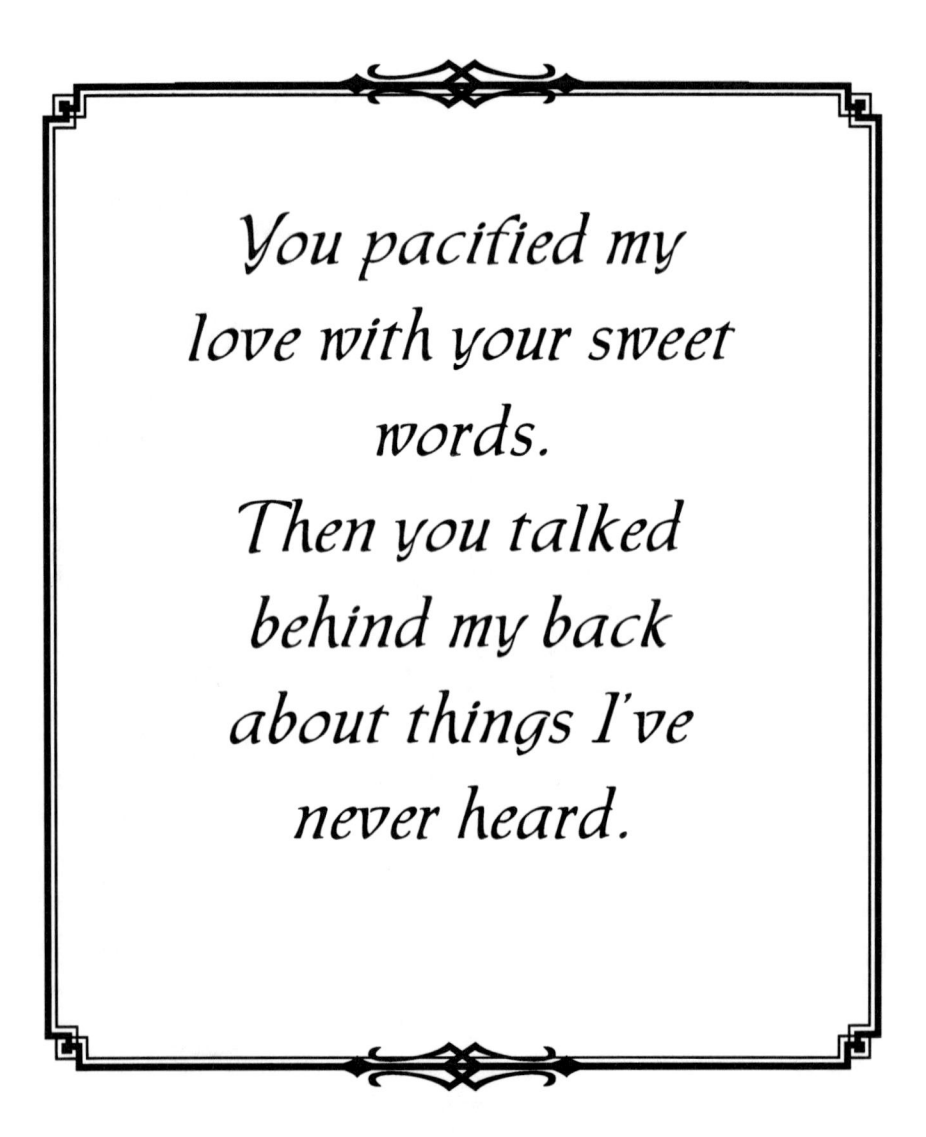

*You pacified my love with your sweet words.
Then you talked behind my back about things I've never heard.*

I'M OUT OF HERE

For years I tried to give you my love, but all you did was push me away. Now that I'm leaving, you have the nerve to beg me to stay.

IMPORTANT

*I've heard time
heals
a broken heart.
Please have mercy
and don't tear mine
apart.*

MERCY, MERCY

*Love hurts
the hurter.*

THINK ABOUT IT

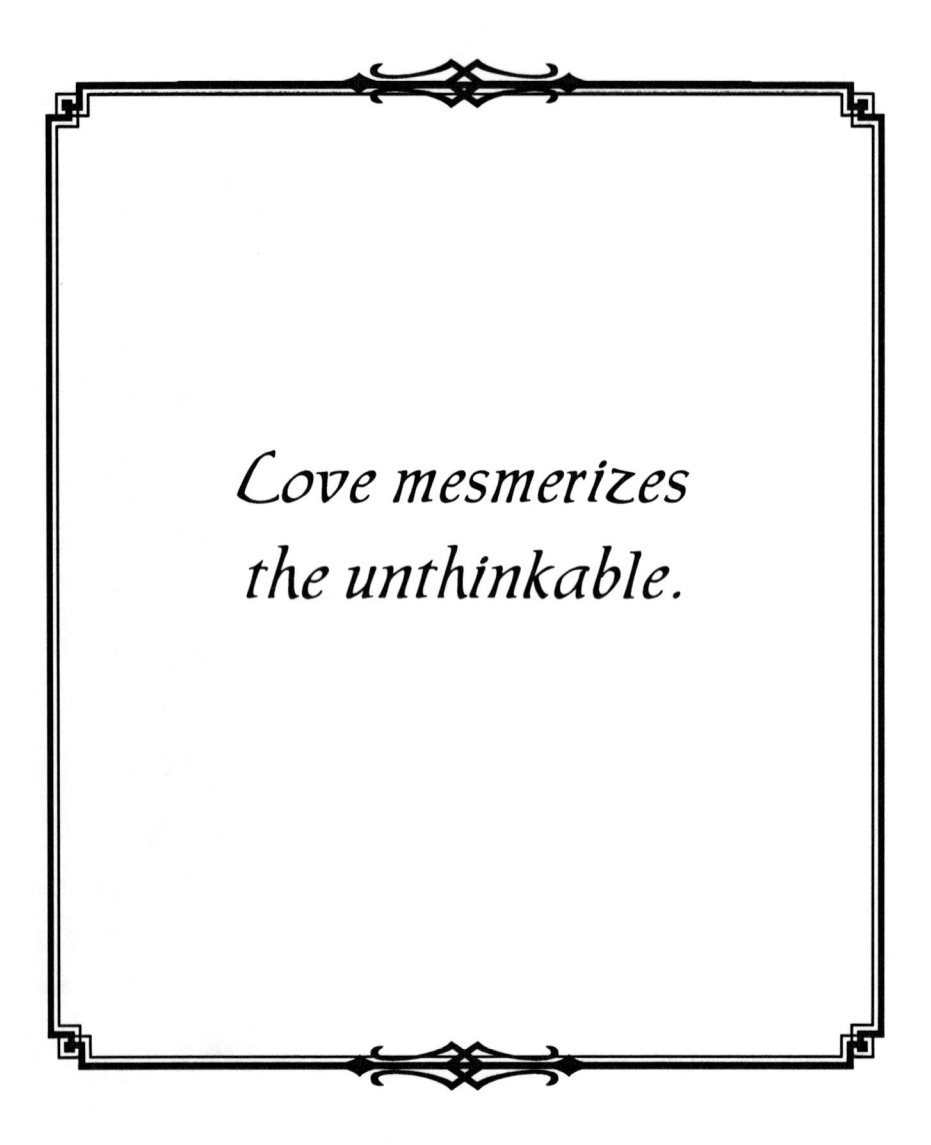

Love mesmerizes the unthinkable.

DO GOOD THINGS

*Love is here,
there and
everywhere.*

YOU SHOULD

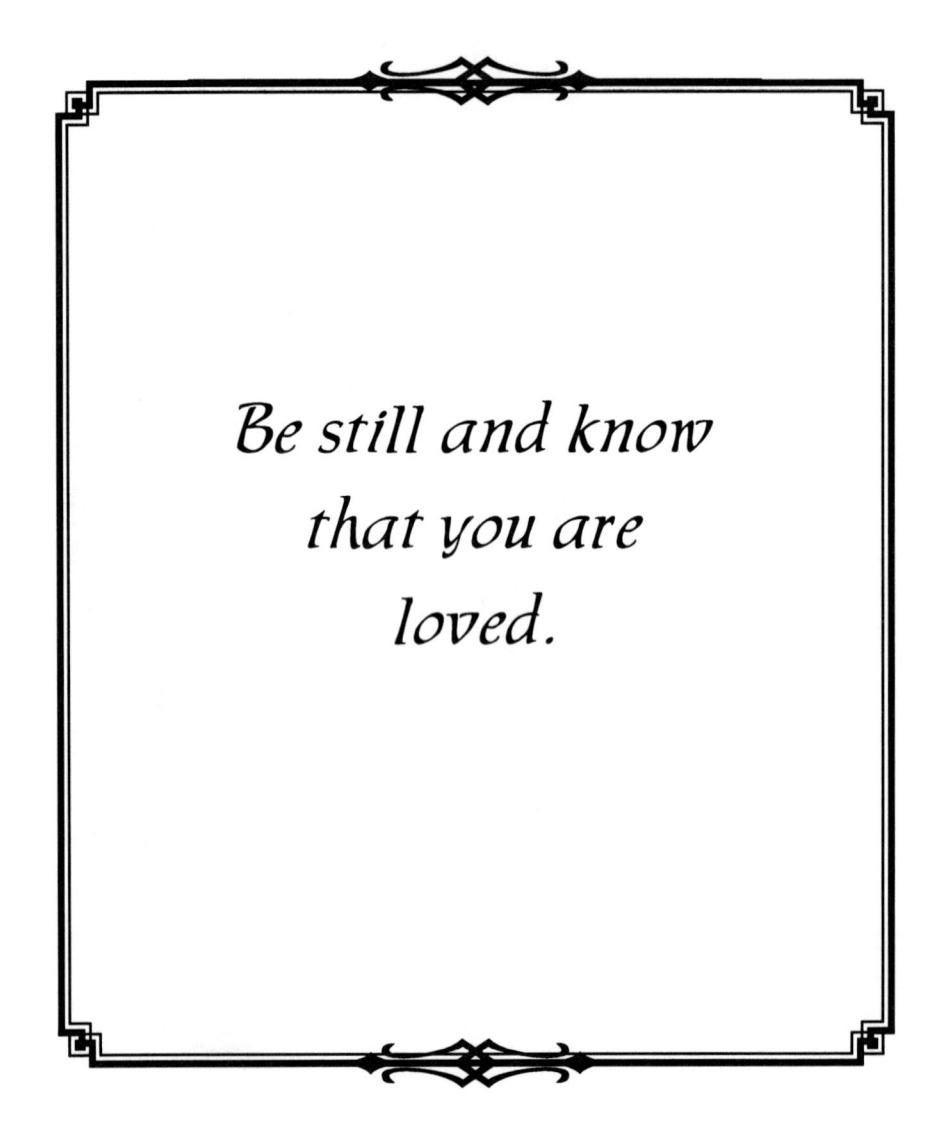

Be still and know that you are loved.

SUBMIT

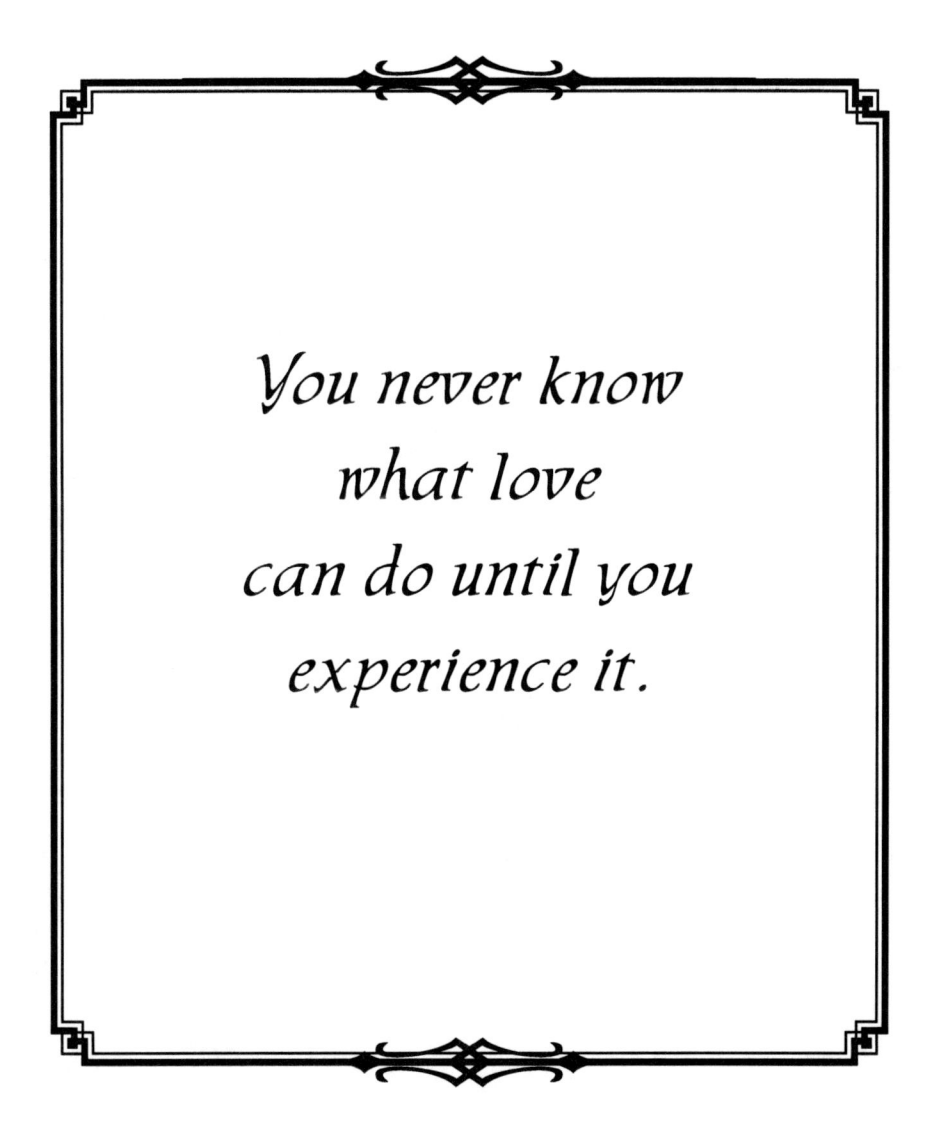

*You never know
what love
can do until you
experience it.*

MISTAKE

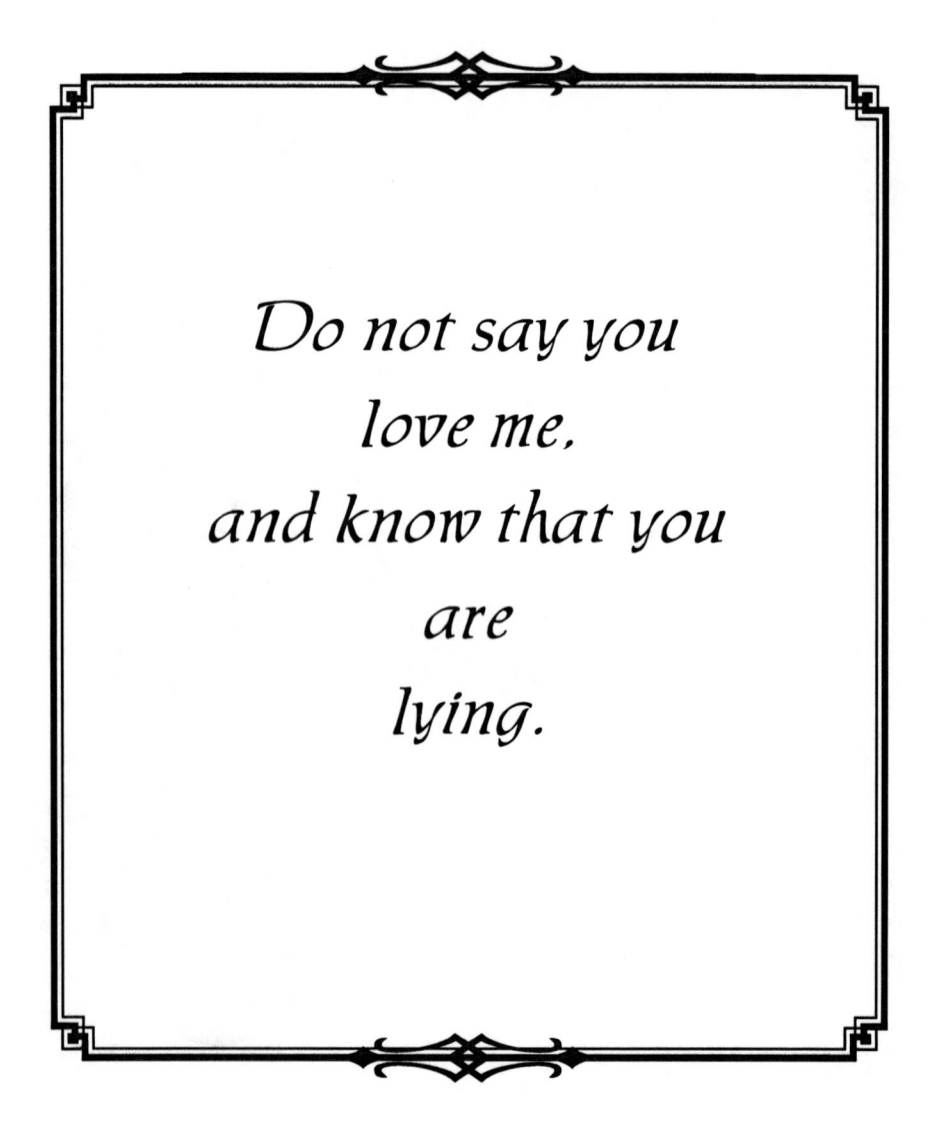

*Do not say you
love me,
and know that you
are
lying.*

WATCH YOURSELF

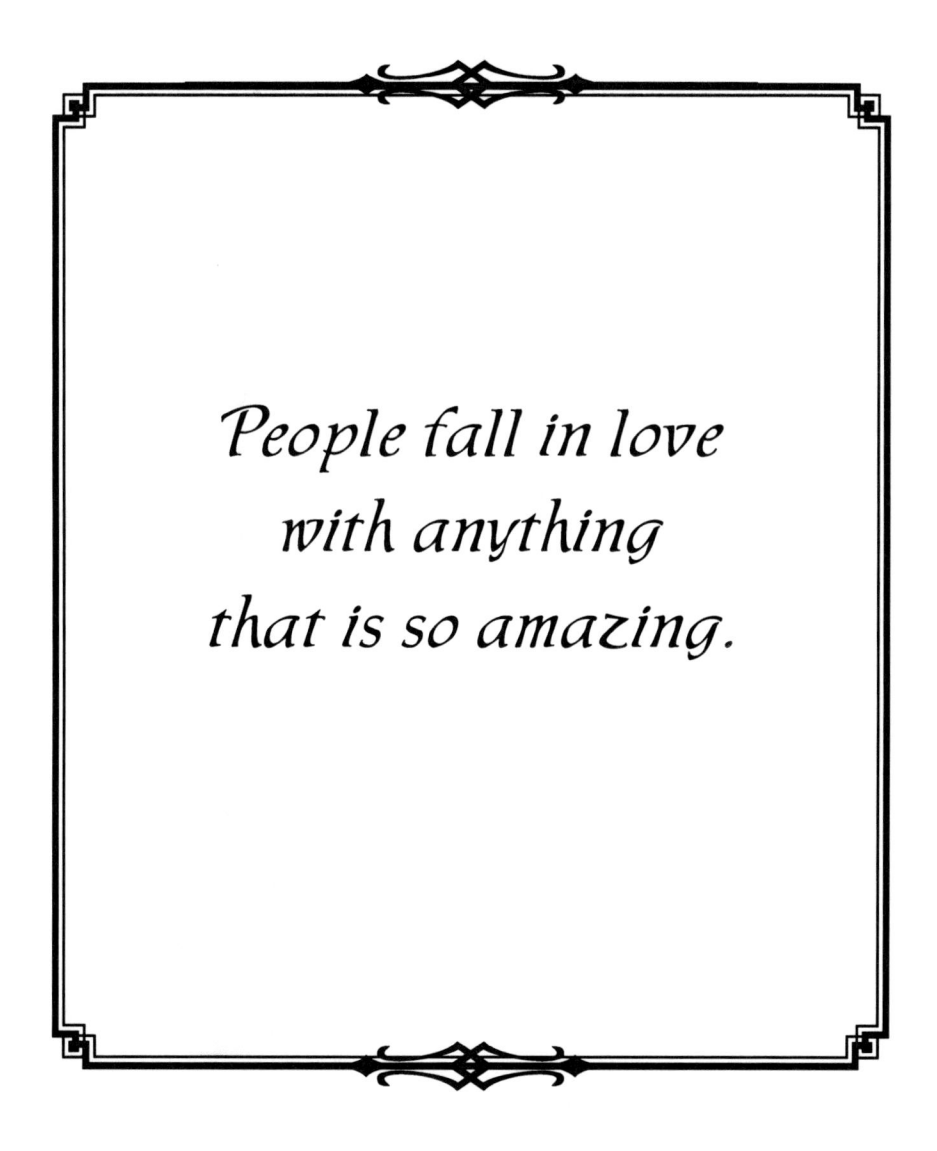

*People fall in love
with anything
that is so amazing.*

IF YOU BELIEVE

*Believe not with thy mind,
but with thy loving heart.*

REQUEST

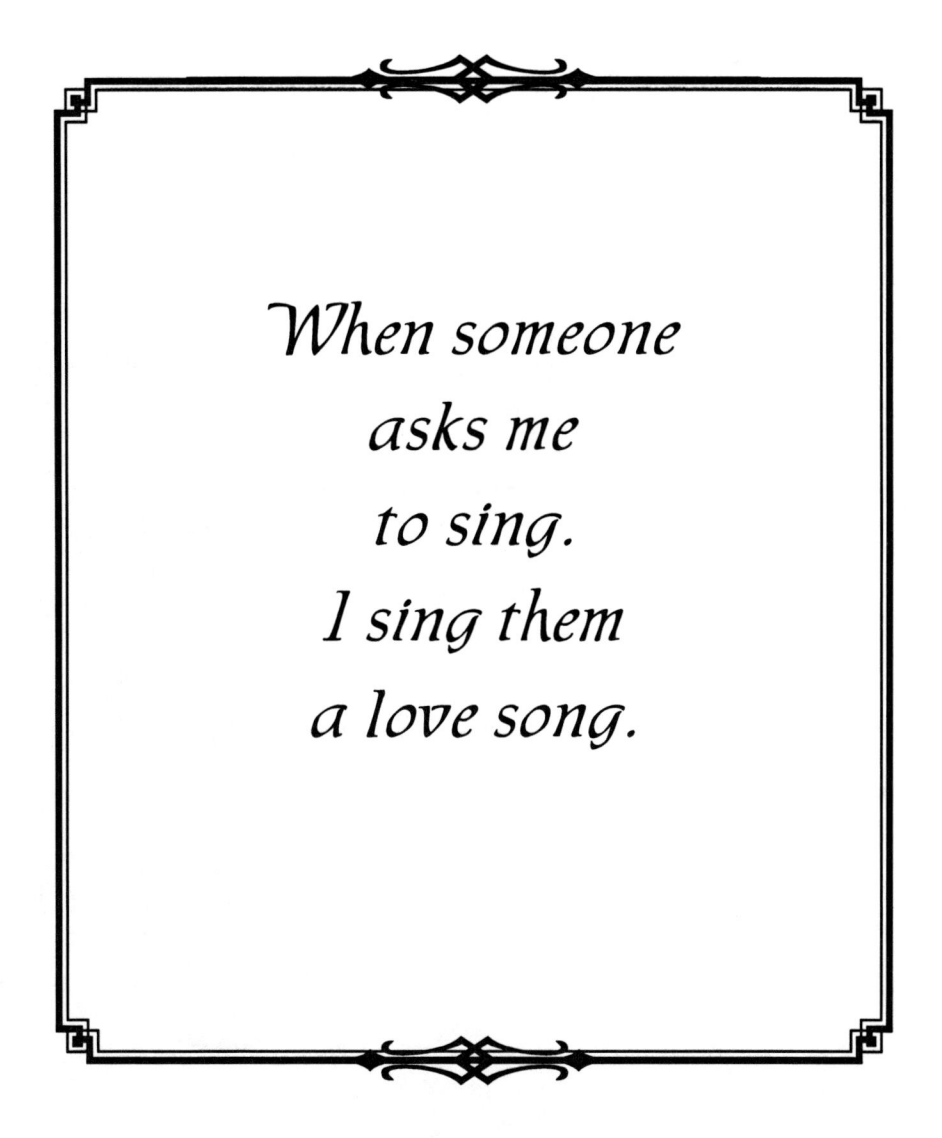

*When someone
asks me
to sing.
I sing them
a love song.*

SMILE IN

Love keeps a smile on my face.

LOVE HEALS

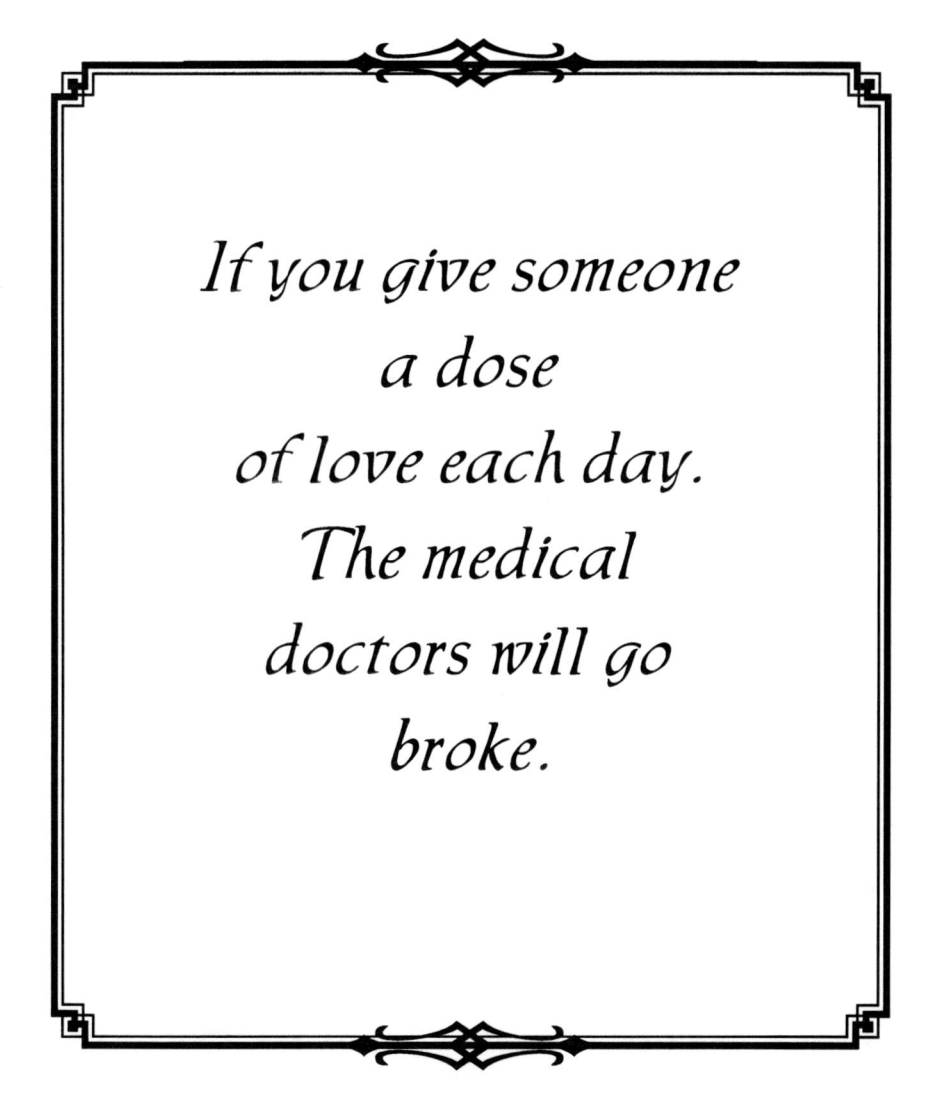

If you give someone a dose of love each day. The medical doctors will go broke.

GREETINGS

*This is the season of love.
Please make yourself accessible
to everyone.*

YOU GOT IT

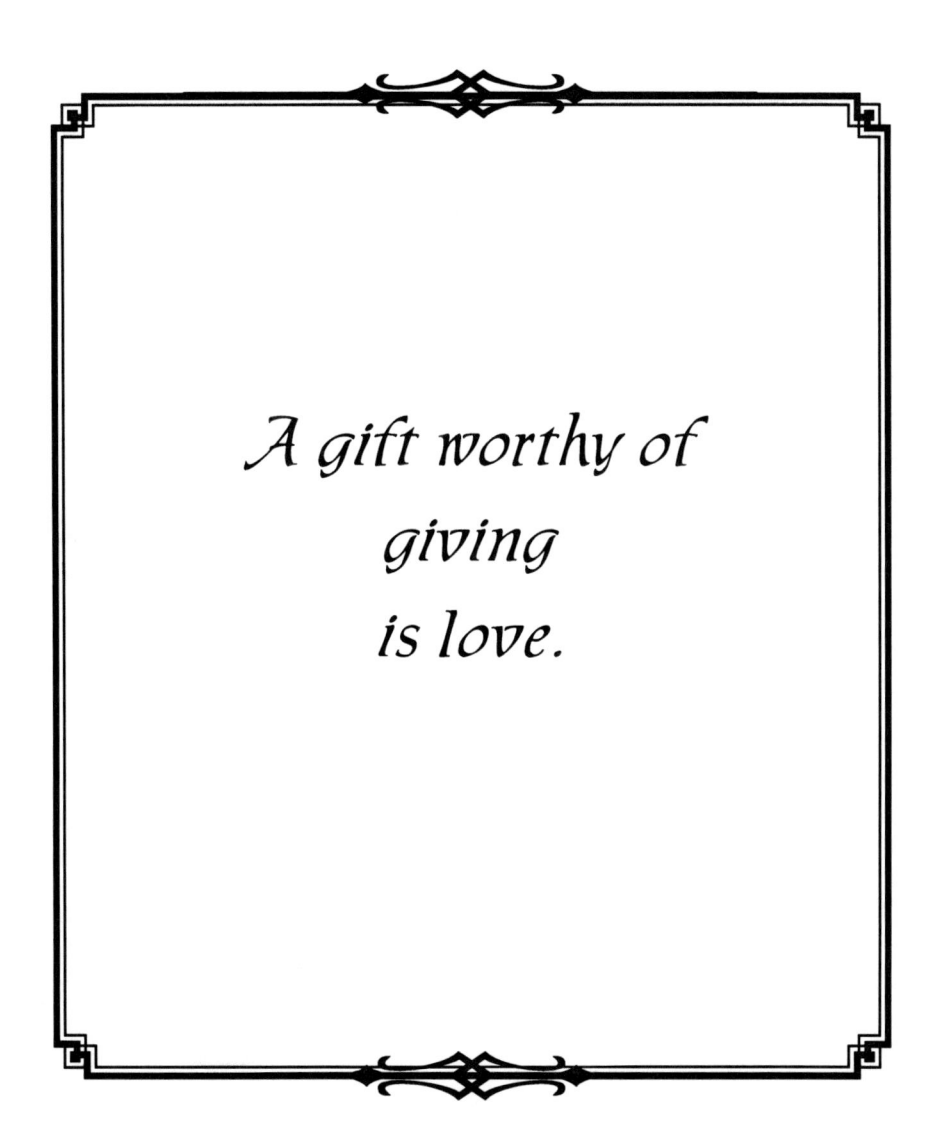

*A gift worthy of
giving
is love.*

INSEPARABLE

*Love sees beauty,
beauty sees love.*

BURN, BABY BURN

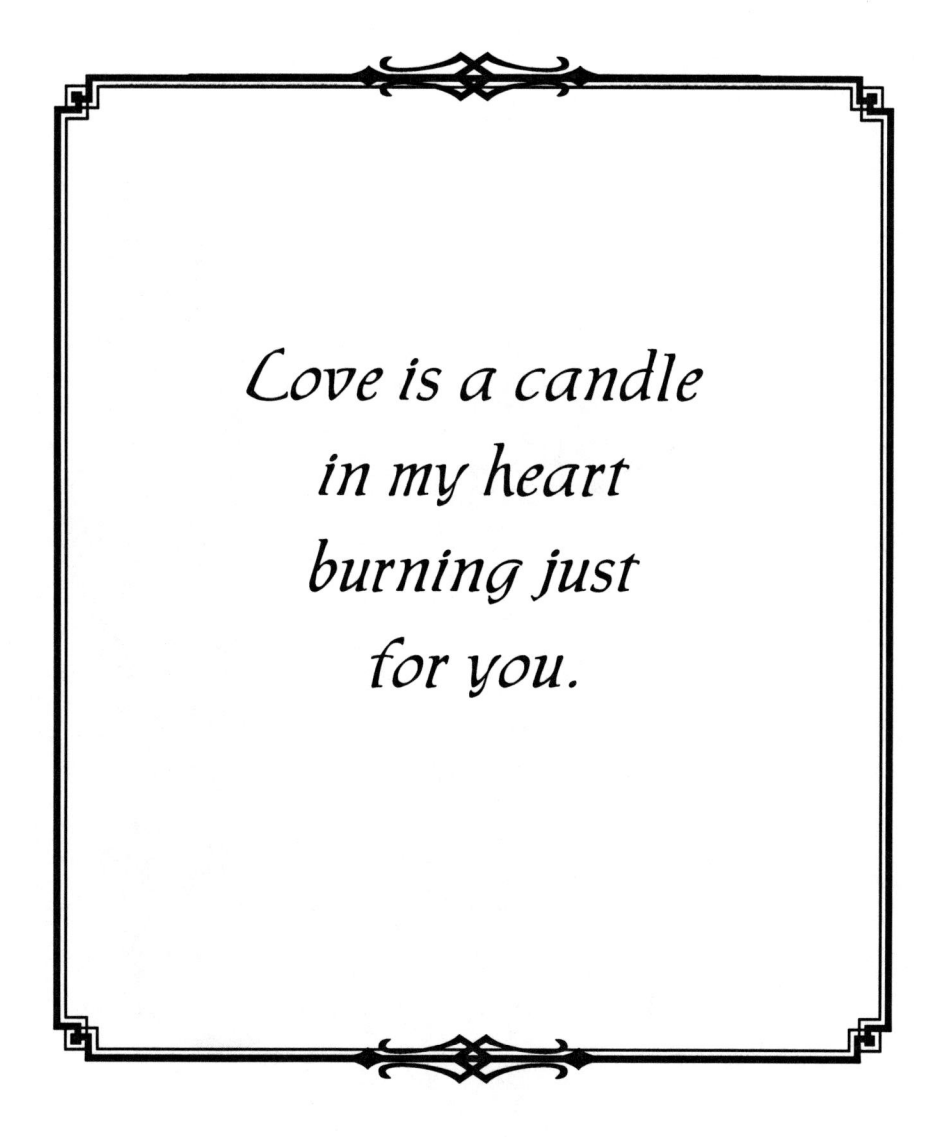

*Love is a candle
in my heart
burning just
for you.*

YOU ARE CRAZY

*Love is sweet.
Love is sour.
Don't get caught
without love
in the midnight
hour.*

ON THIS DAY

I'm sending you one and a million love poems.

WHISPER

I hear your voice in the wind when love whispers.

FOREVER

*Love could be a blast
if you commit
to make it last.*

WE GONNA MAKE IT

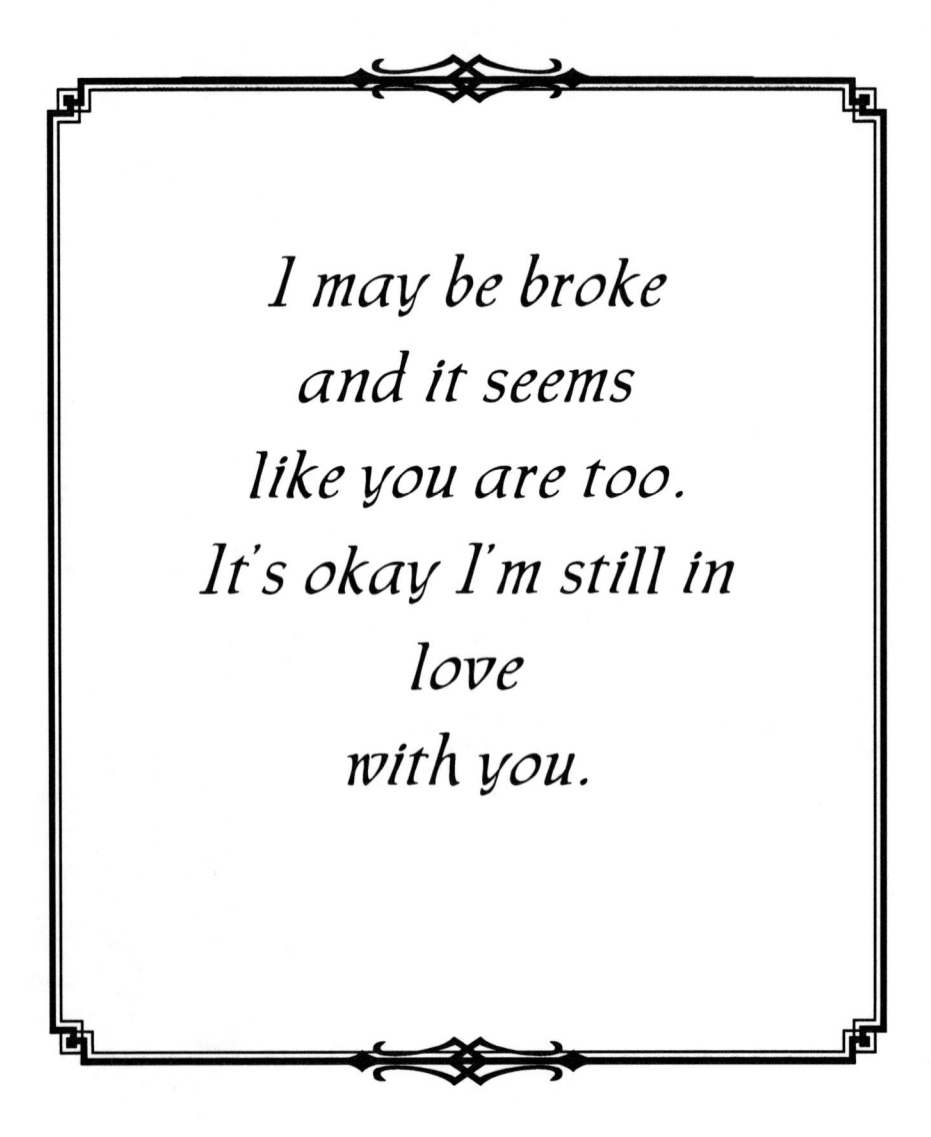

*I may be broke
and it seems
like you are too.
It's okay I'm still in
love
with you.*

MOMENTS ALONE

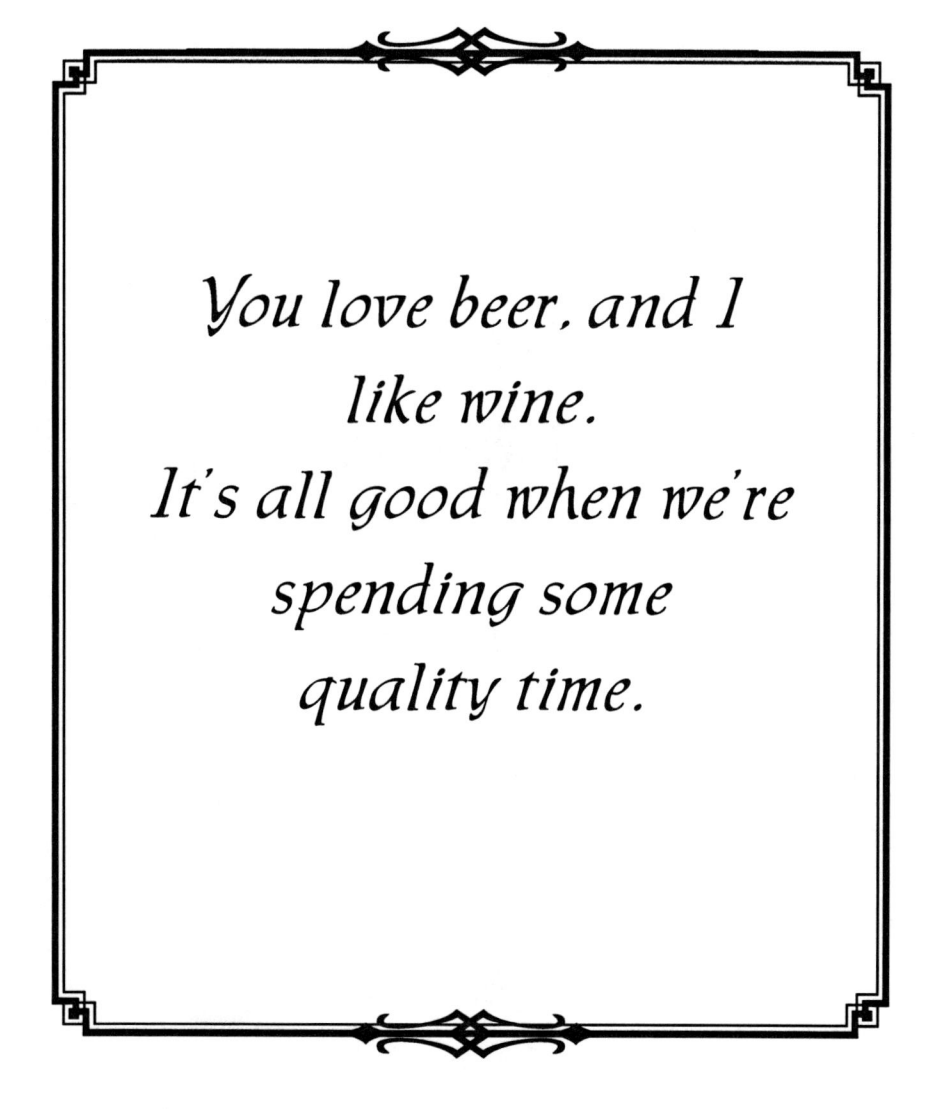

*You love beer, and I like wine.
It's all good when we're spending some quality time.*

REASSURING

The most exhilarating love I ever felt came from you.

FANTASY

*Beside the river
I sat with love.*

Dadisi Mwende Netifnet

THE JOY OF LIFE

*Love restores
laughter
in my soul.*

BE LOVABLE

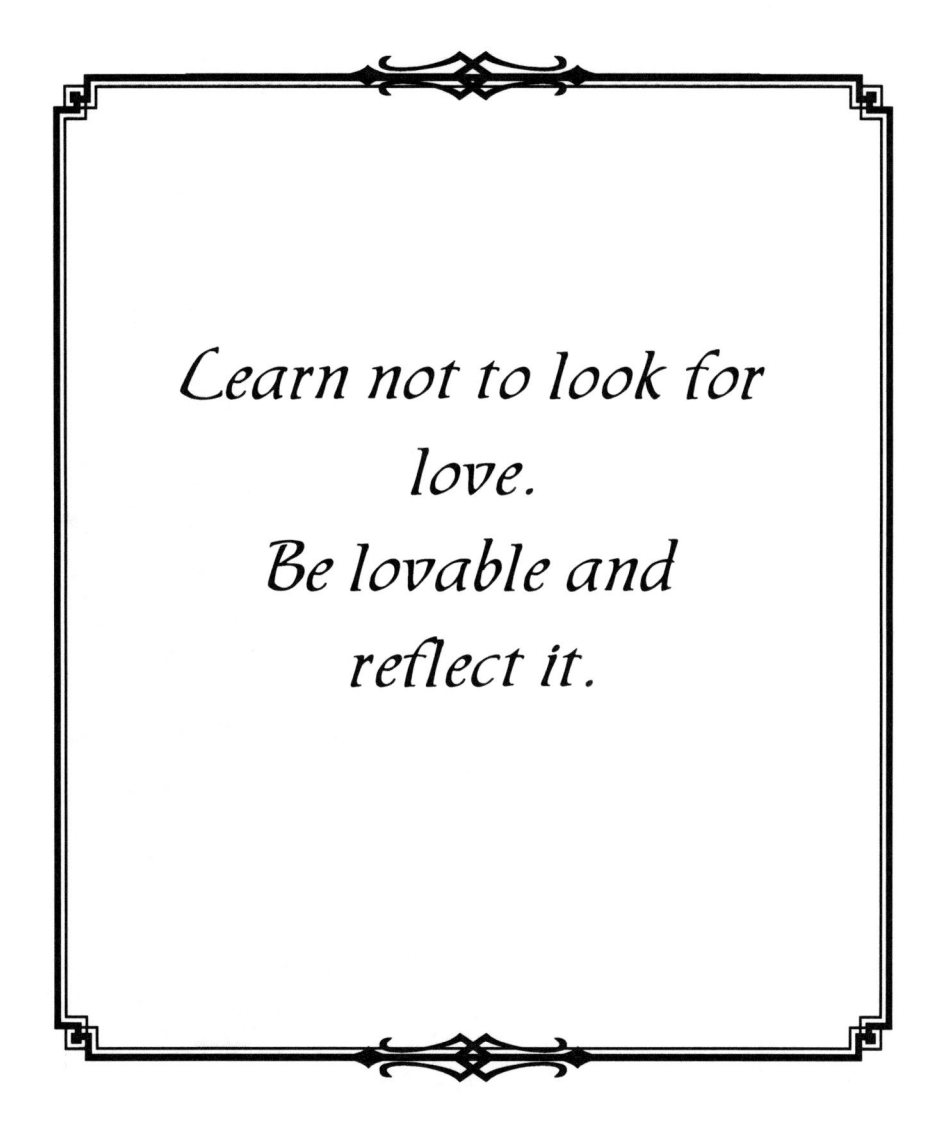

*Learn not to look for love.
Be lovable and reflect it.*

LEGEND SAYS

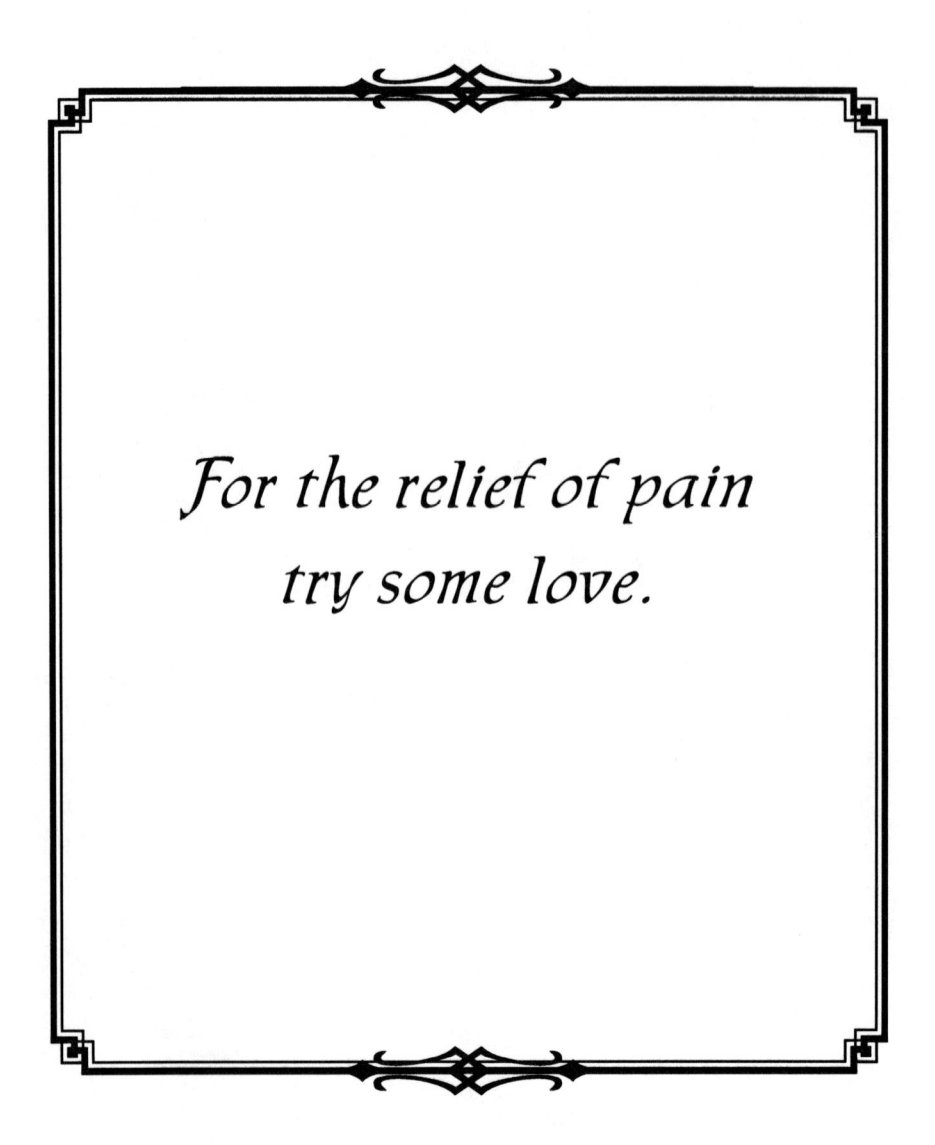

*For the relief of pain
try some love.*

WE'RE GOING TO GROW

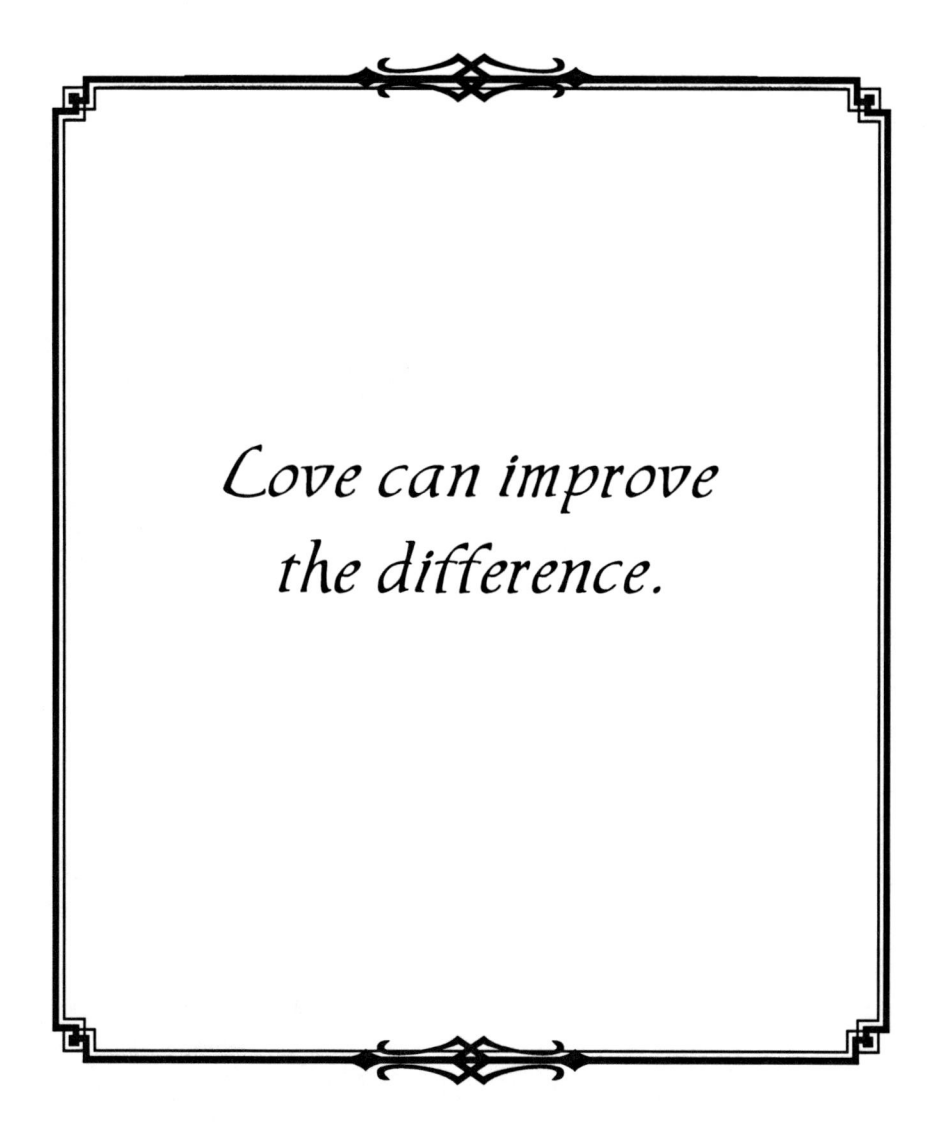

*Love can improve
the difference.*

BE SMART

Give love abundantly and it will not let you down.

COME ON IN

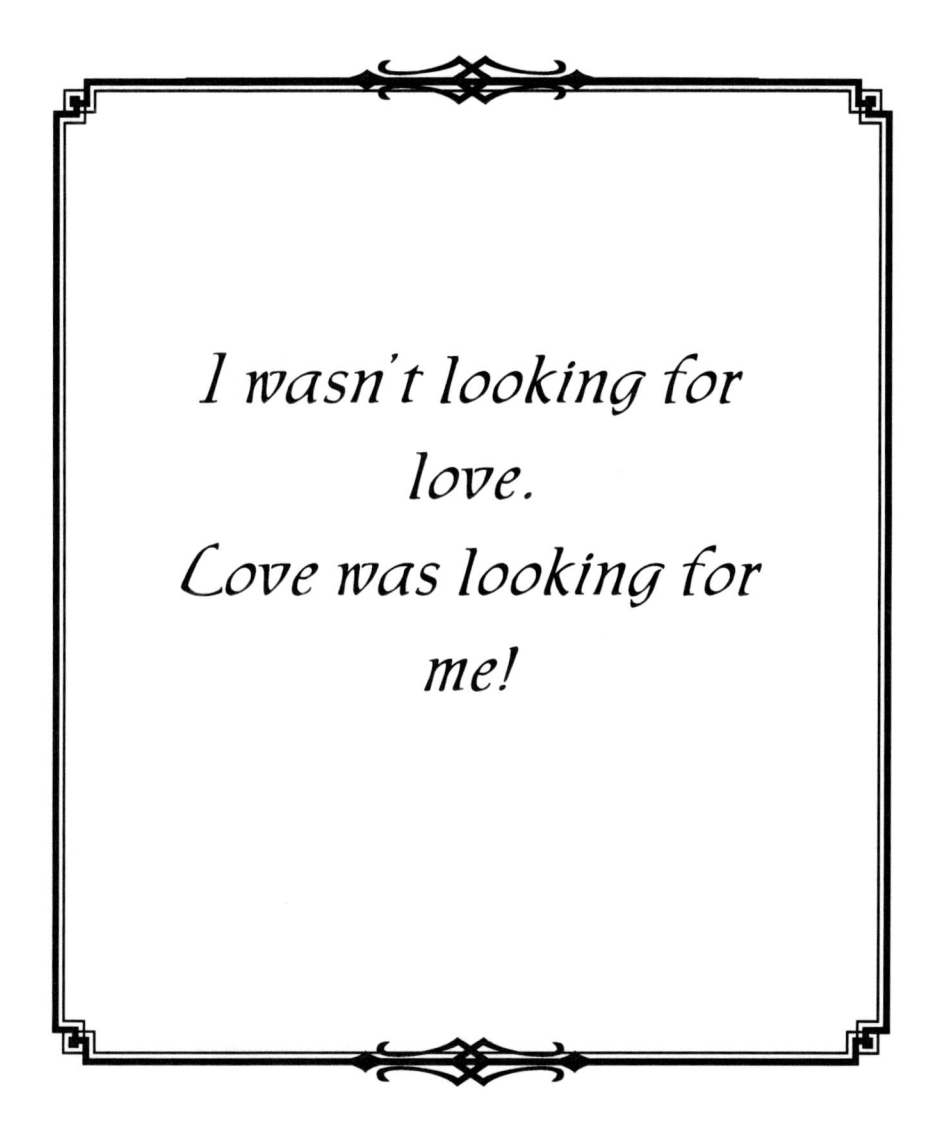

*I wasn't looking for love.
Love was looking for me!*

WHY LOVE MORE?

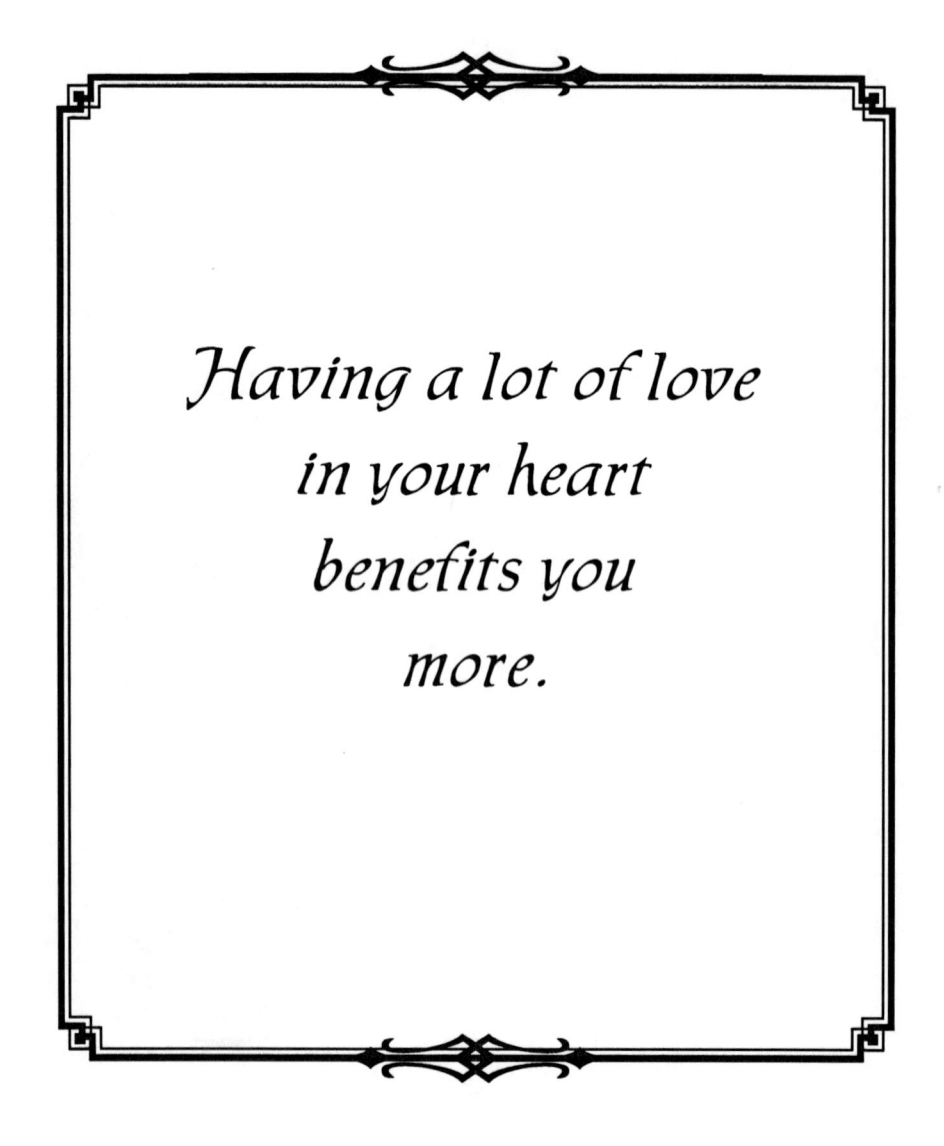

Having a lot of love in your heart benefits you more.

SELF LOVE

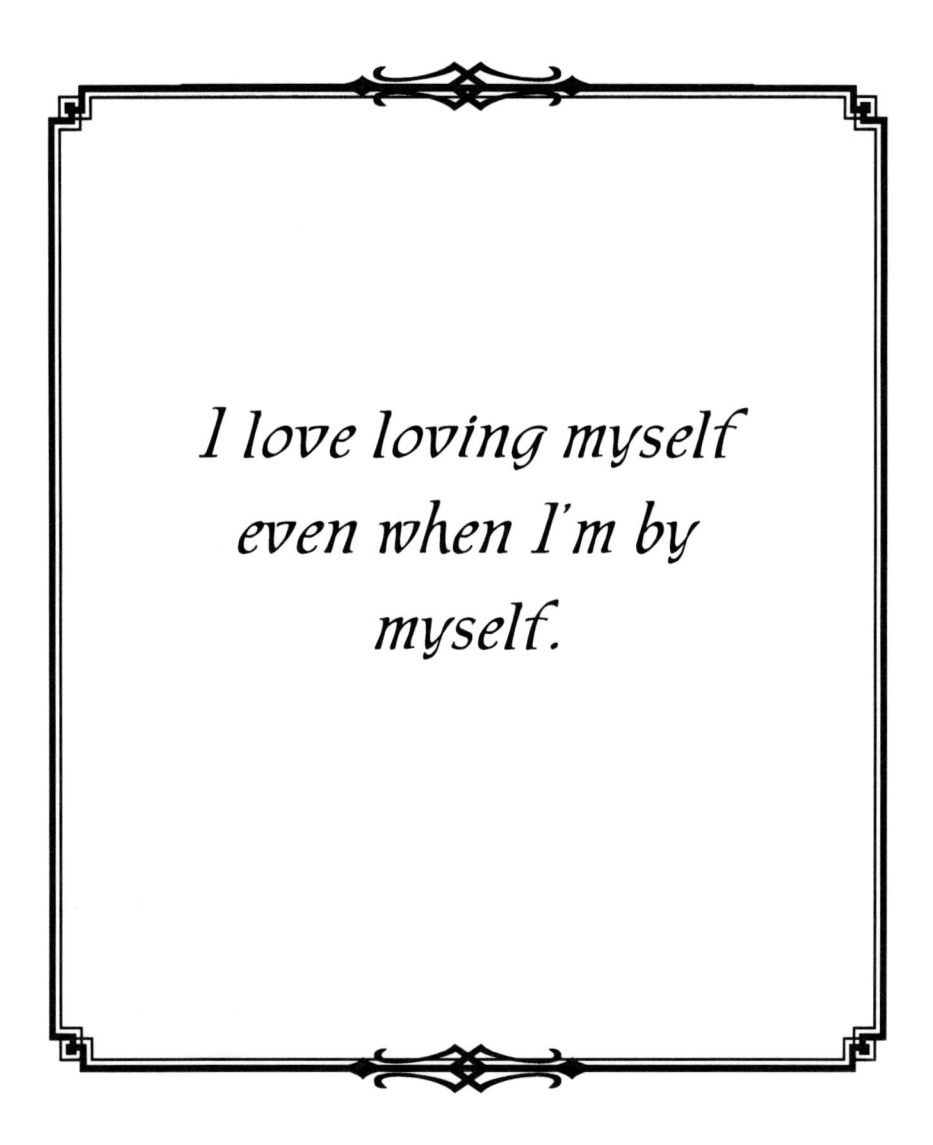

I love loving myself even when I'm by myself.

FEARMINDED

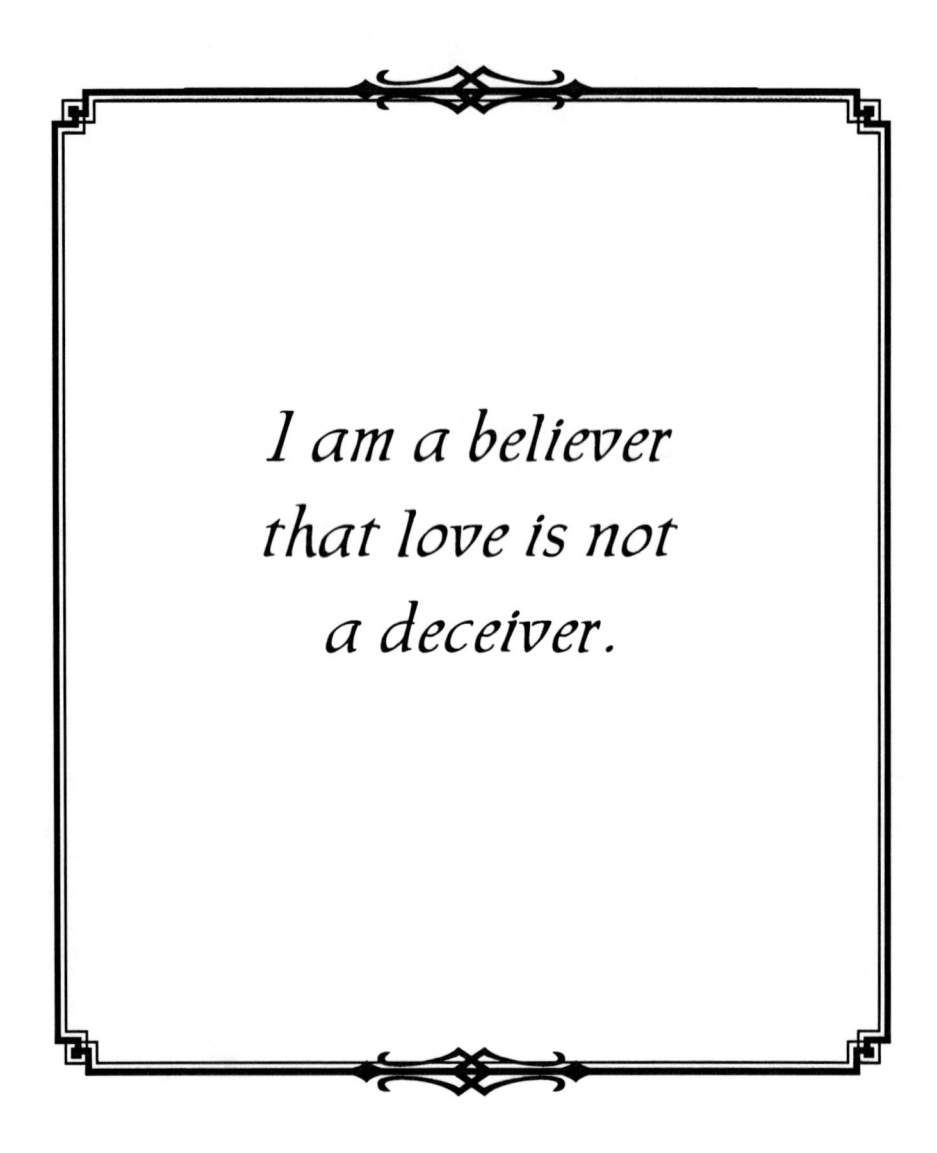

*I am a believer
that love is not
a deceiver.*

REMEMBER

Love respects a silent moment.

EXCITEMENT

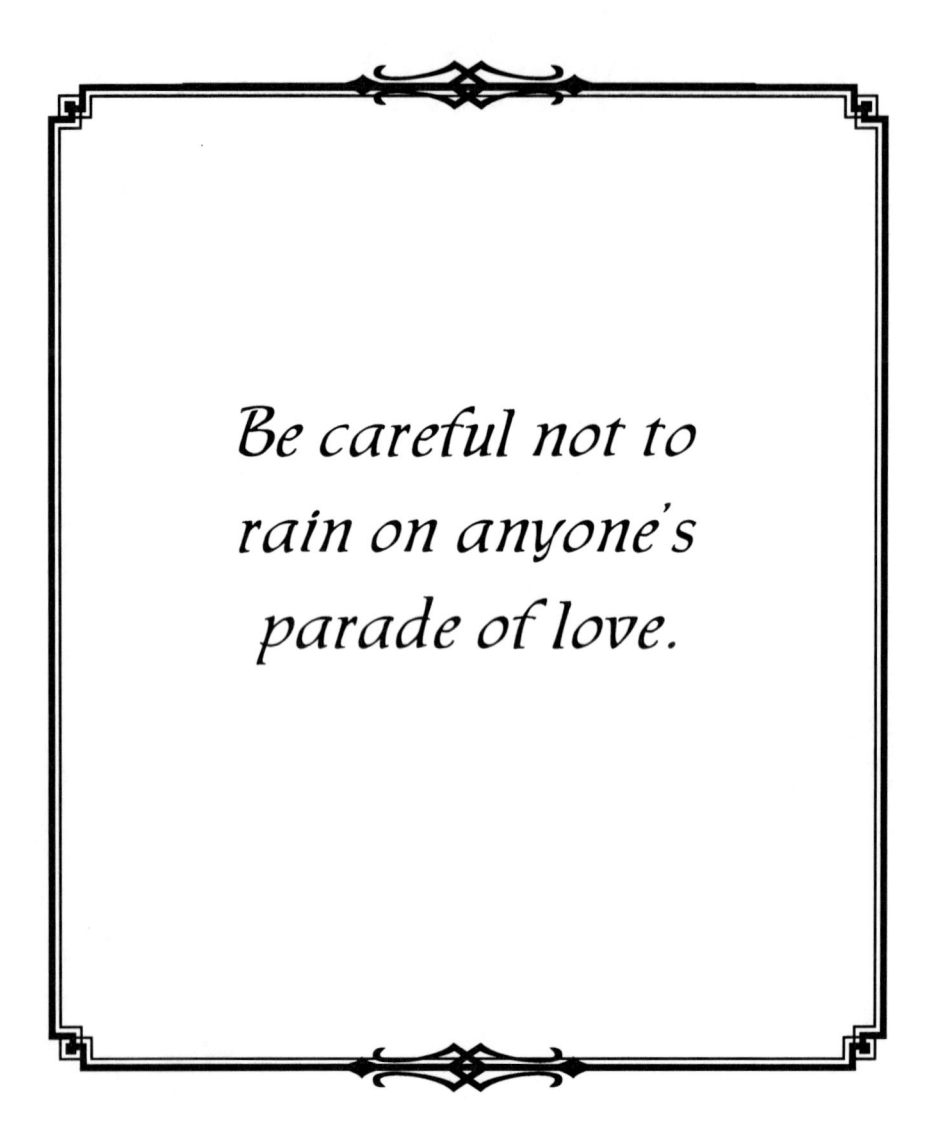

Be careful not to rain on anyone's parade of love.

PROGRAM

Notice to all students: activate your love before stepping into my classroom.

WAIT A MINUTE

*Give me love the way
love should be given.*

VISUALIZE IT

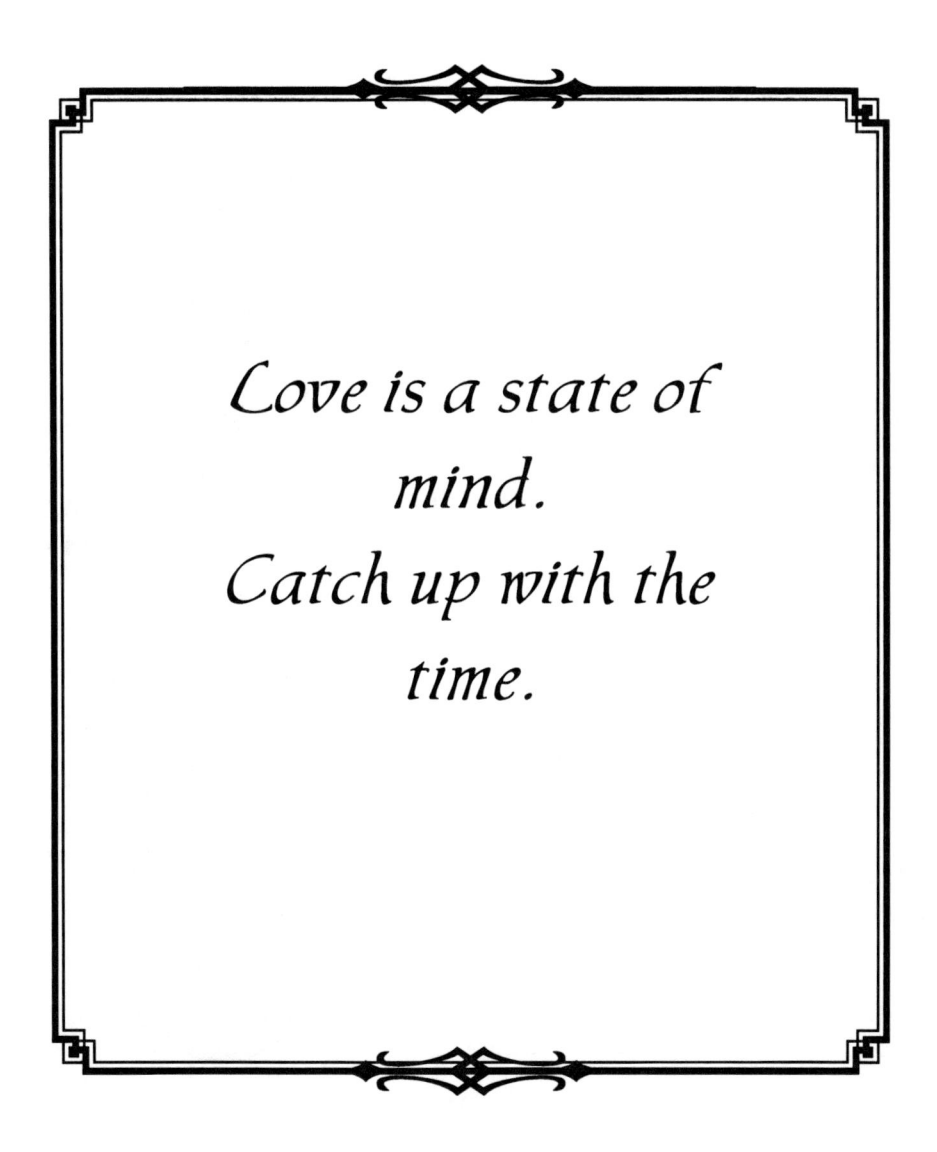

Love is a state of mind. Catch up with the time.

ACCOMMODATE

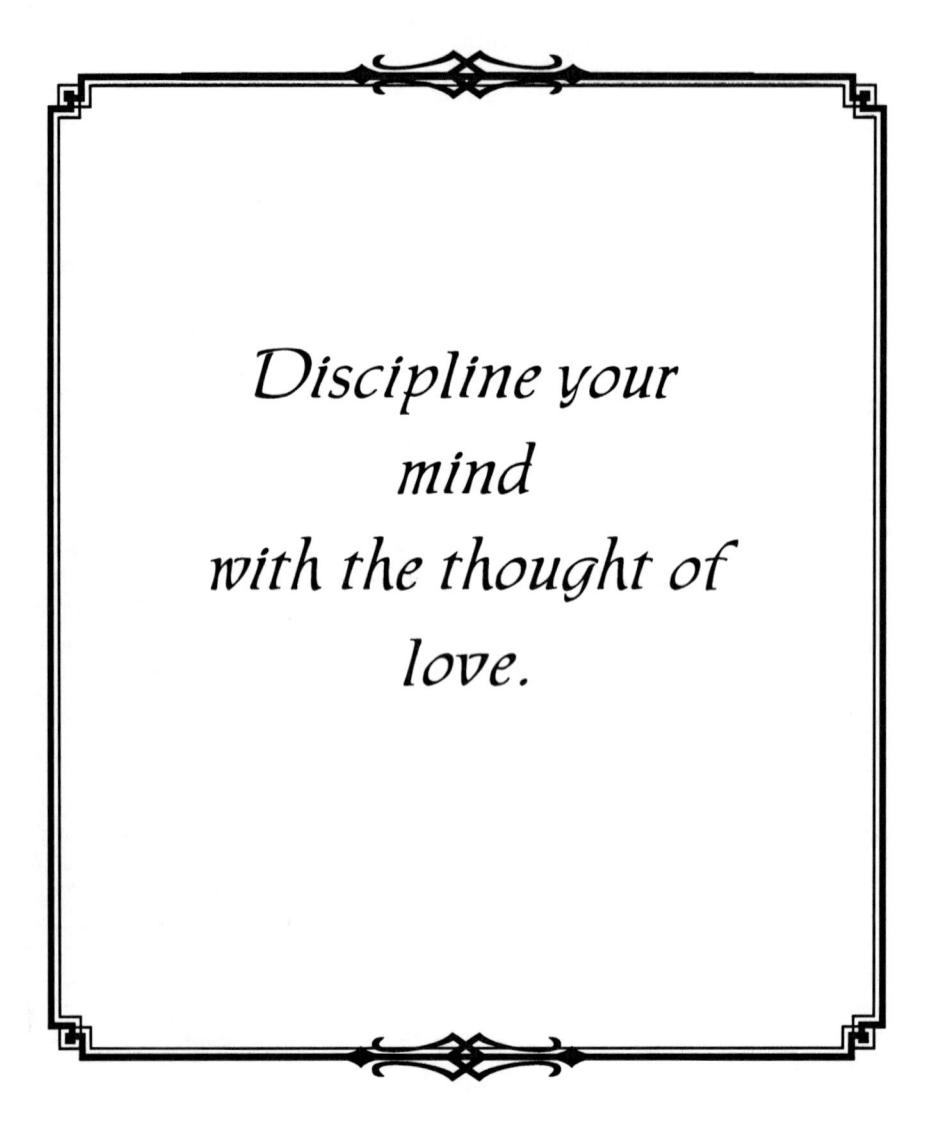

Discipline your mind with the thought of love.

HEAT

*On a cold night
I dreamt of heat
that only love
can bring.*

QUEST

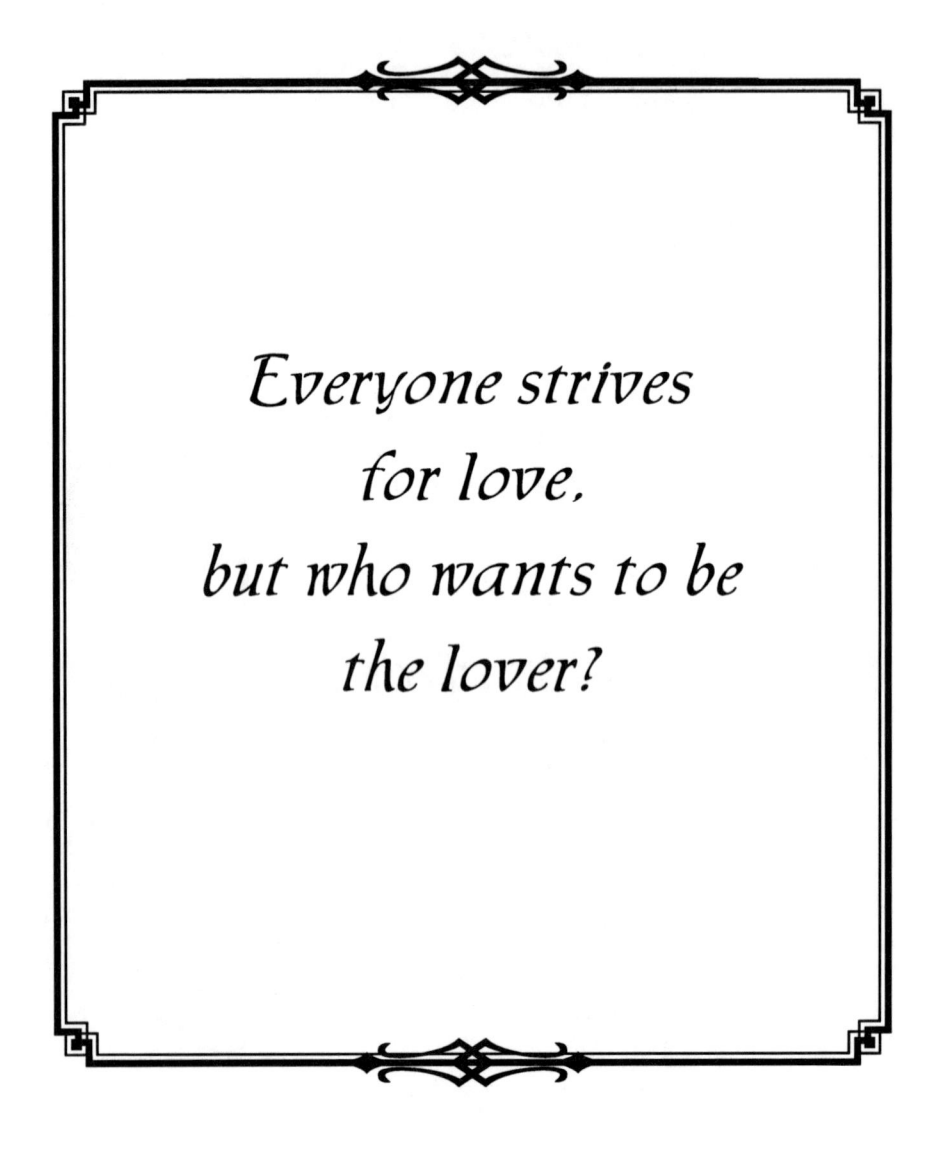

*Everyone strives
for love,
but who wants to be
the lover?*

I SAY

*Love has style
sometimes
it takes awhile.*

DON'T SHY AWAY

Make training your heart to love convenient.

LISTEN

Love never lose sight of your goal.

REALLY

It's fun to be in love.

CONFLICT

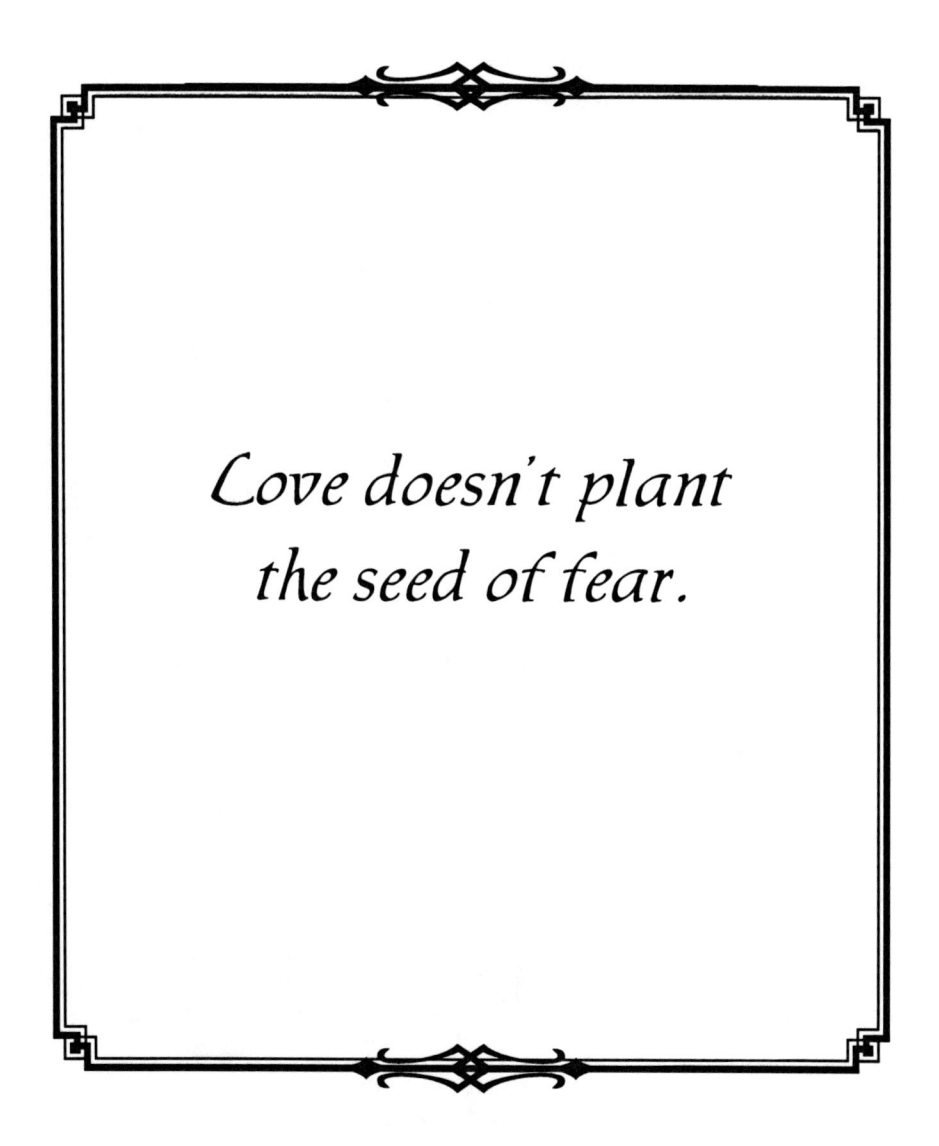

Love doesn't plant the seed of fear.

MORE TIMES WITHIN

*Please make sure
your heart
is sincere before we
begin
this deep
conversation.*

ADMIT

*Due to the fact that
you don't
love me anymore,
I will admit
that I hate to see
you go.
So long my beloved.*

TRUE TO THYSELF

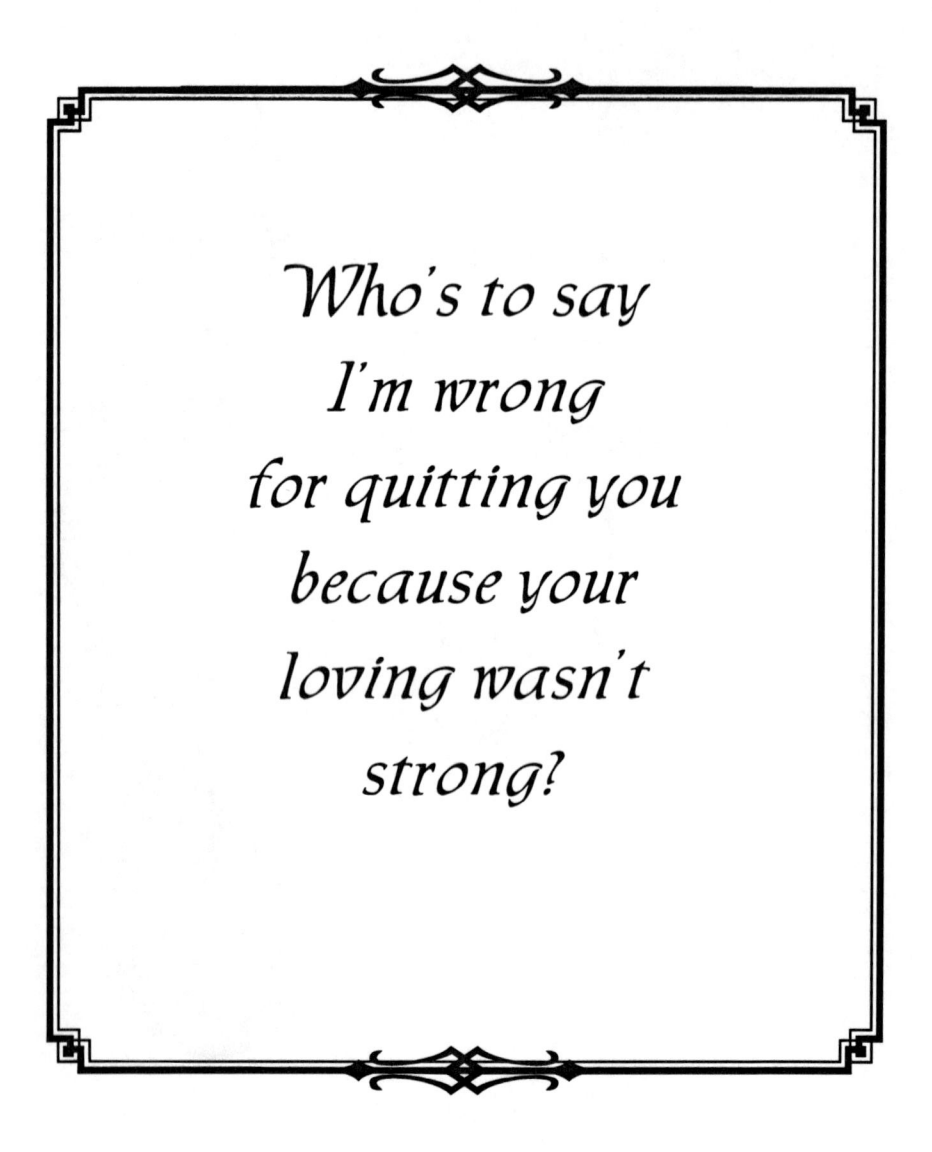

*Who's to say
I'm wrong
for quitting you
because your
loving wasn't
strong?*

DON'T FORGET

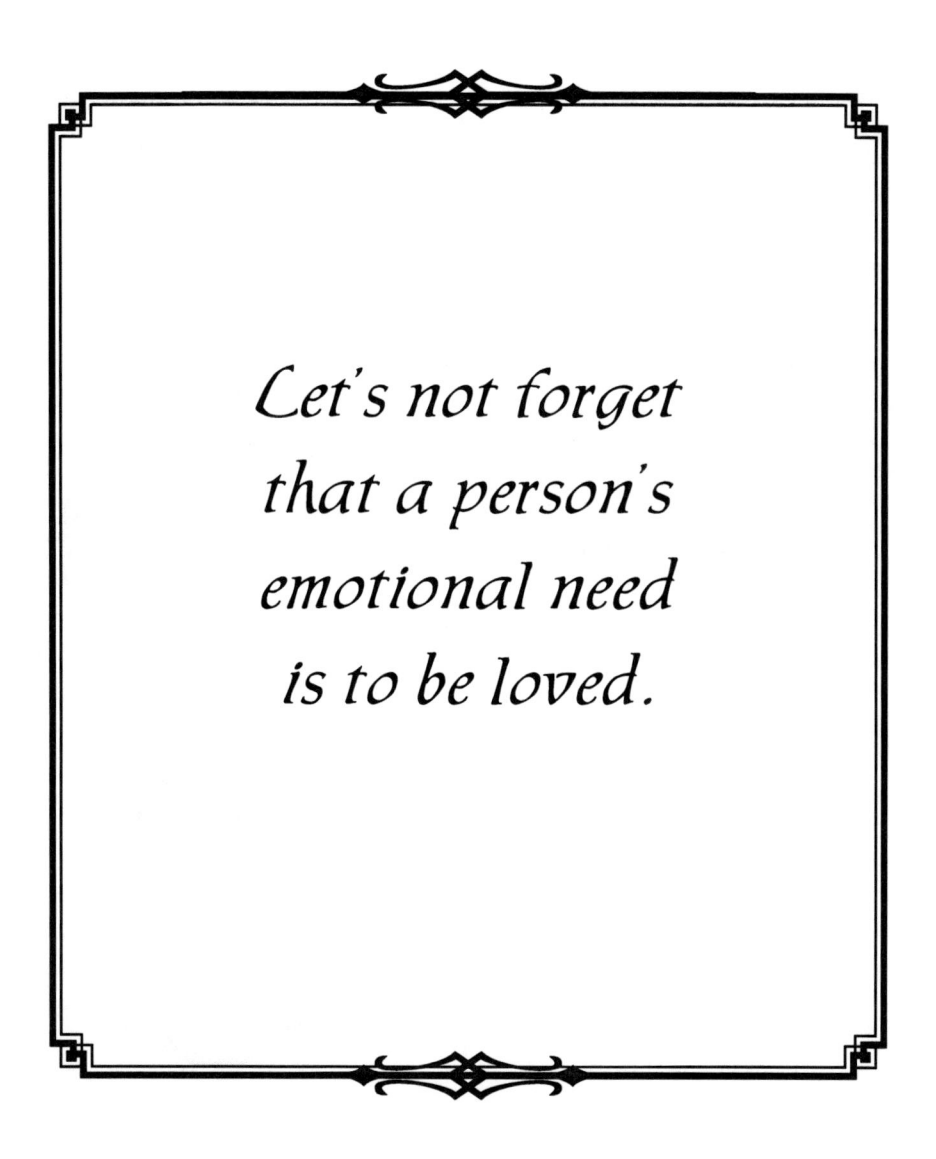

Let's not forget that a person's emotional need is to be loved.

LOVE POLICY

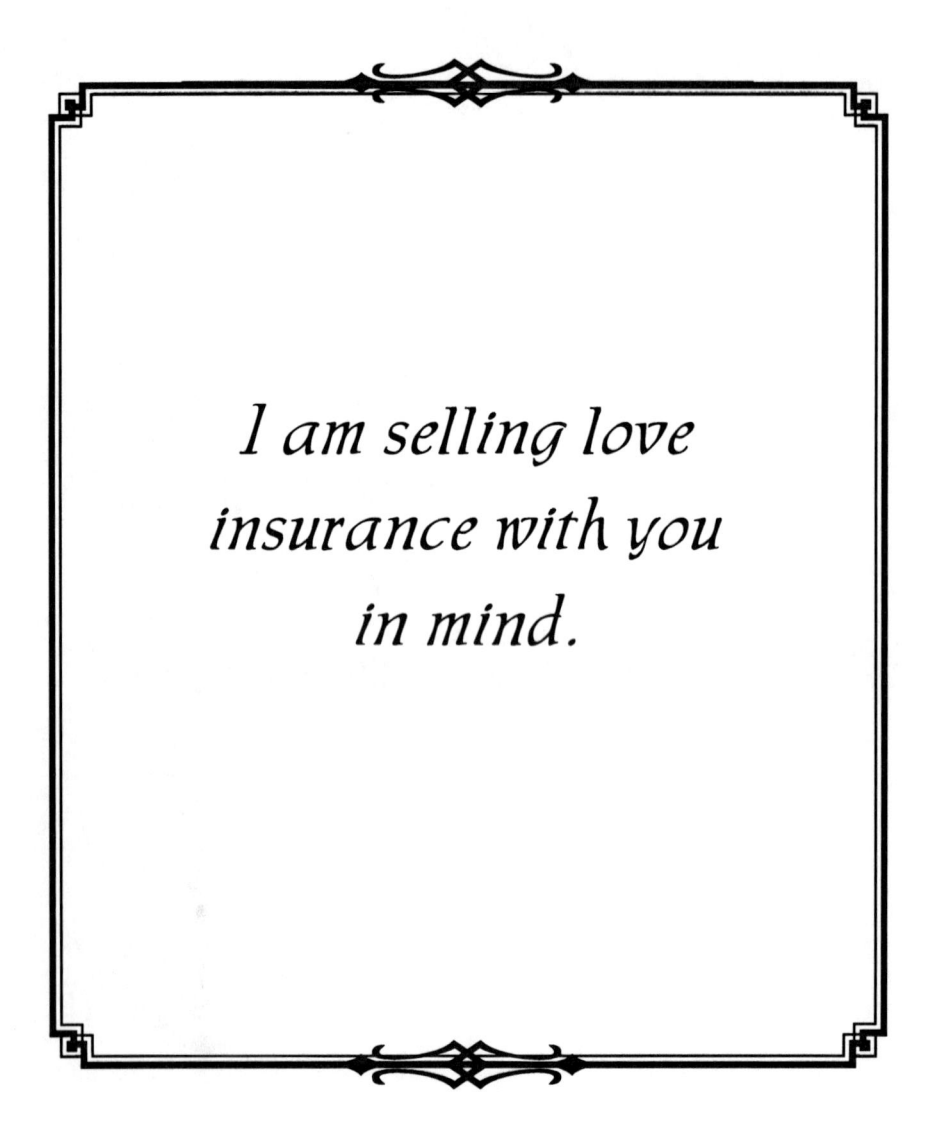

I am selling love insurance with you in mind.

YOUR GROUP

Cash in on your circle of love.

BEST FRIENDS

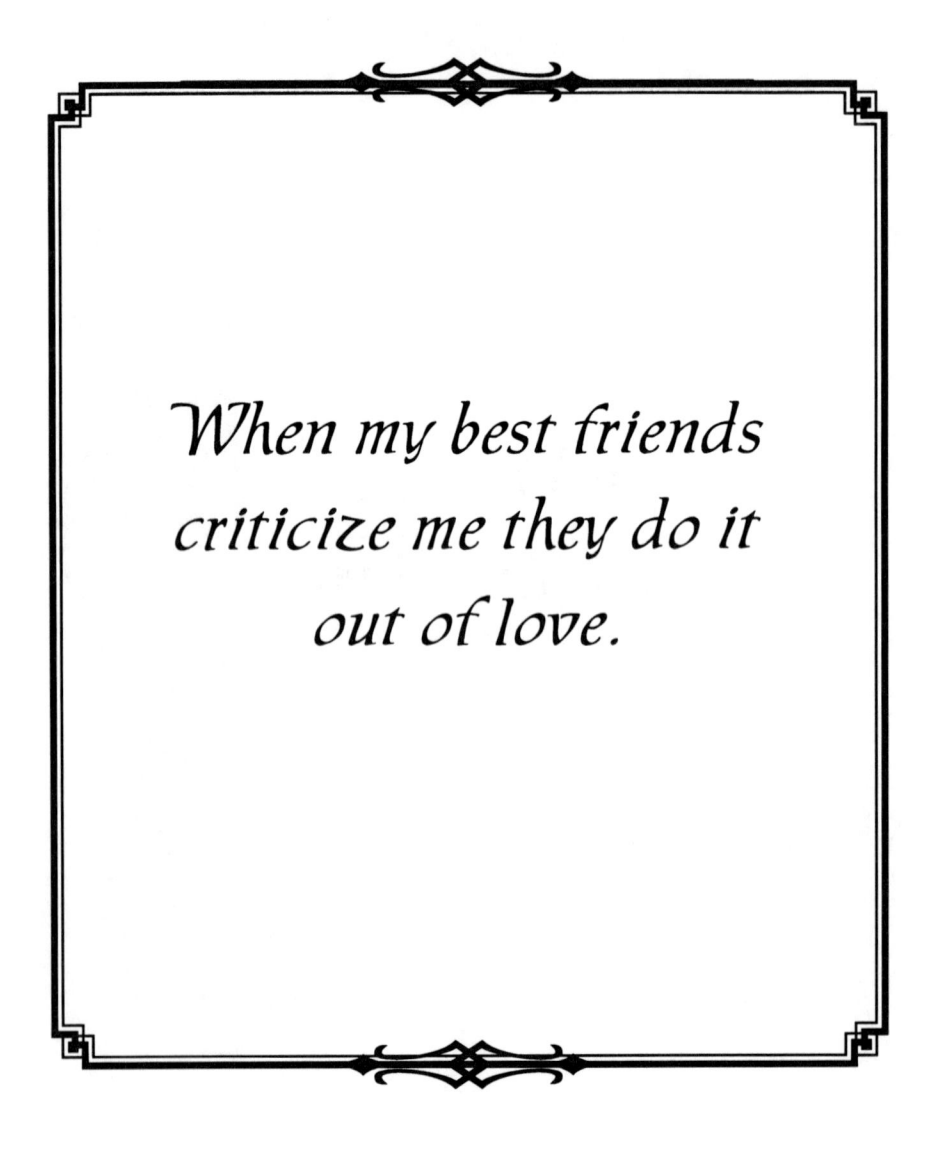

When my best friends criticize me they do it out of love.

THE HUMAN SOUL

Nothing is impossible to love.

EXTINGUSISH

Strive to minimize the love you lost.

MY OPINION

*Forget your lover
of the past.
You see it
didn't last.*

YOU KNOW

*I've heard it said,
"It's cheaper to keep her".
But what if he/she doesn't
love you anymore?*

EMPATHIZE

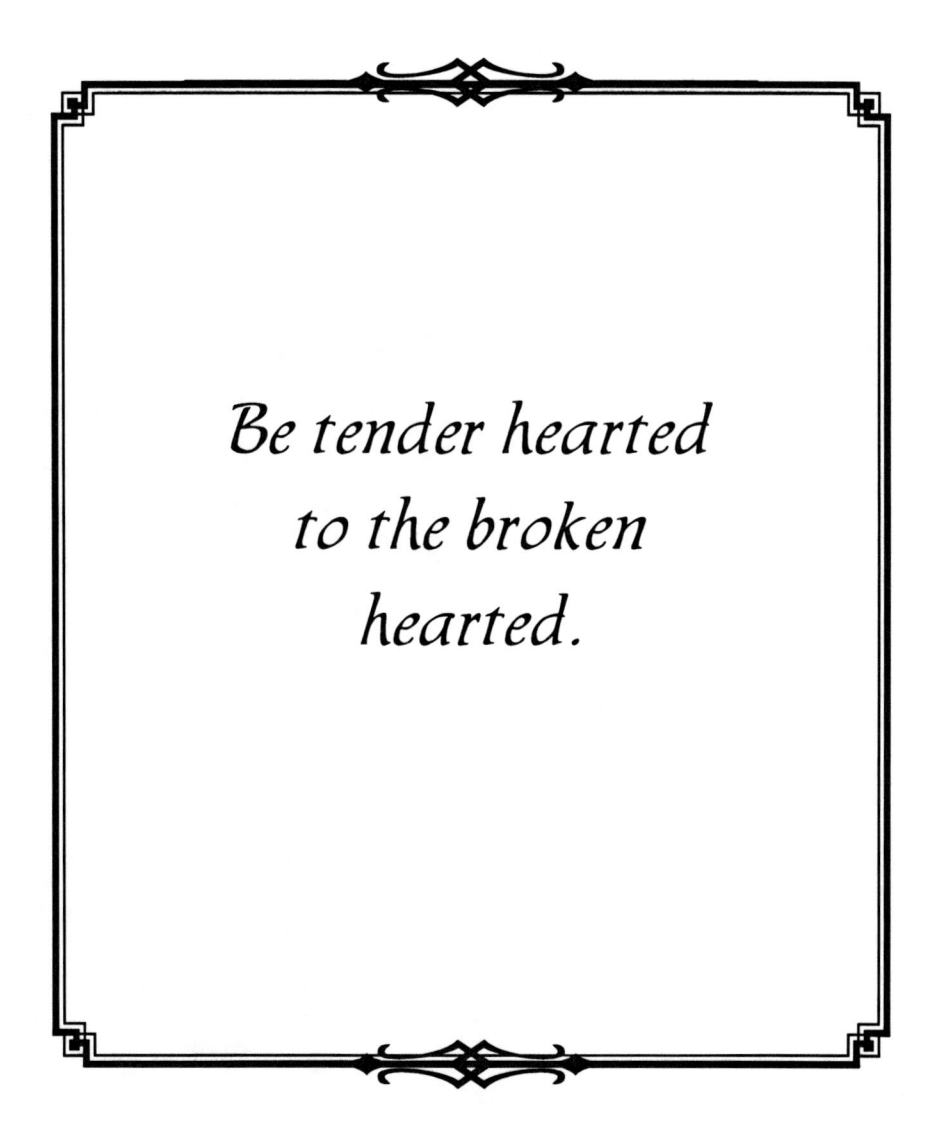

Be tender hearted to the broken hearted.

WAIT

*Before you fall in love
wait for further
instructions
from your heart.*

LONELY ONE

Believe in love and love will believe in you.

NO SECOND GUESS

Learn more about this new lover you have found.

CONFRONTING

*Seek and you shall find.
Love isn't blind.*

PRESCRIBE

Share new developments with the ones you love.

RADIANCE OF THE SOUL

*I see love in
your eyes whenever you
pass me by.*

IT'S GOOD TO KNOW

Love comes in all sizes.
Some like them big.
Some like them small.
Who me? I love them all.

DISASTER

Love can be sweeter than apple pie. But it can be a disaster if one is shy. So don't be shy be willing to try.

BREATHE EASY

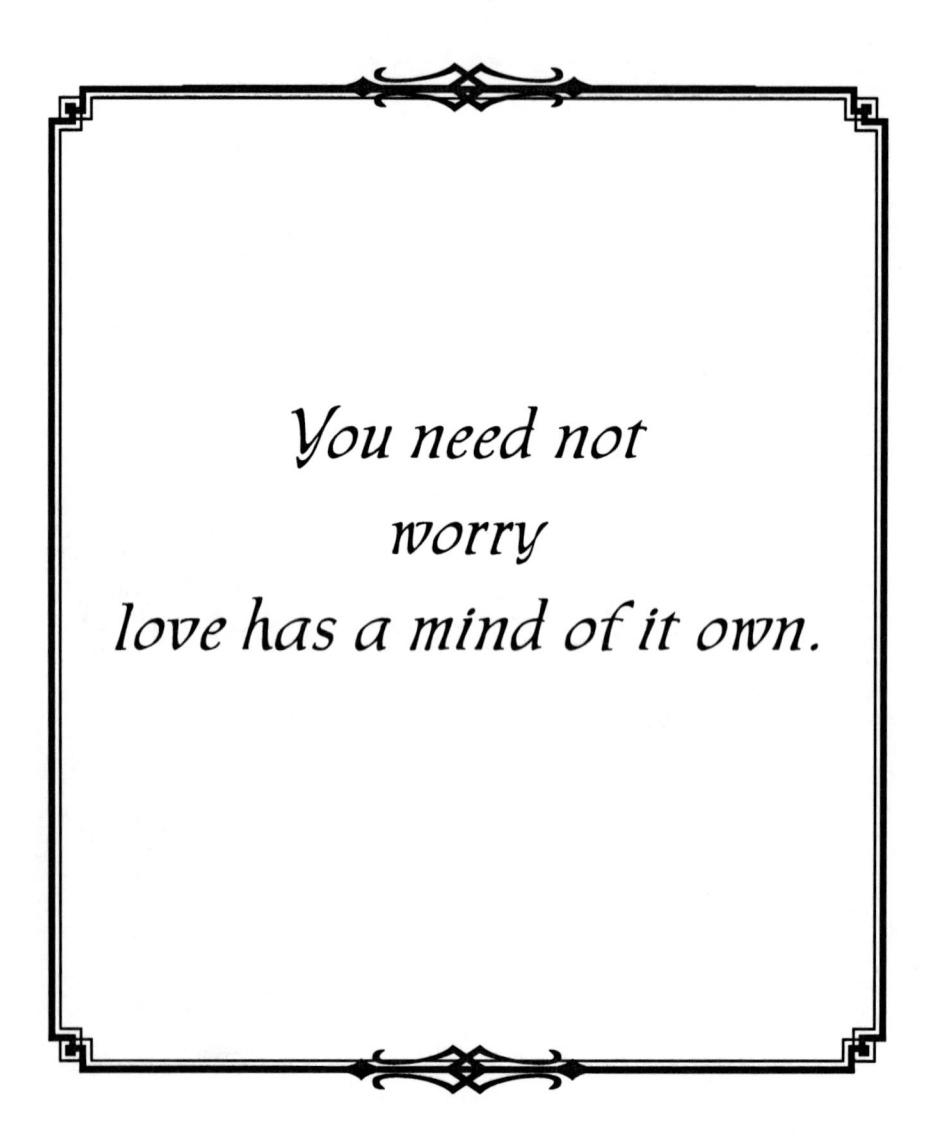

*You need not
worry
love has a mind of it own.*

NEVER FORGET TO

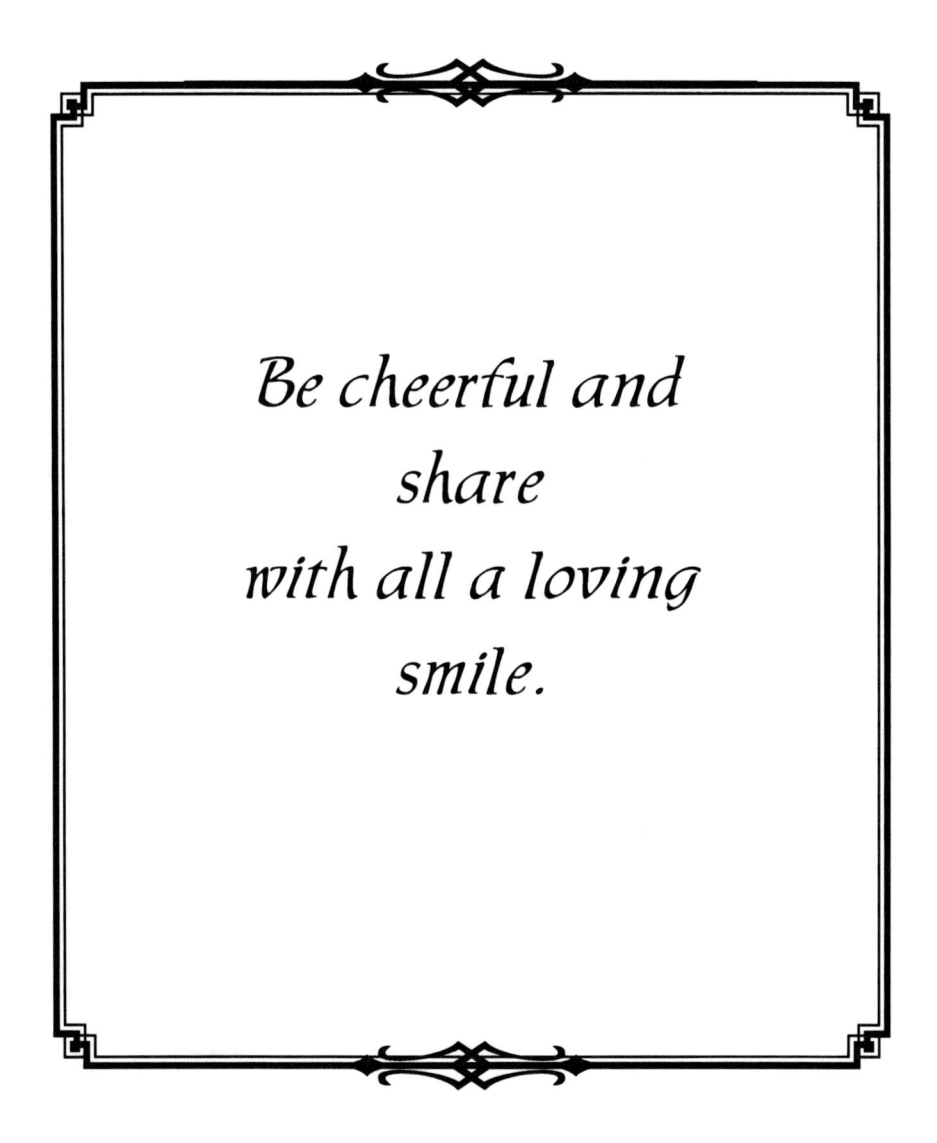

Be cheerful and share with all a loving smile.

FULFILLMENT

*You fill me up with
joy
and I love it.*

PASSPORT

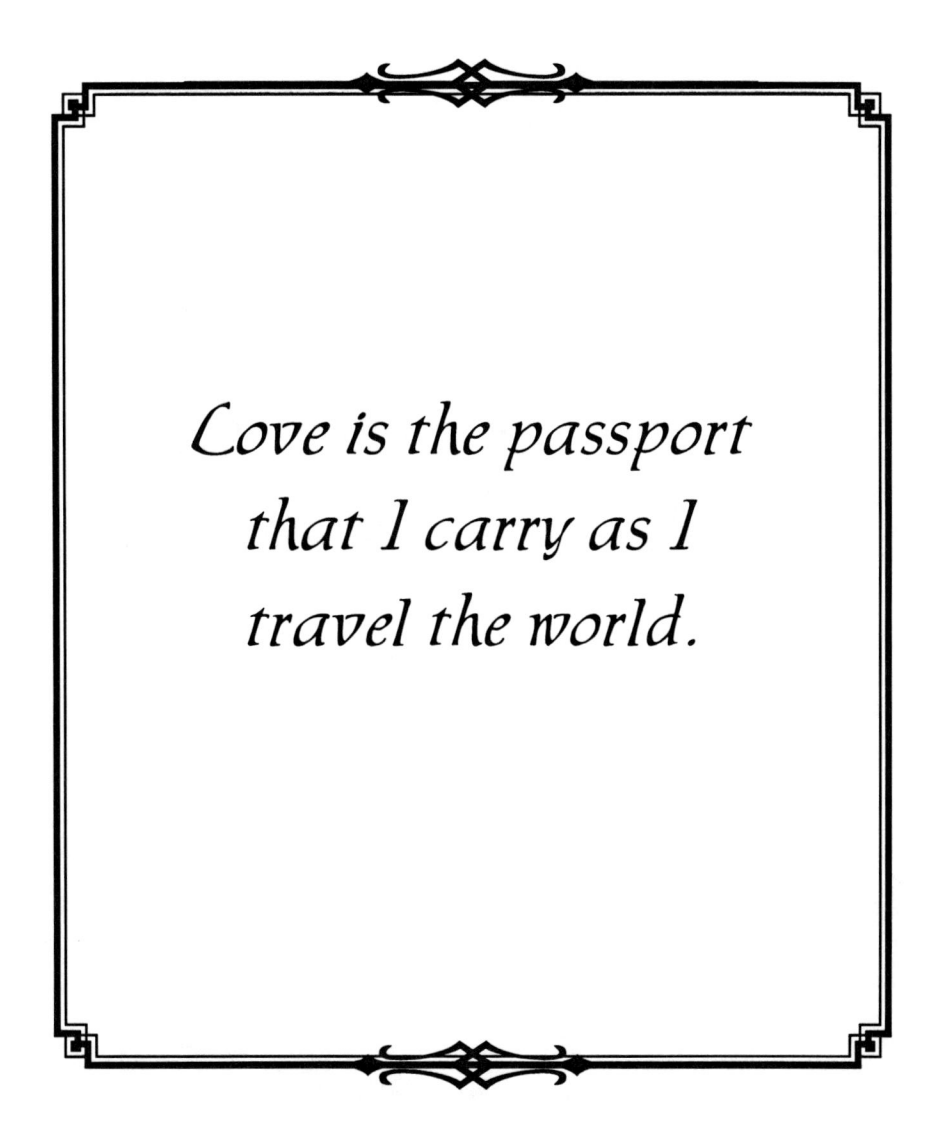

Love is the passport that I carry as I travel the world.

SACRED LOVE

*Love sees no enemy.
Love feels a broken heart.*

HEAVY CASE

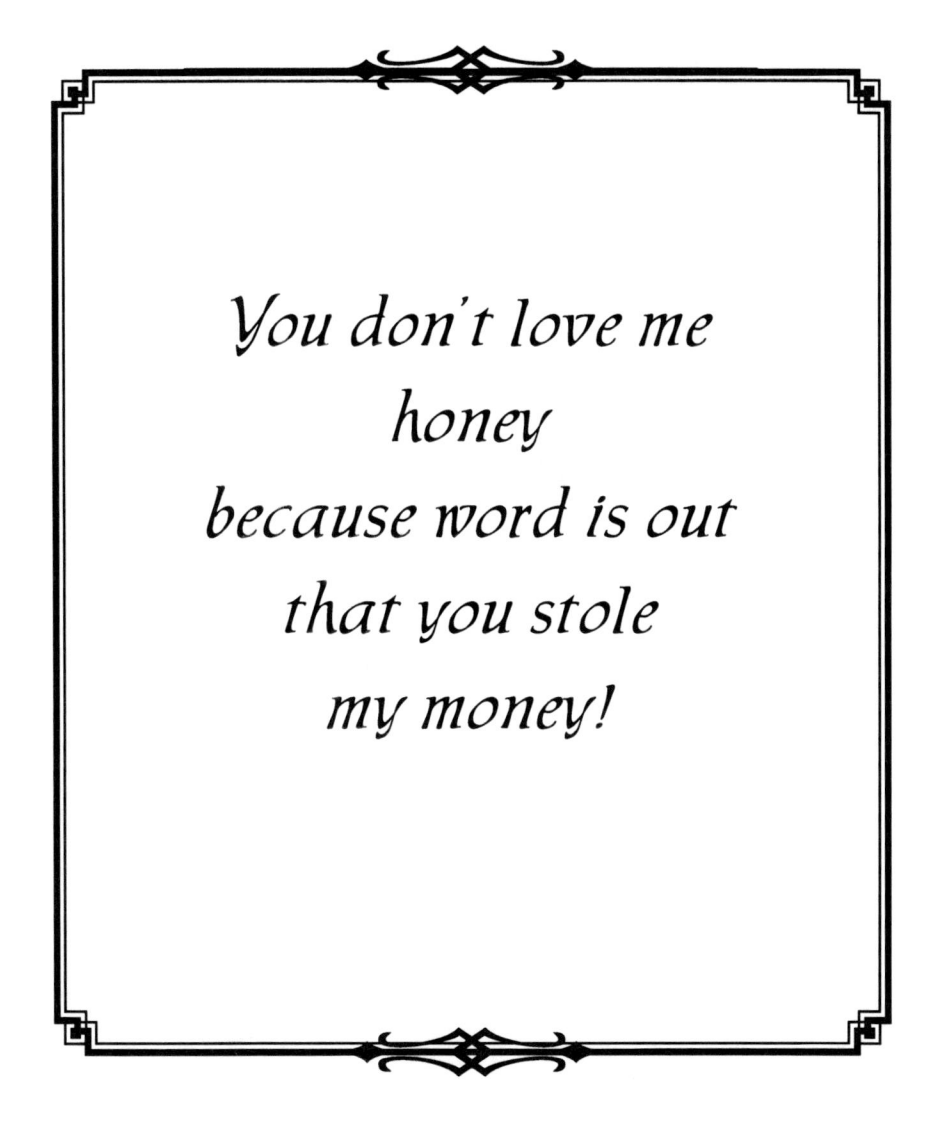

*You don't love me
honey
because word is out
that you stole
my money!*

TAKE INTO CONSIDERATION

Listen carefully to the voice that says "I love you".

PROVE IT TO ME

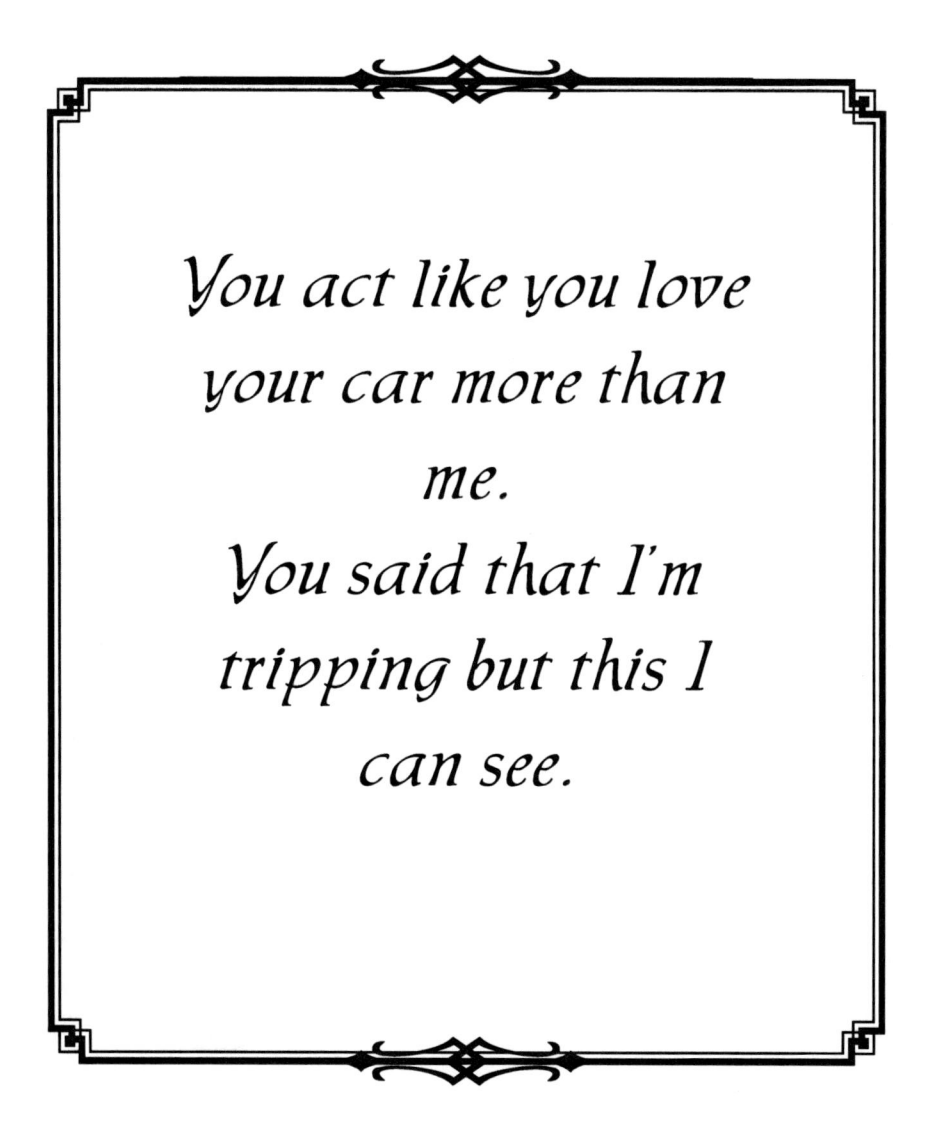

*You act like you love your car more than me.
You said that I'm tripping but this I can see.*

CHOCOLATE

Chocolate cover strawberries, cheese and fine wine and a full body massage may heal a dying relationship.

IT'S UP TO YOU

*The love in my heart
I long to share
with anyone
who's dear.*

LOVINGNESS

Love is a bright ideal ready to be released.

DONE DEAL

If you can believe it love can achieve it.

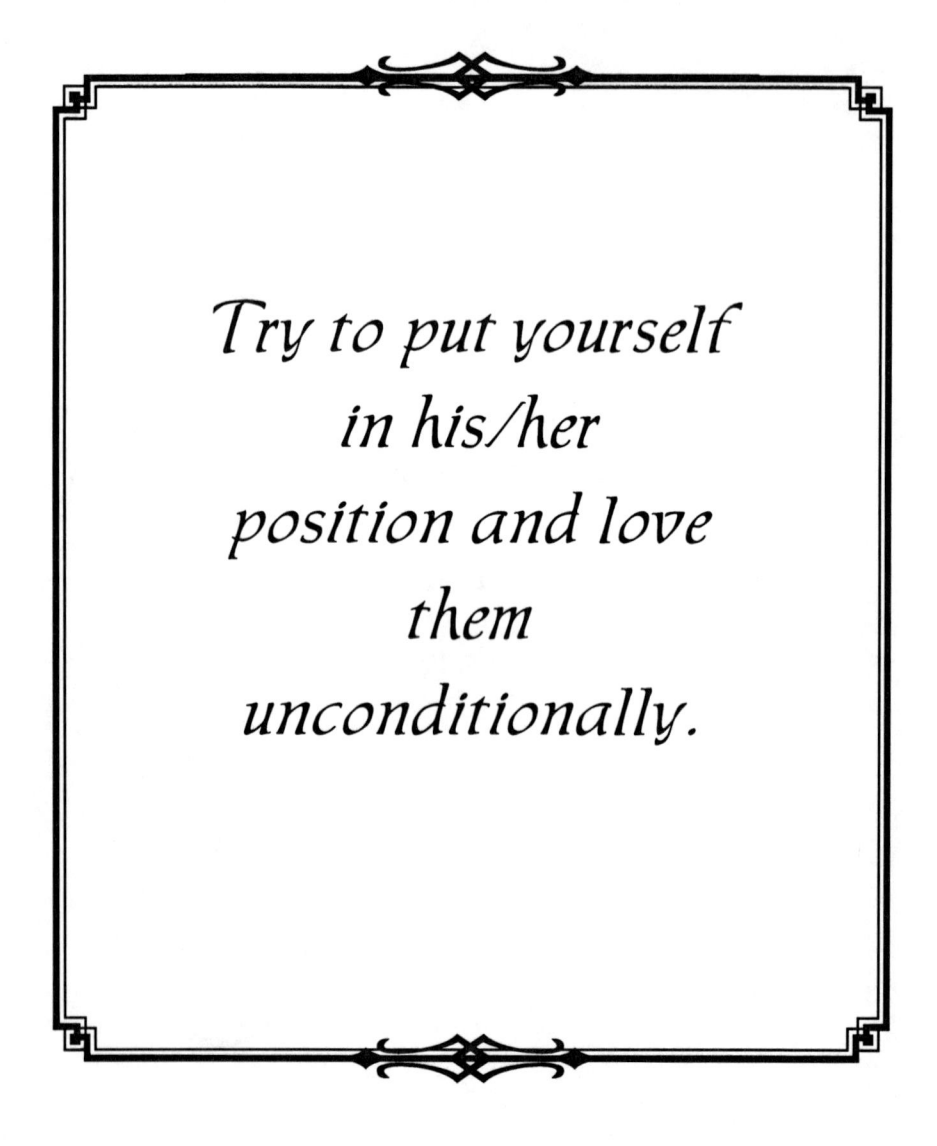

UNCONDITIONALLY

Try to put yourself in his/her position and love them unconditionally.

TRUTH ABOUT LOVE

Love consoles me whenever you hold me.

PERMIT

My heart is licensed to love.

MEDITATION

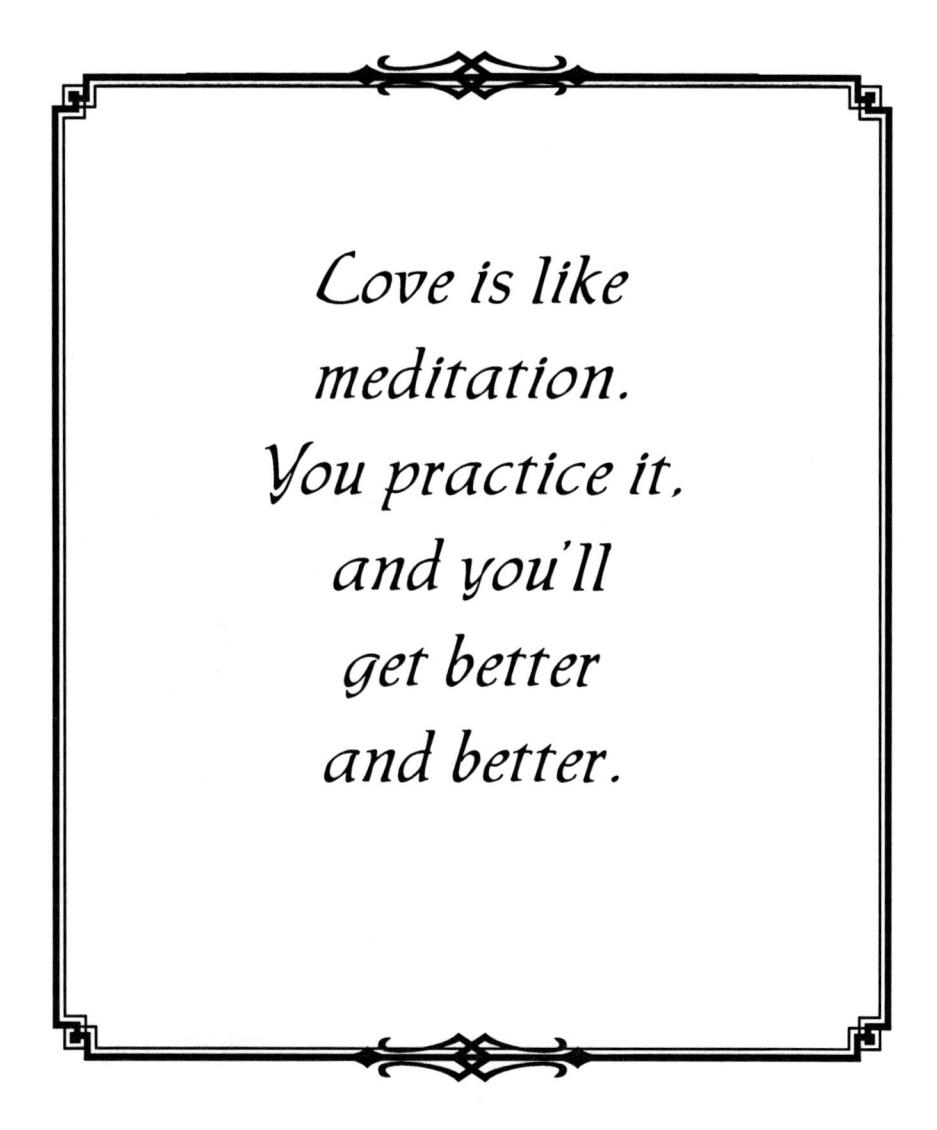

Love is like meditation. You practice it, and you'll get better and better.

FOR THE RECORD

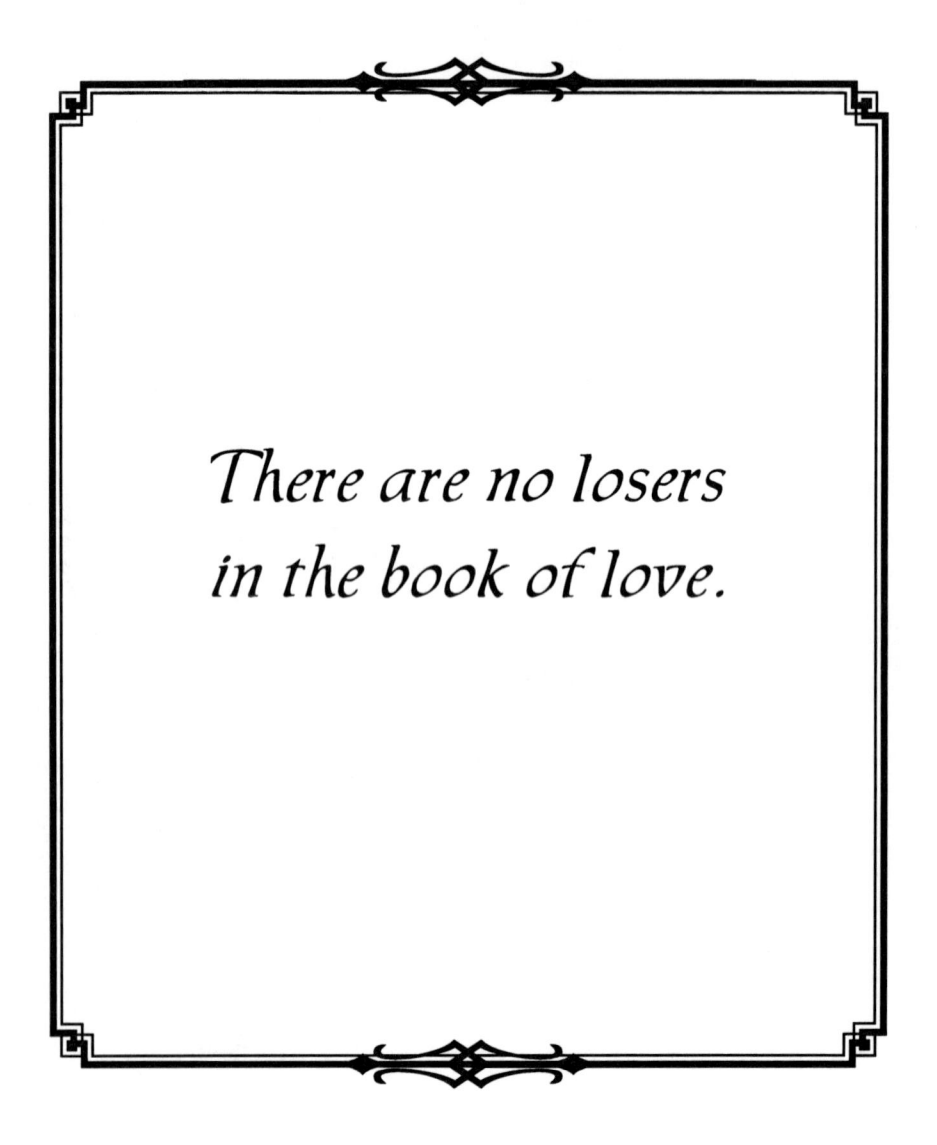

There are no losers in the book of love.

KISS AND MAKE UP

Thanks for sharing your love with me.

SURRENDER

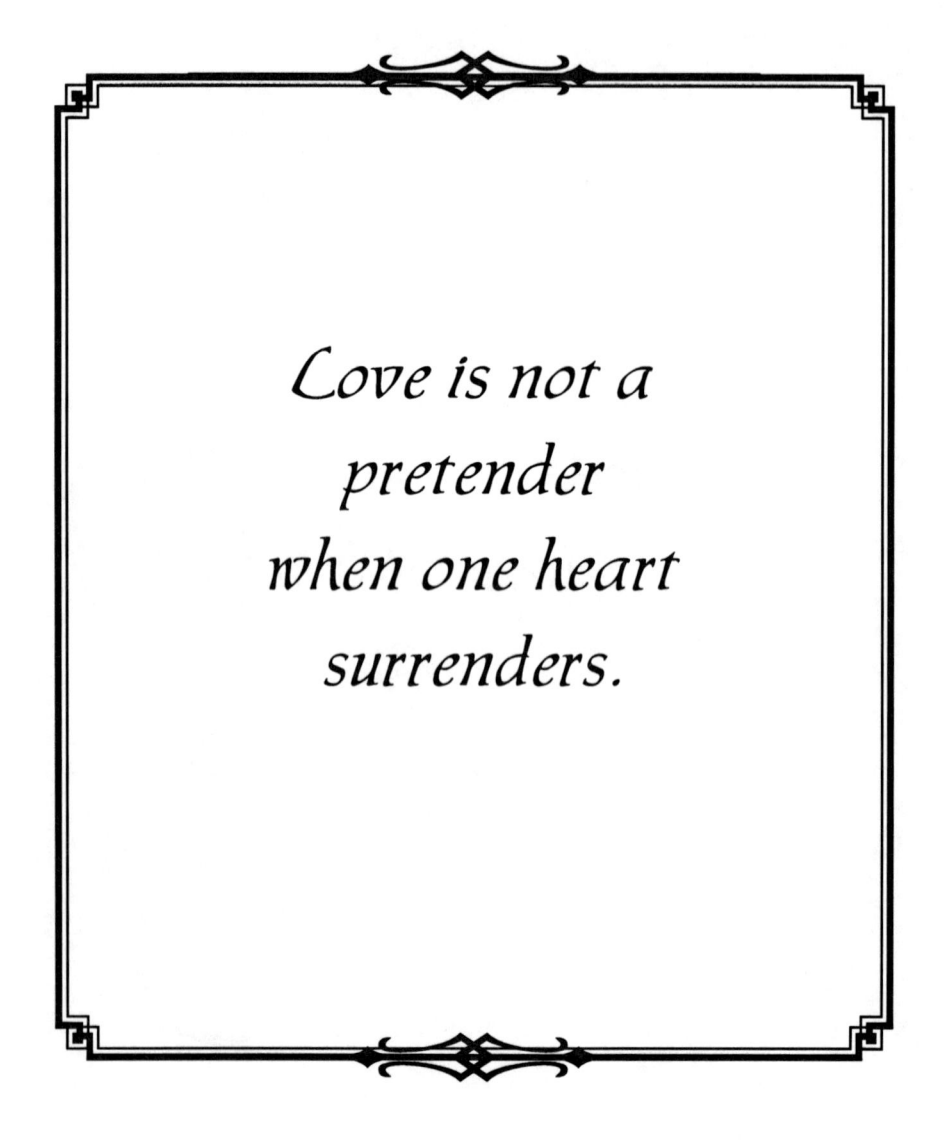

Love is not a pretender when one heart surrenders.

PERSONAL

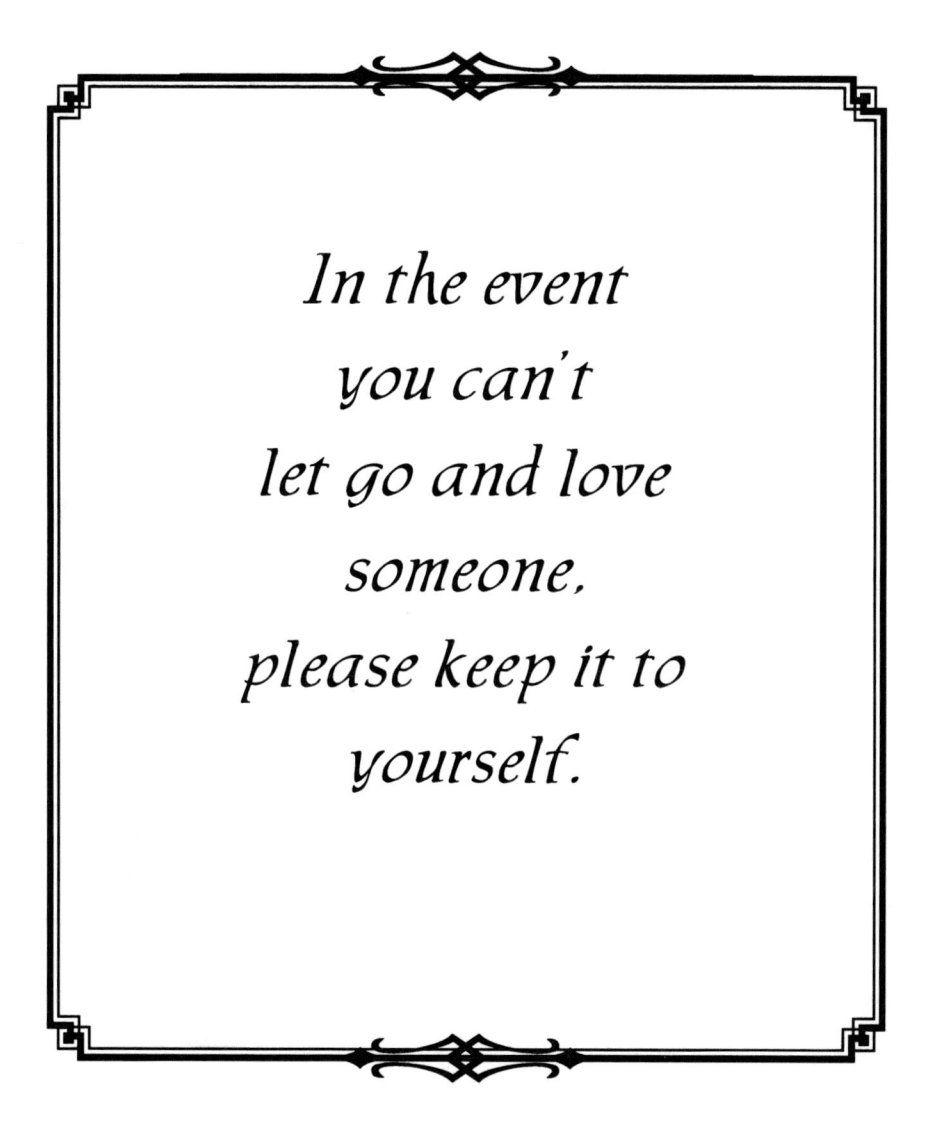

In the event you can't let go and love someone, please keep it to yourself.

REPRESENT

Have a safe and happy love life.

LET'S TALK

Love is all I know. Everything else just has to go.

MY PERSPECTIVE

Love is the meaning of my wonderful life.

ROSES

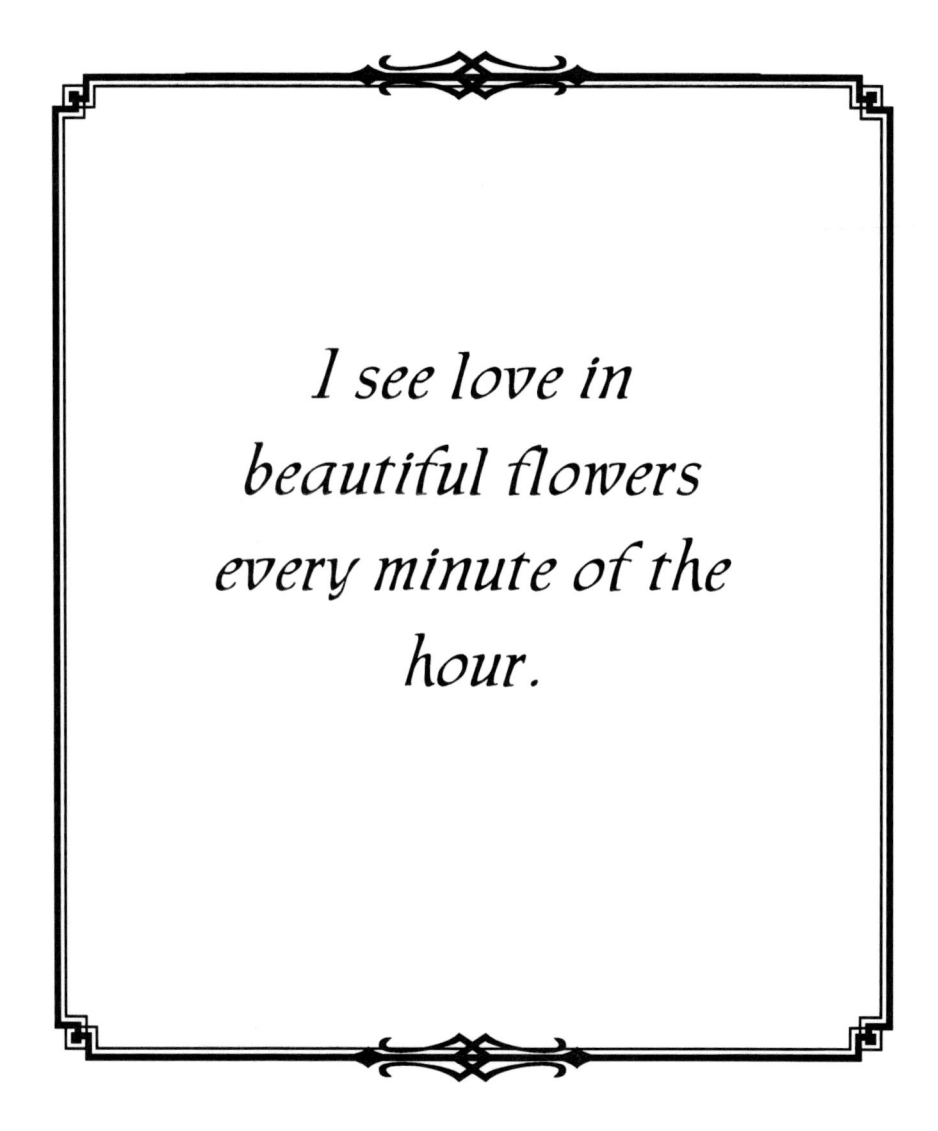

I see love in beautiful flowers every minute of the hour.

BOOK SMART

*My love for a great book
is like a baby with candy.
I can't let it go.*

MYSTERY

Love is a mystery that sometimes we just can't understand.

ANIMAL LOVERS

Some people love their animals more than they love their friends. That's why many loving relationships come to an end.

IMAGINE THAT

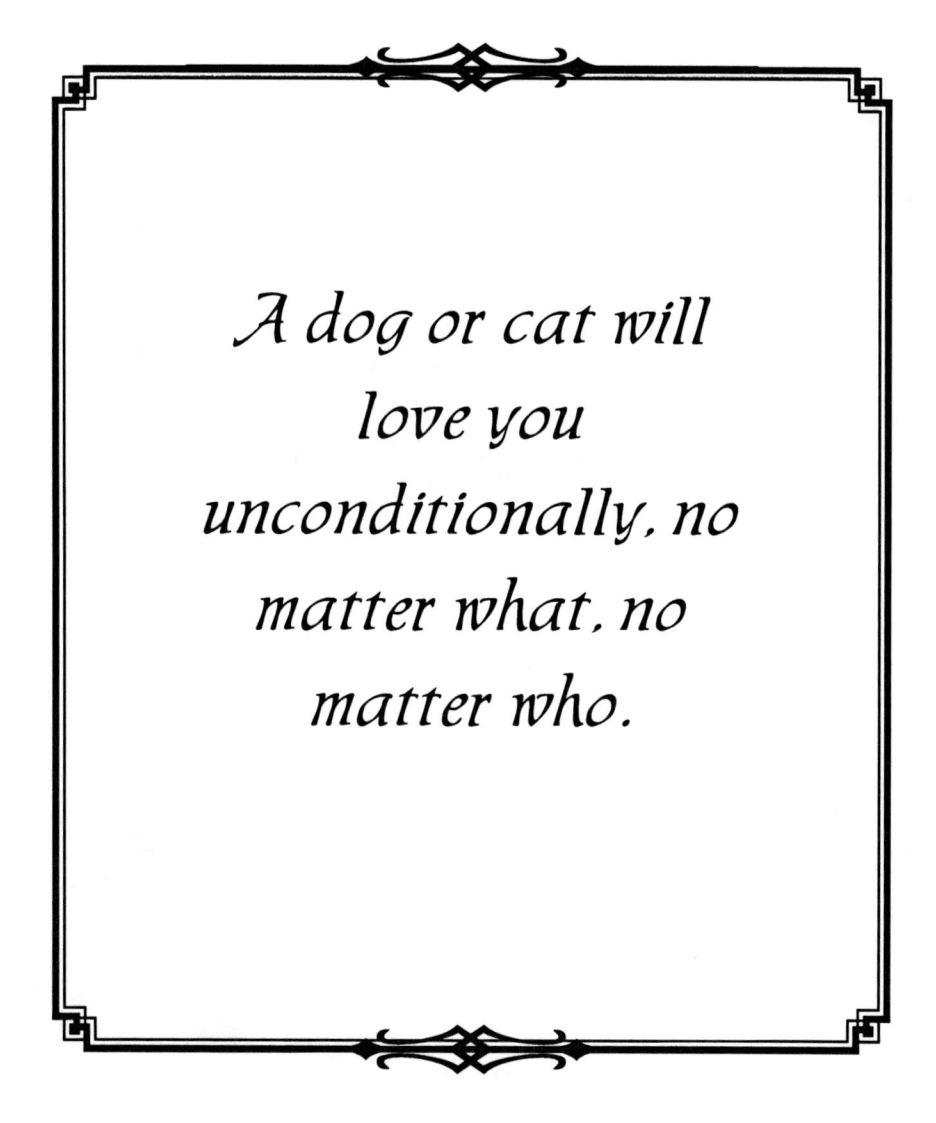

A dog or cat will love you unconditionally, no matter what, no matter who.

BOUNTIFUL

*There is an abundance of
love in the air
if only you take time
out and care.*

JAZZY LOVE

*Love is my song.
I love every note
that I play on.*

RECOGNITION

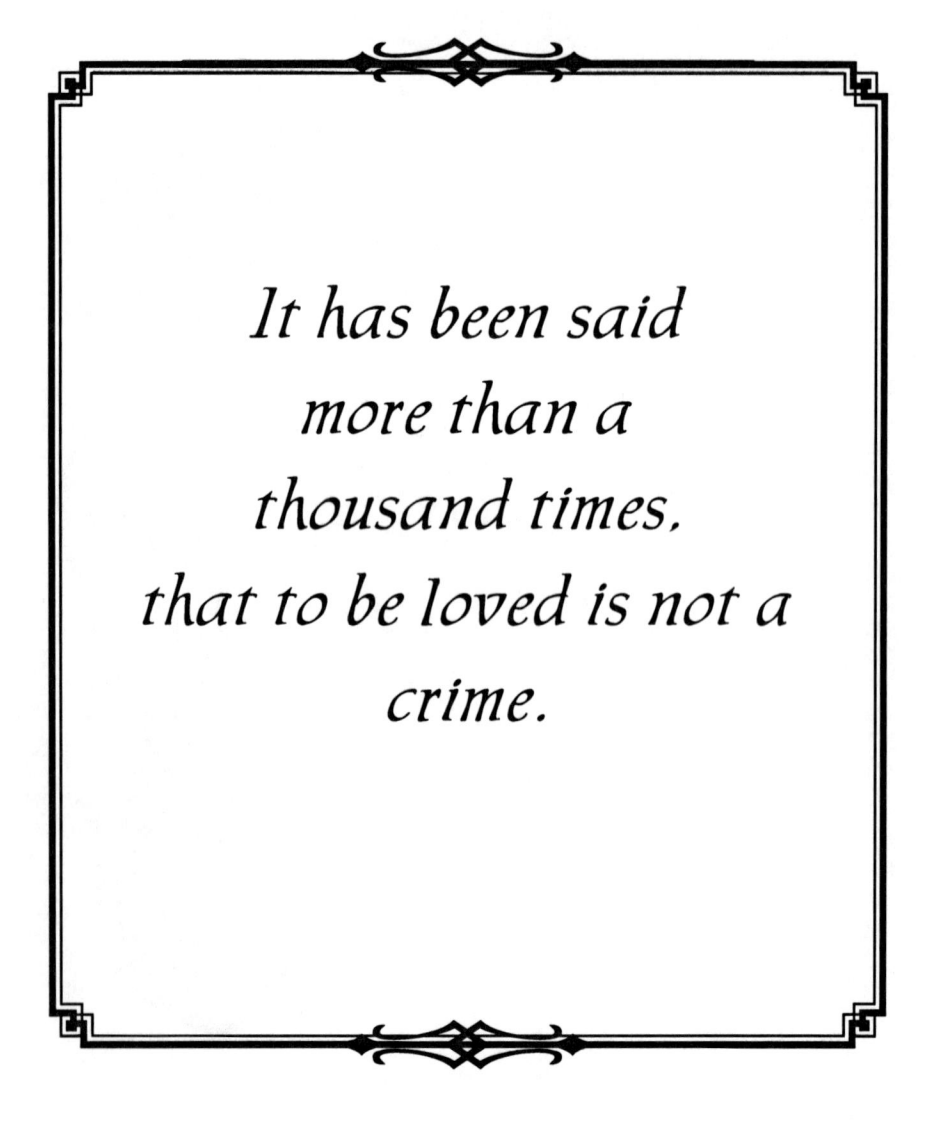

It has been said more than a thousand times, that to be loved is not a crime.

RELEASE YOURSELF

I love you, but I wish you would speak from your heart.

NO PROBLEMS

Love can handle all challenges.

YES

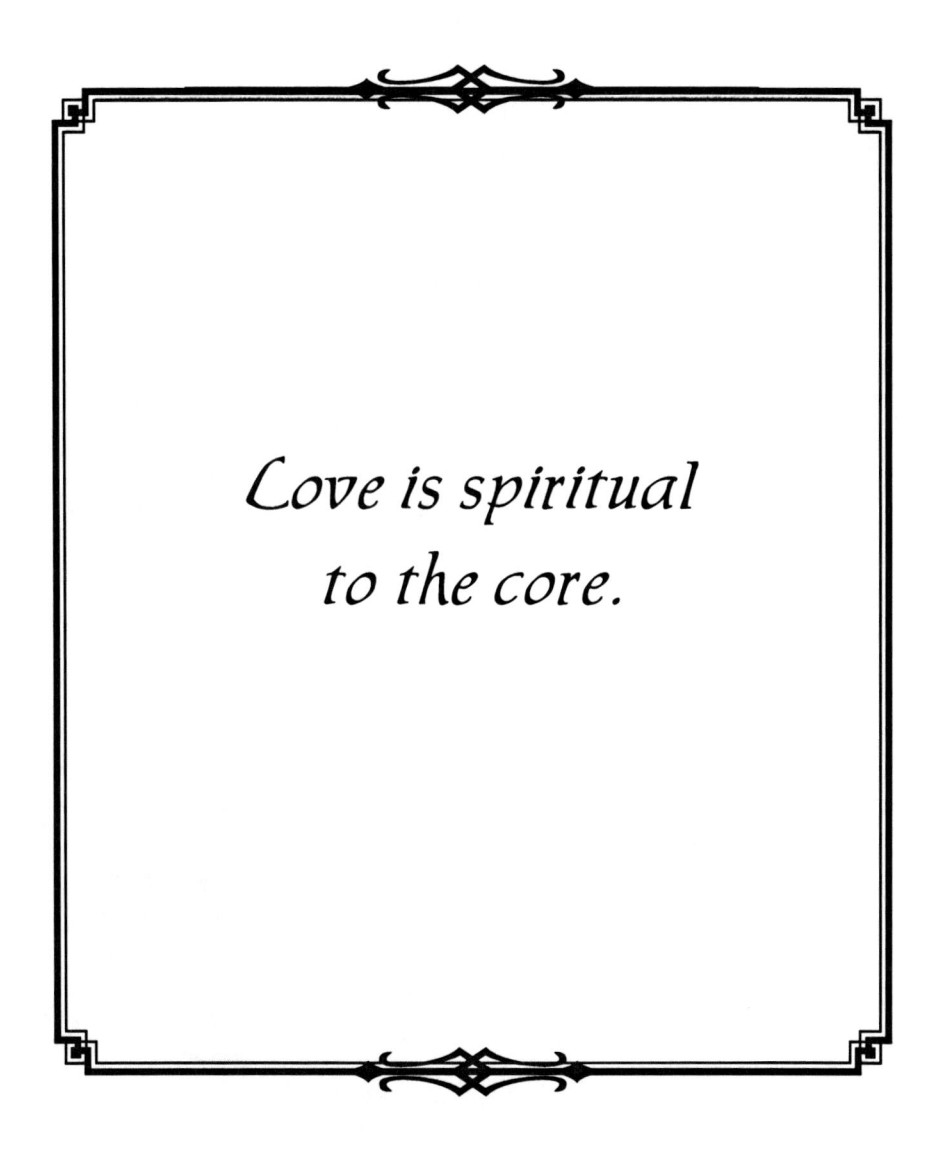

Love is spiritual to the core.

KISS

*Kiss me with your sweet lips.
Adore me with your smile.
Once I make love to you,
you will be feeling mighty proud.*

PLAYER, PLAYER

*Love is a game and
I am the player.*

SLEEPING BEAUTY

I called you last night to let you know that your loving was out of sight.

THE GLOW OF LOVE

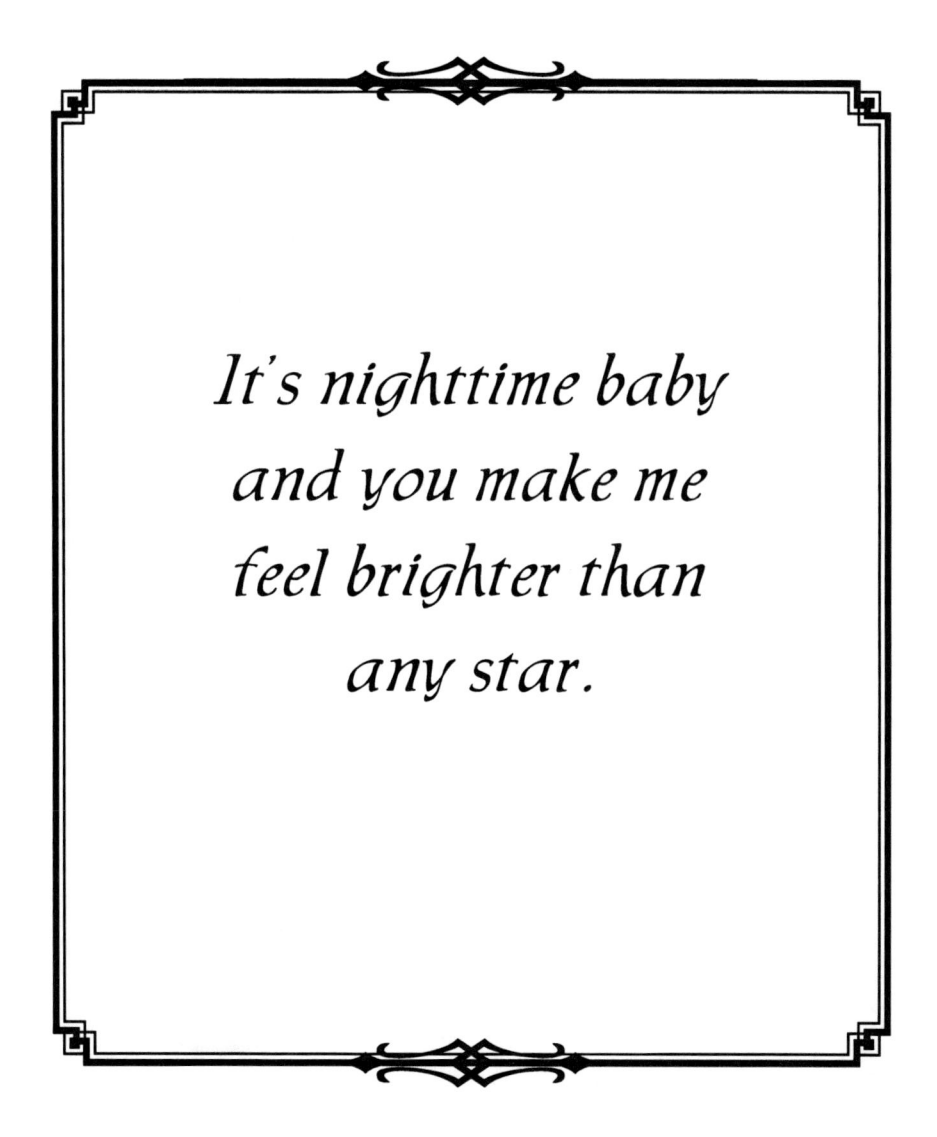

It's nighttime baby and you make me feel brighter than any star.

LOOKING BACK

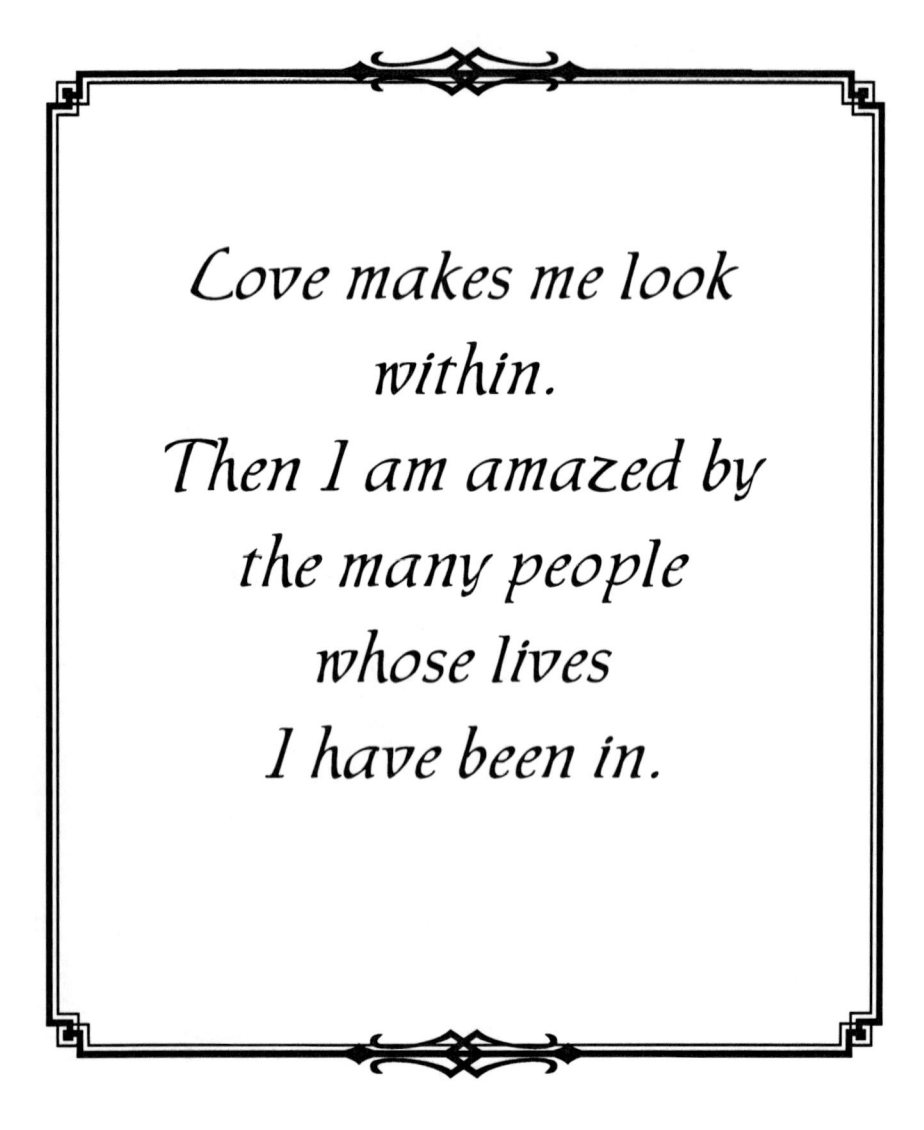

*Love makes me look within.
Then I am amazed by the many people whose lives I have been in.*

GENTLE

*Love is never forced upon thee.
Love is as kind as can be.*

I FEEL FOR YOU

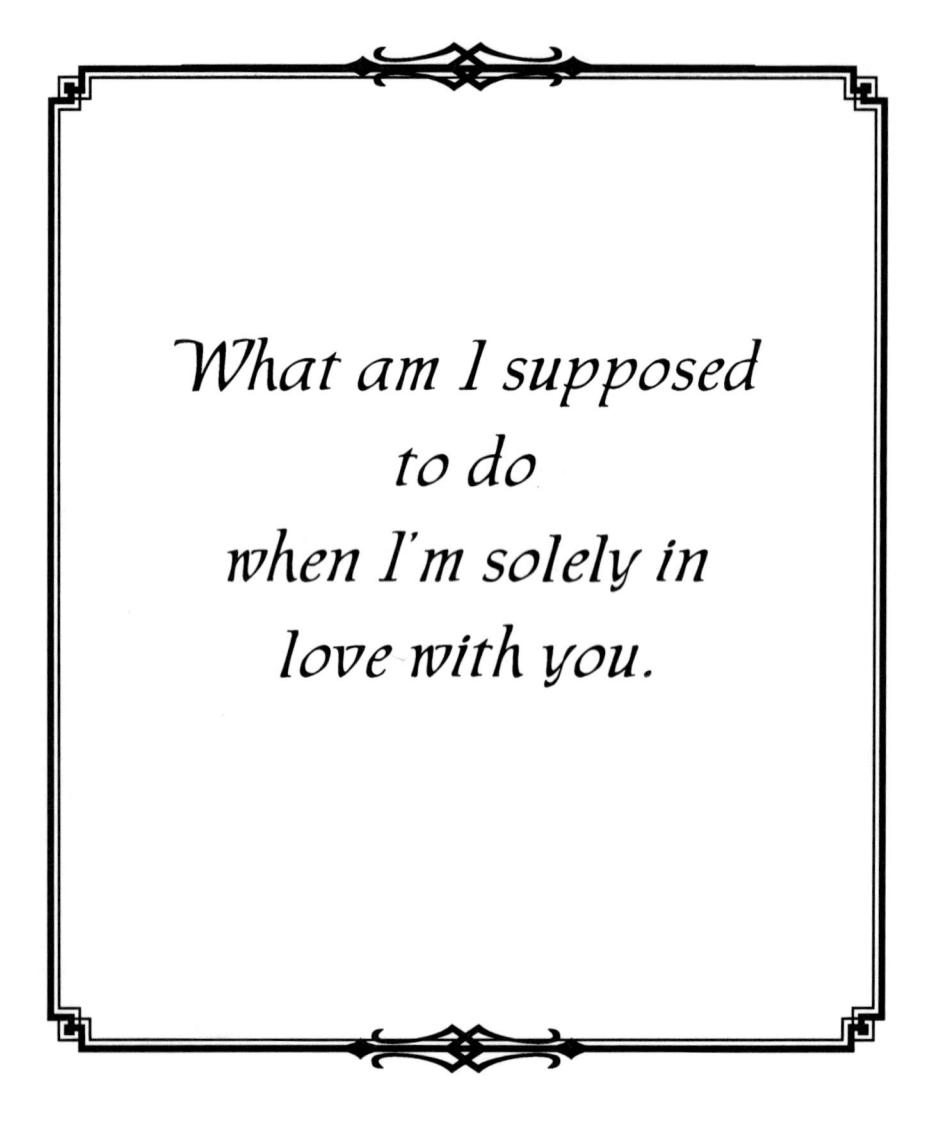

*What am I supposed
to do
when I'm solely in
love with you.*

I REPEAT

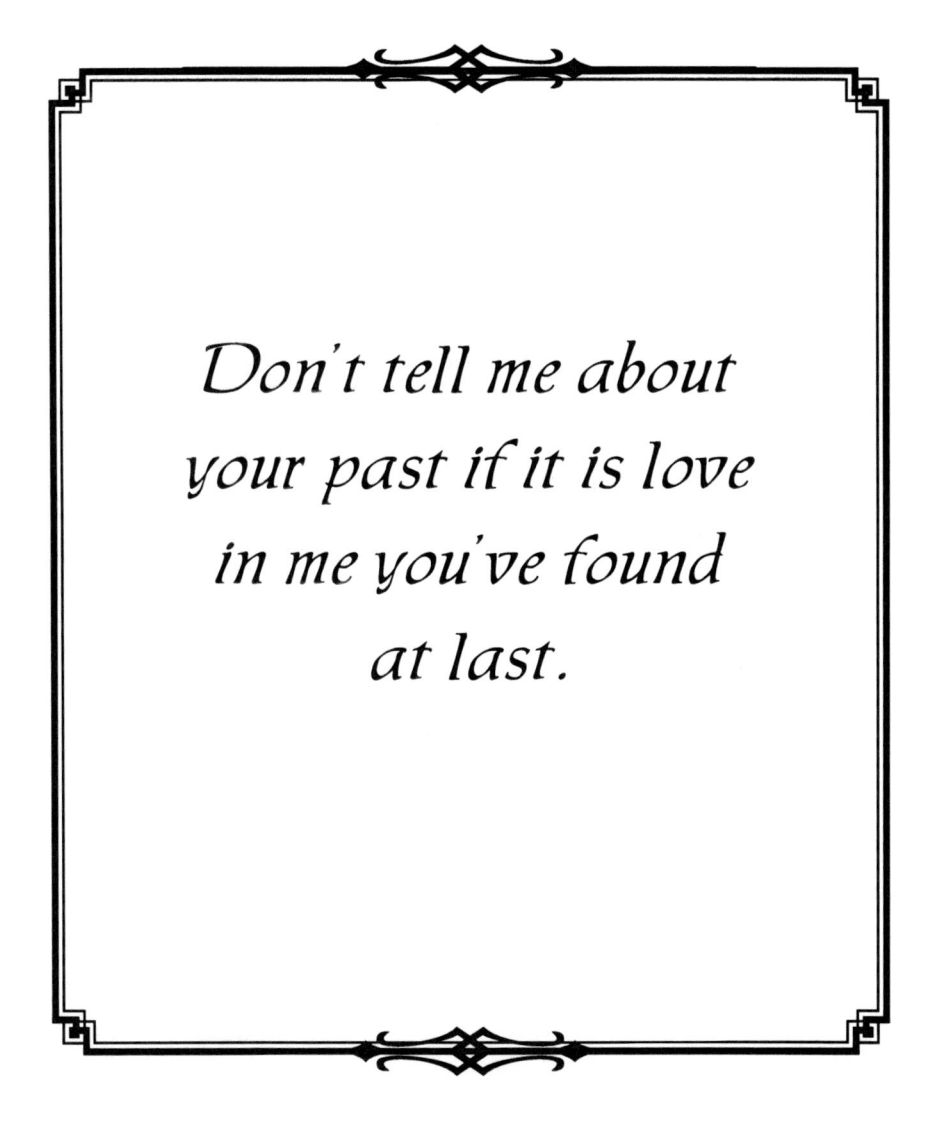

Don't tell me about your past if it is love in me you've found at last.

A CRY FOR LOVE

I cried last night as I thought about the betrayal of your love all night.

APPALLING

Love can be mean when the sex isn't clean.

DANGER

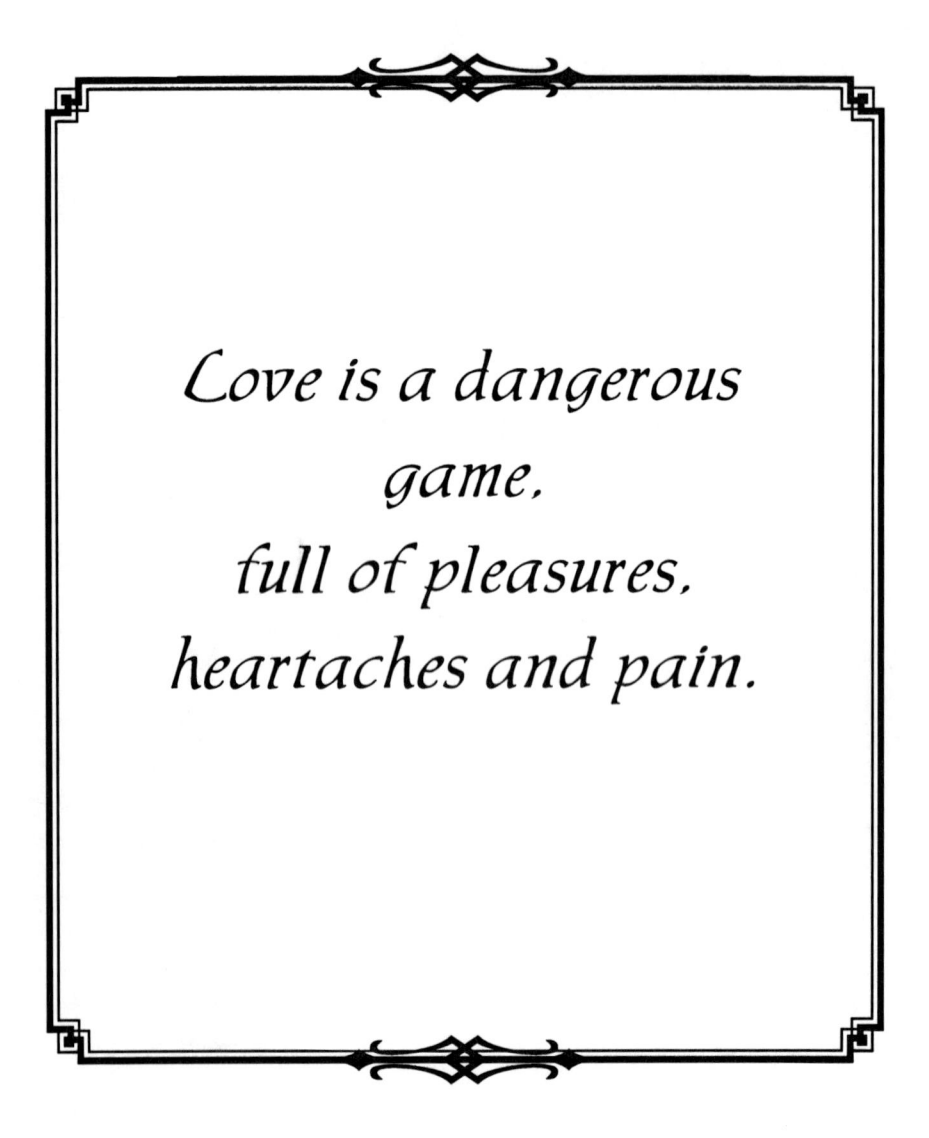

*Love is a dangerous game,
full of pleasures,
heartaches and pain.*

INSPECT YOURSELF

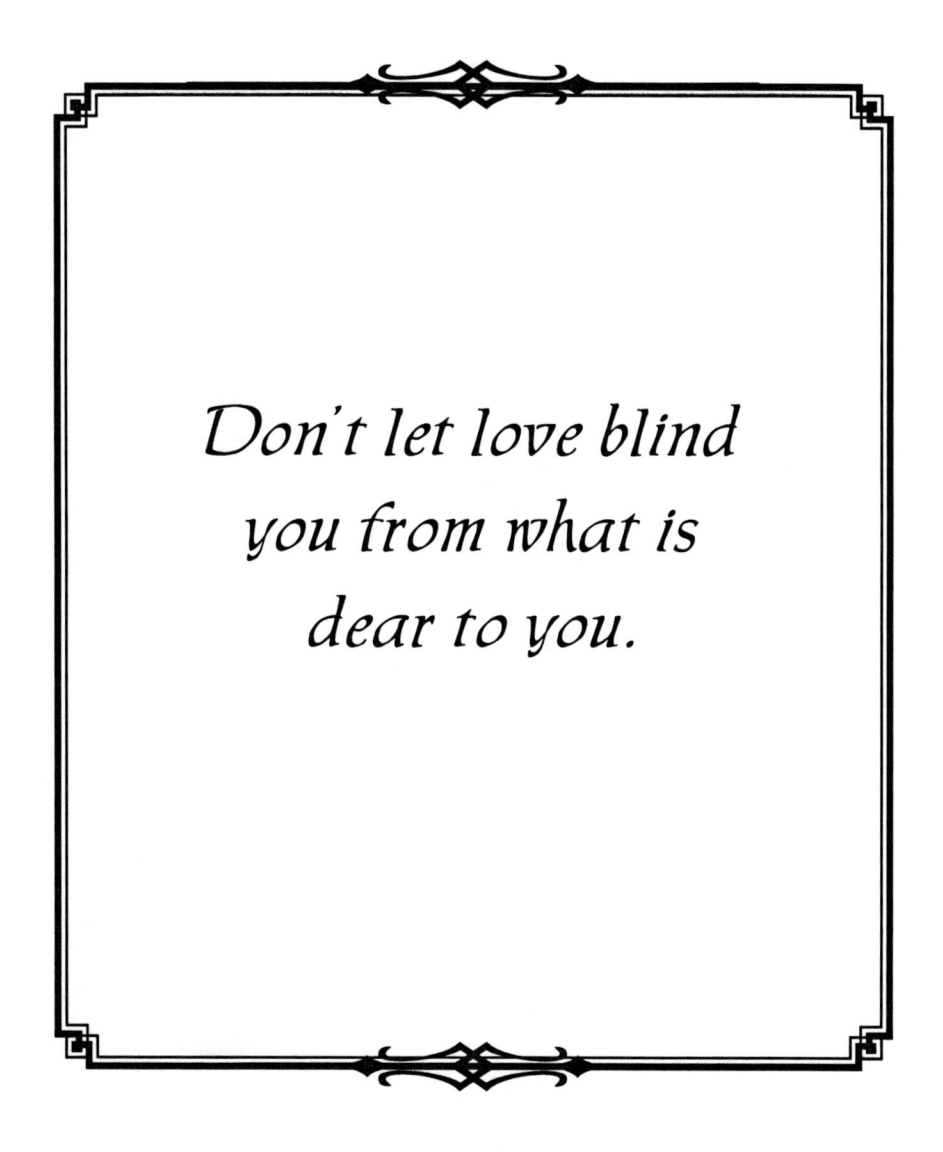

Don't let love blind you from what is dear to you.

Dadisi Mwende Netifnet

L-O-V-E

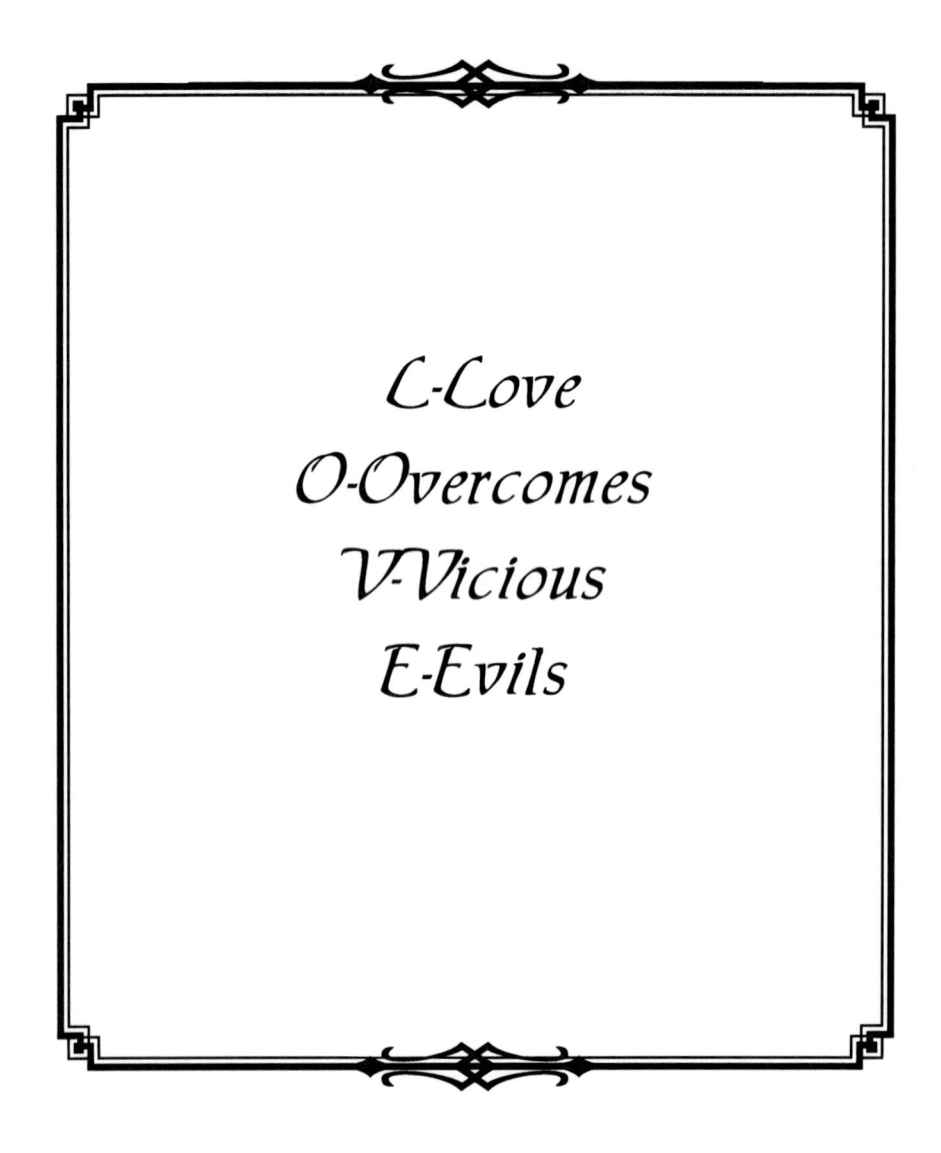

L-Love
O-Overcomes
V-Vicious
E-Evils

FAIRGROUND

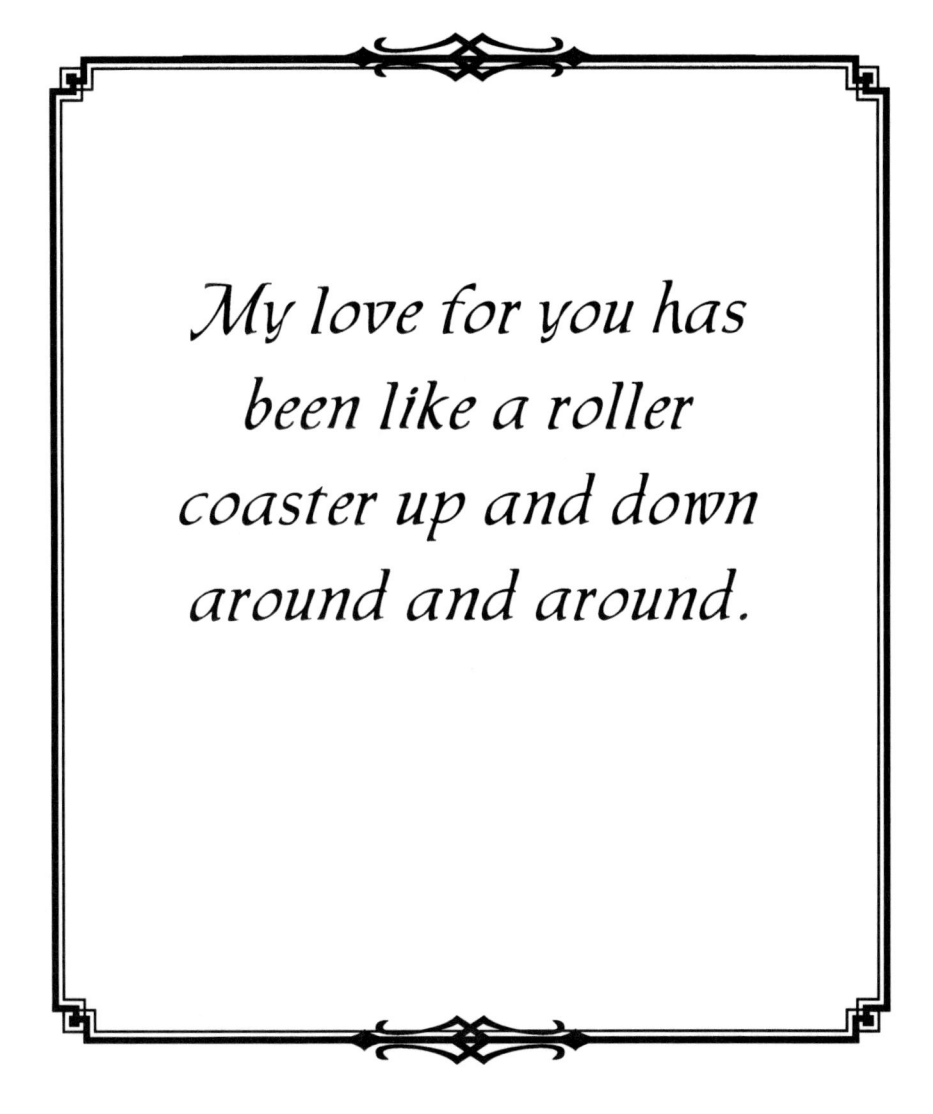

My love for you has been like a roller coaster up and down around and around.

HONESTY

*I said I don't love you.
You said, "It hurts you inside".
I'm trying to be honest.
Would you prefer that I lie?*

THERE WERE PROBLEMS

I never wanted this love affair to end. But gee there were so many fights between us that I would not want to go through that again.

QUESTION

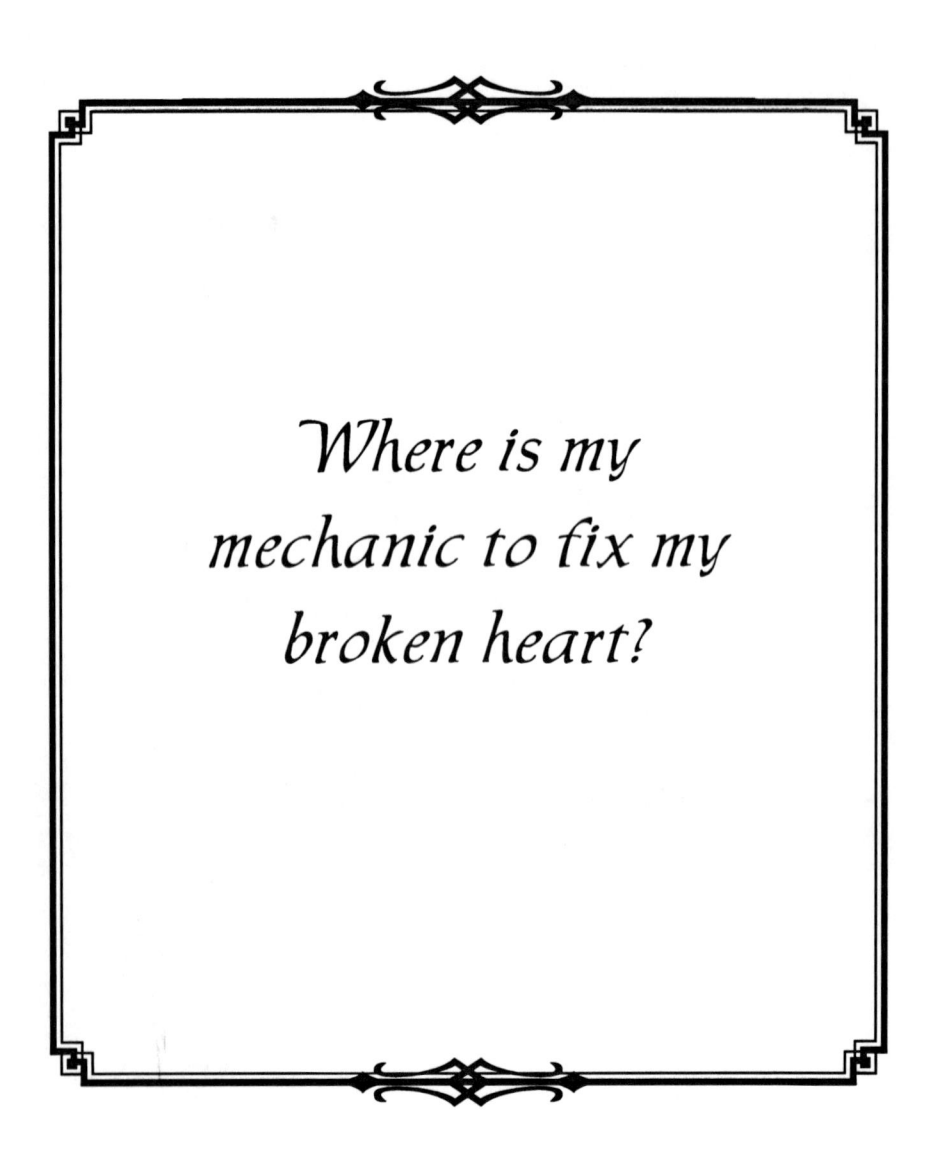

Where is my mechanic to fix my broken heart?

MY GOD

*Let the truth be told.
The love we had
was getting old.*

I AM SERIOUS

*Pretty woman, don't let your lover slap you and beat you down.
If he can't appreciate your beauty,
get out of town.*

SONG BIRD

I love to hear a bird sing in the early morning.

YOU CAN BE ALL THAT

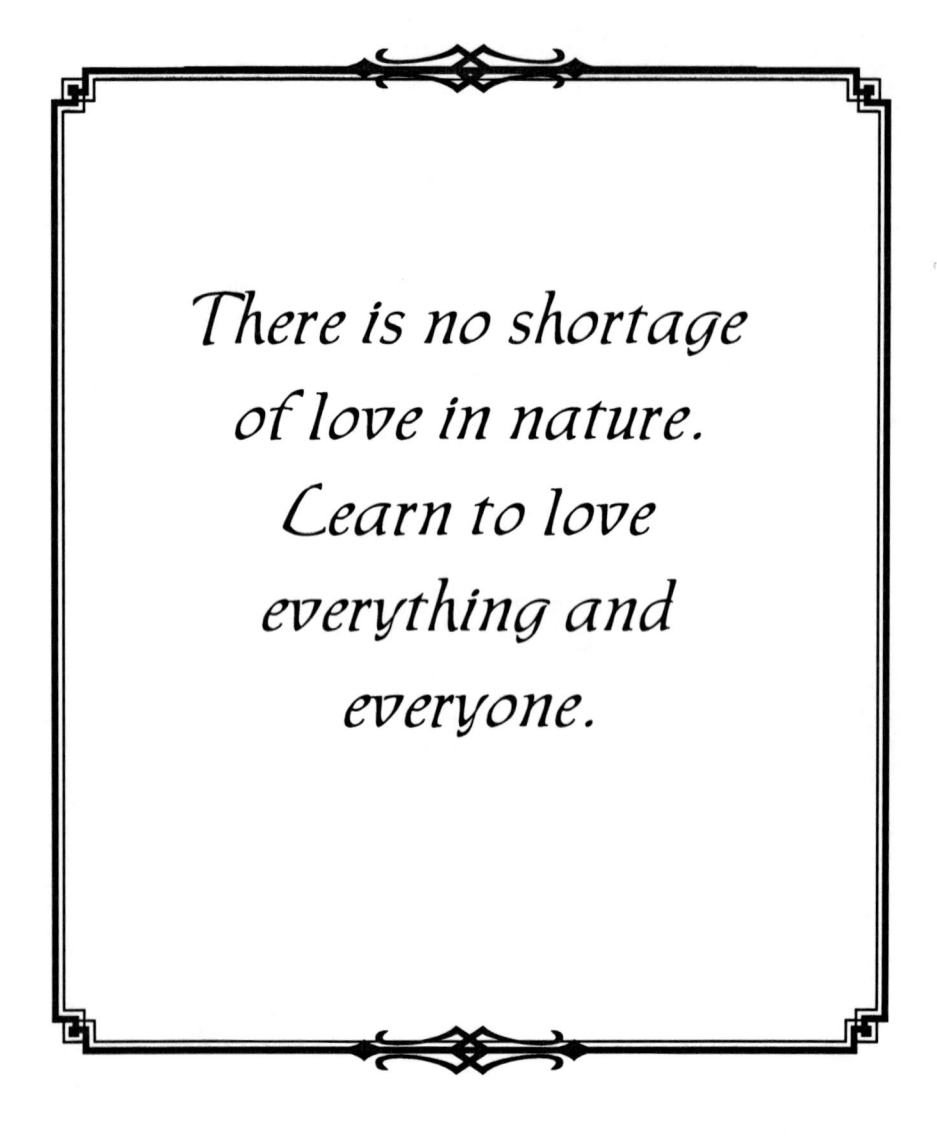

There is no shortage of love in nature. Learn to love everything and everyone.

THE GREAT CONQUERER

*Love makes the world
so much better.*

UNWIND

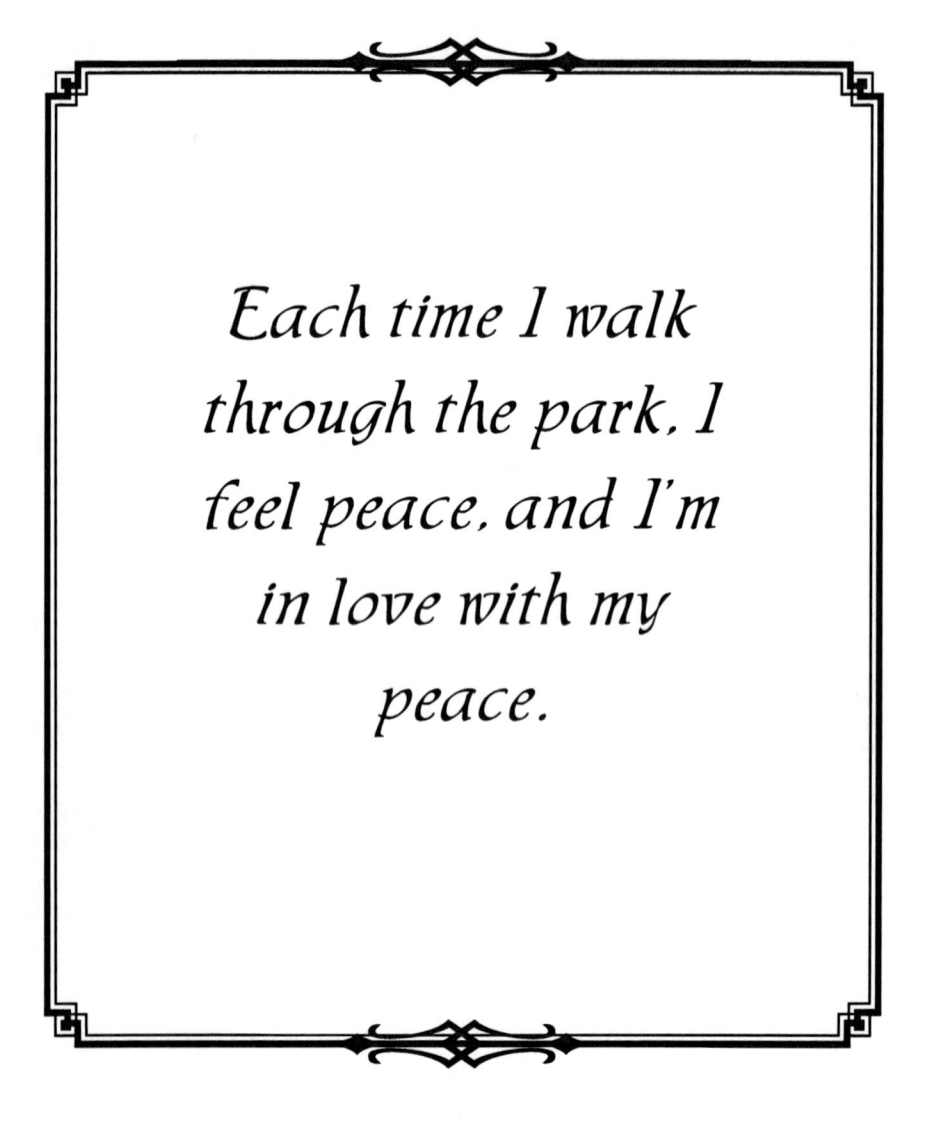

Each time I walk through the park, I feel peace, and I'm in love with my peace.

WARM LOVE

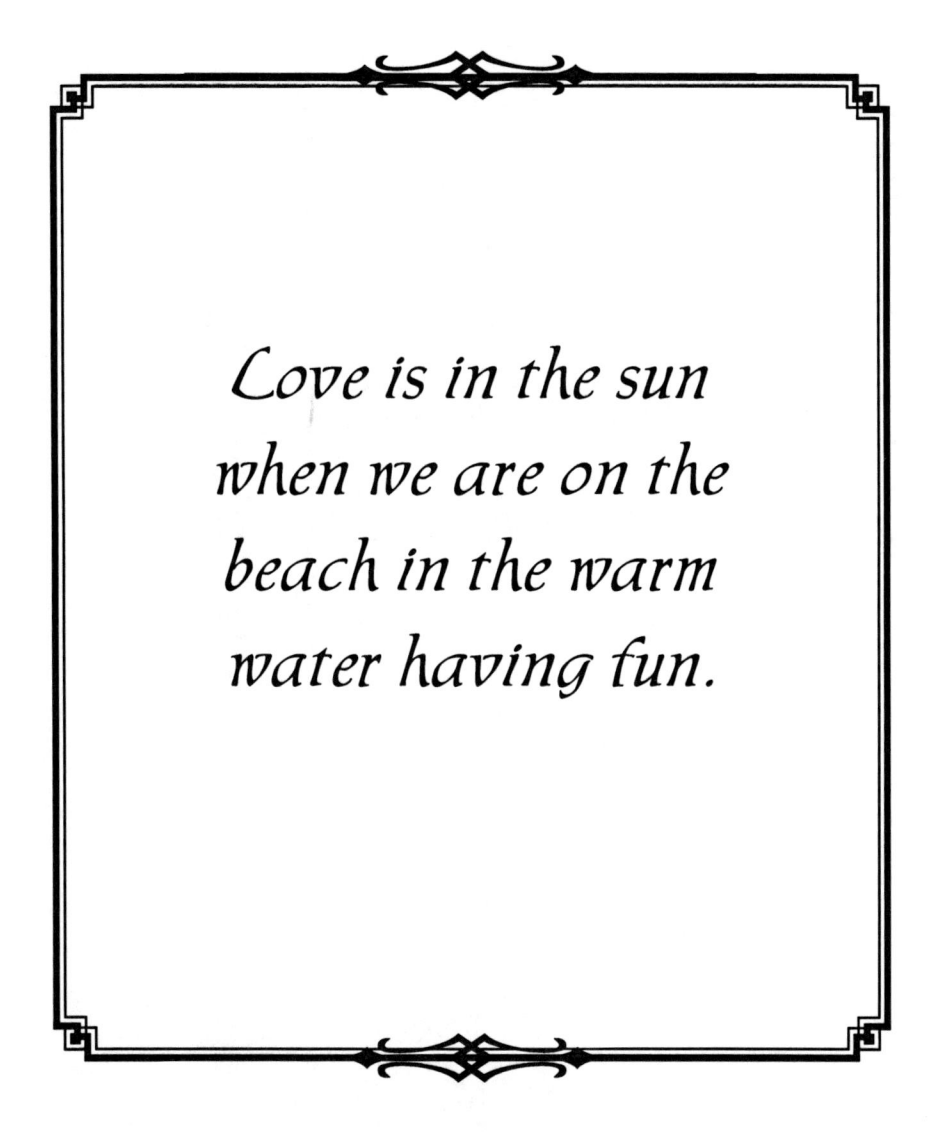

Love is in the sun when we are on the beach in the warm water having fun.

REFINE

*Purify your soul with love.
I do.*

SOMEONE LIKE YOU

*Love is what a child
can feel.
It's so real.*

FOSTER CHILD

Now is the time to love you.

TRANSFUSION

Infuse your love into a child's heart, and you will never be forgotten.

LIKELIHOOD

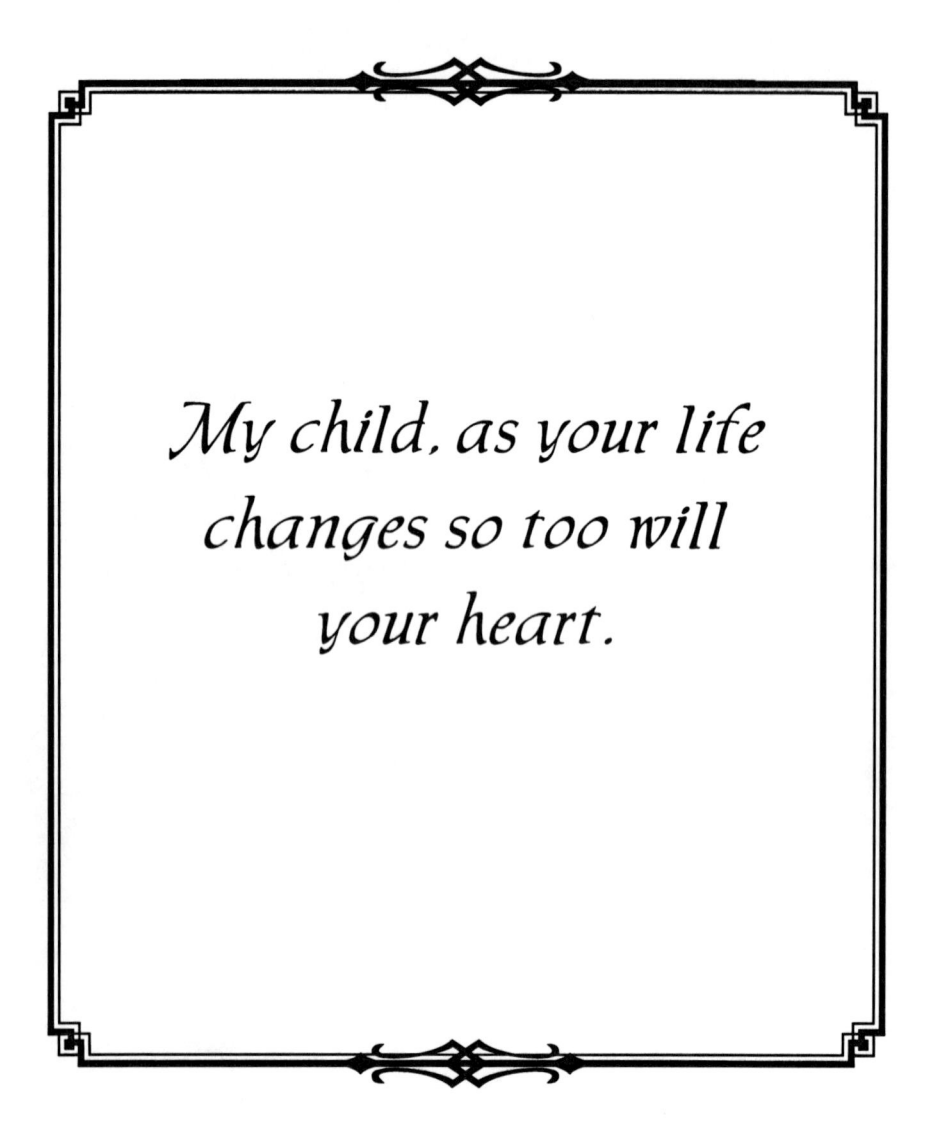

My child, as your life changes so too will your heart.

THE PRINCIPLE

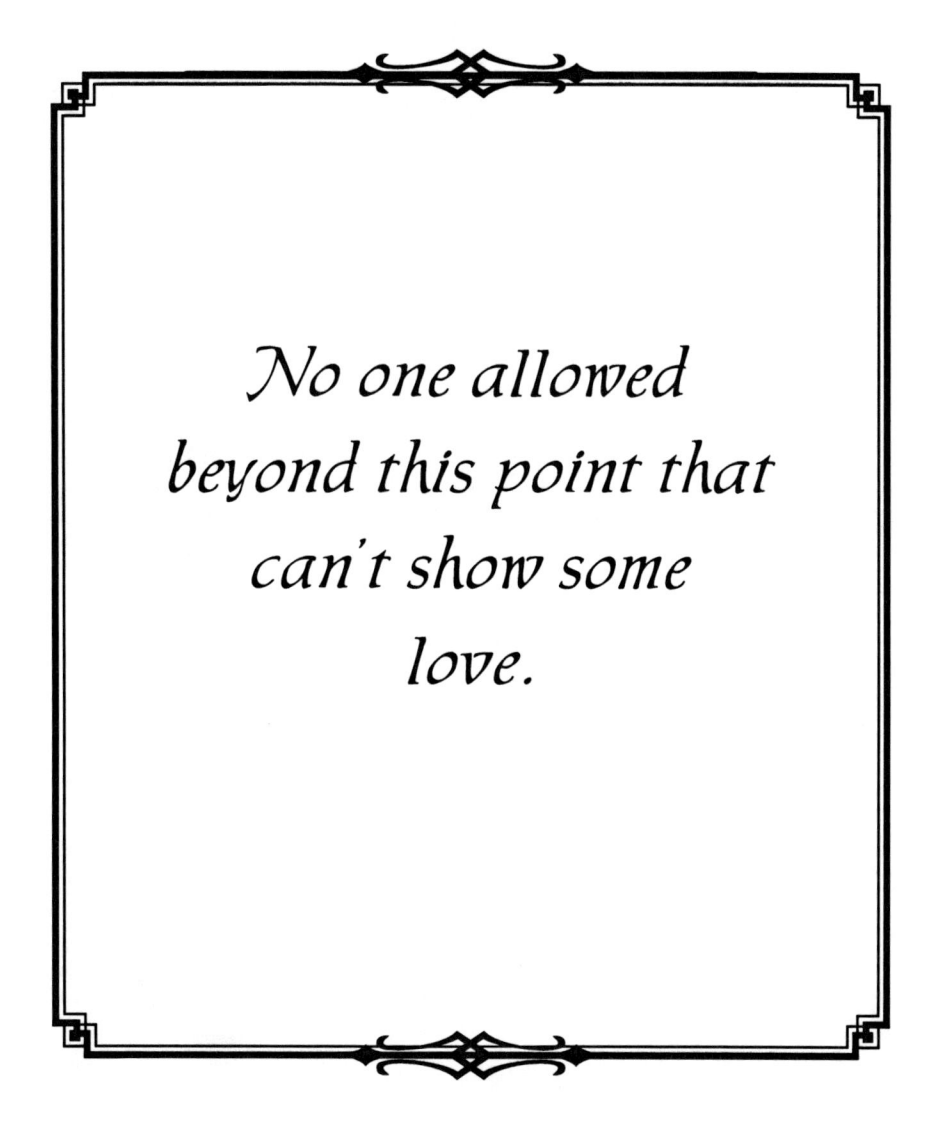

No one allowed beyond this point that can't show some love.

UNTANGLES

Love untangles a barbed wired heart.

ANSWER

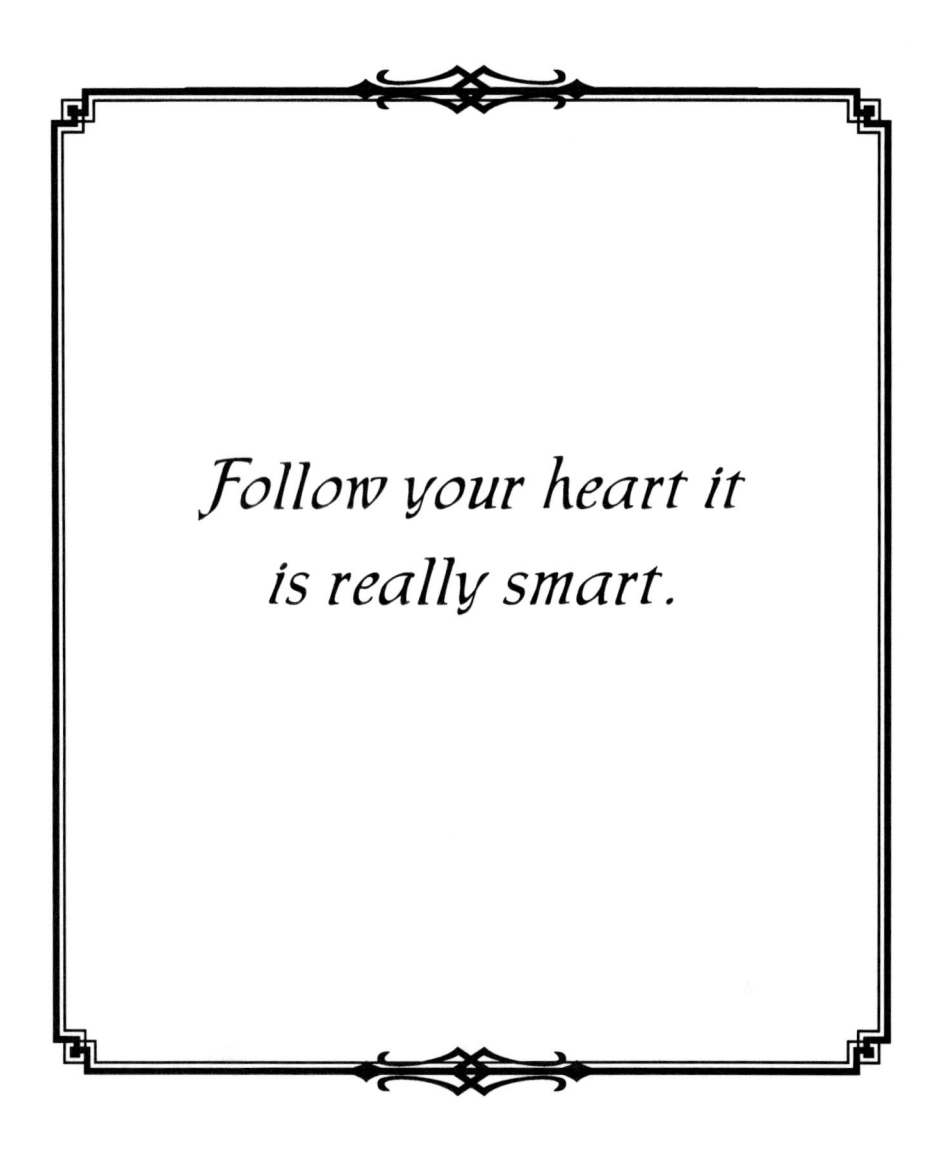

Follow your heart it is really smart.

STOP THINKING ABOUT LOVE

Love has its own divine reason.

DREAM

*Love works like a dream.
It keeps you wondering.*

INCOME

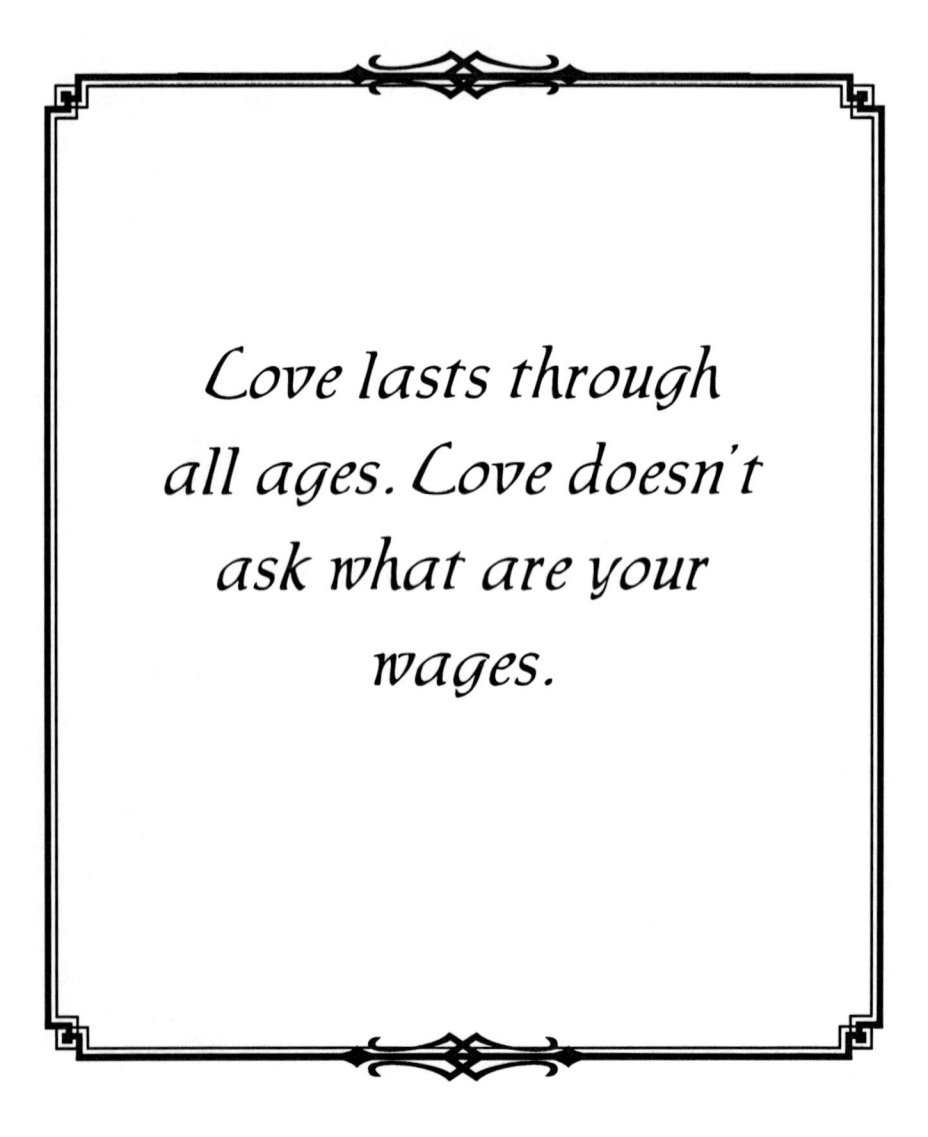

Love lasts through all ages. Love doesn't ask what are your wages.

EVIL

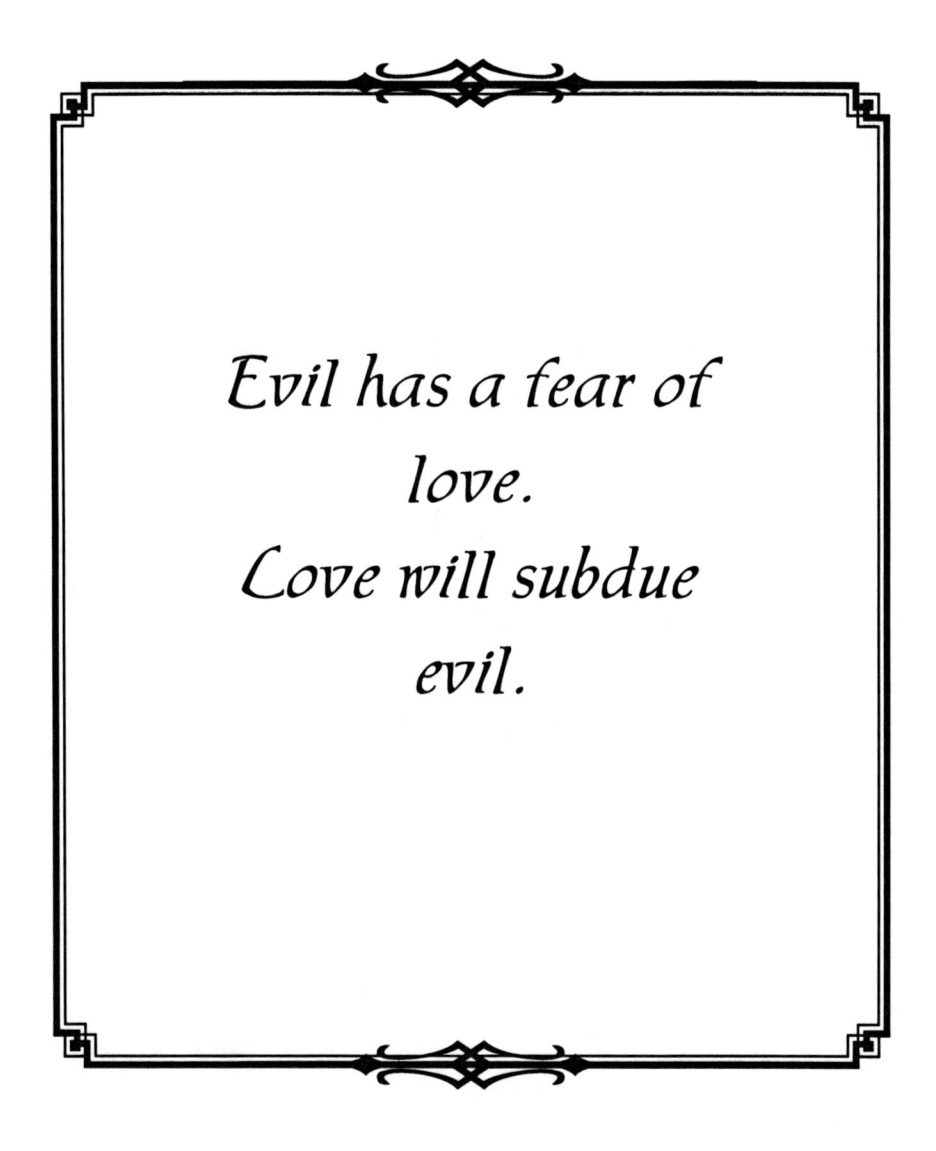

*Evil has a fear of love.
Love will subdue evil.*

GENTLEMEN'S CLUB

I wear the crown because I am the king. I love the way women shake their thangs.

LET IT GO

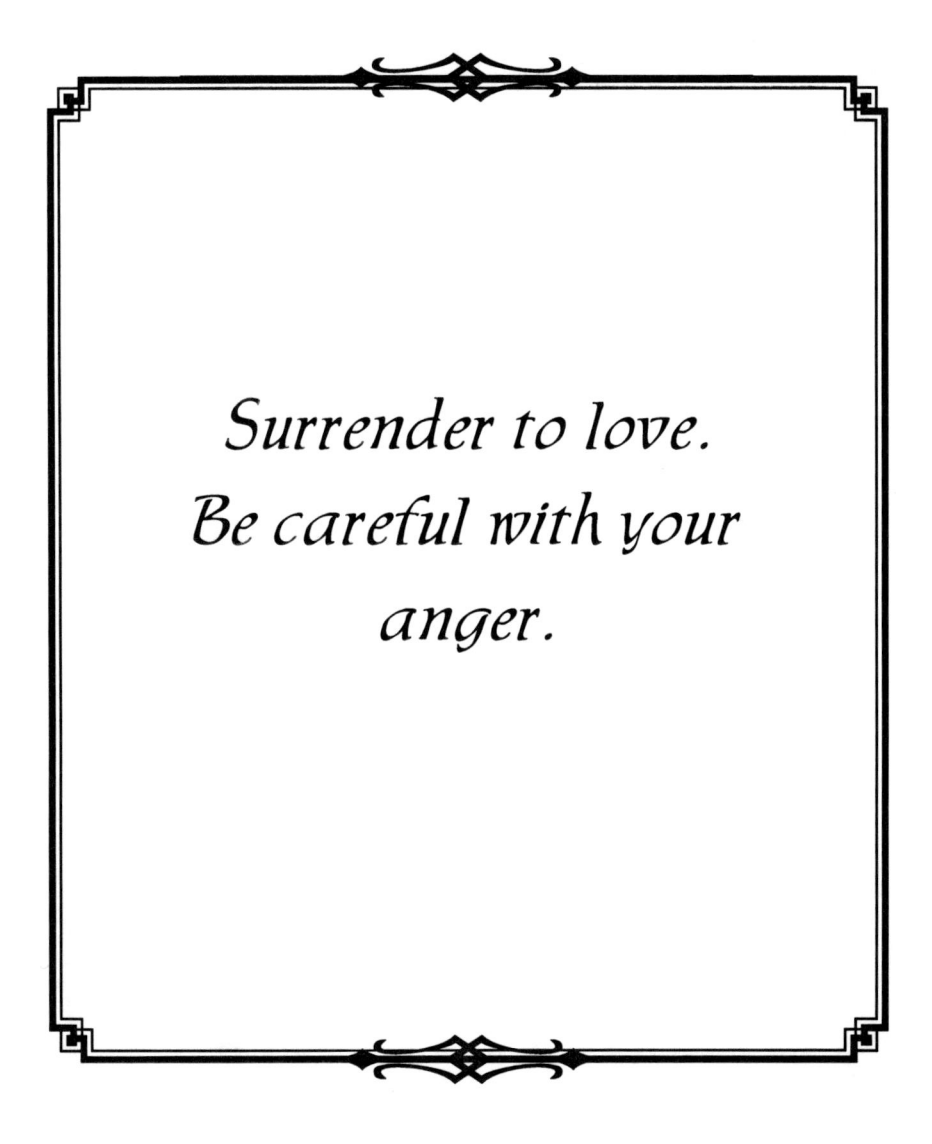

*Surrender to love.
Be careful with your anger.*

THE SOLUTION

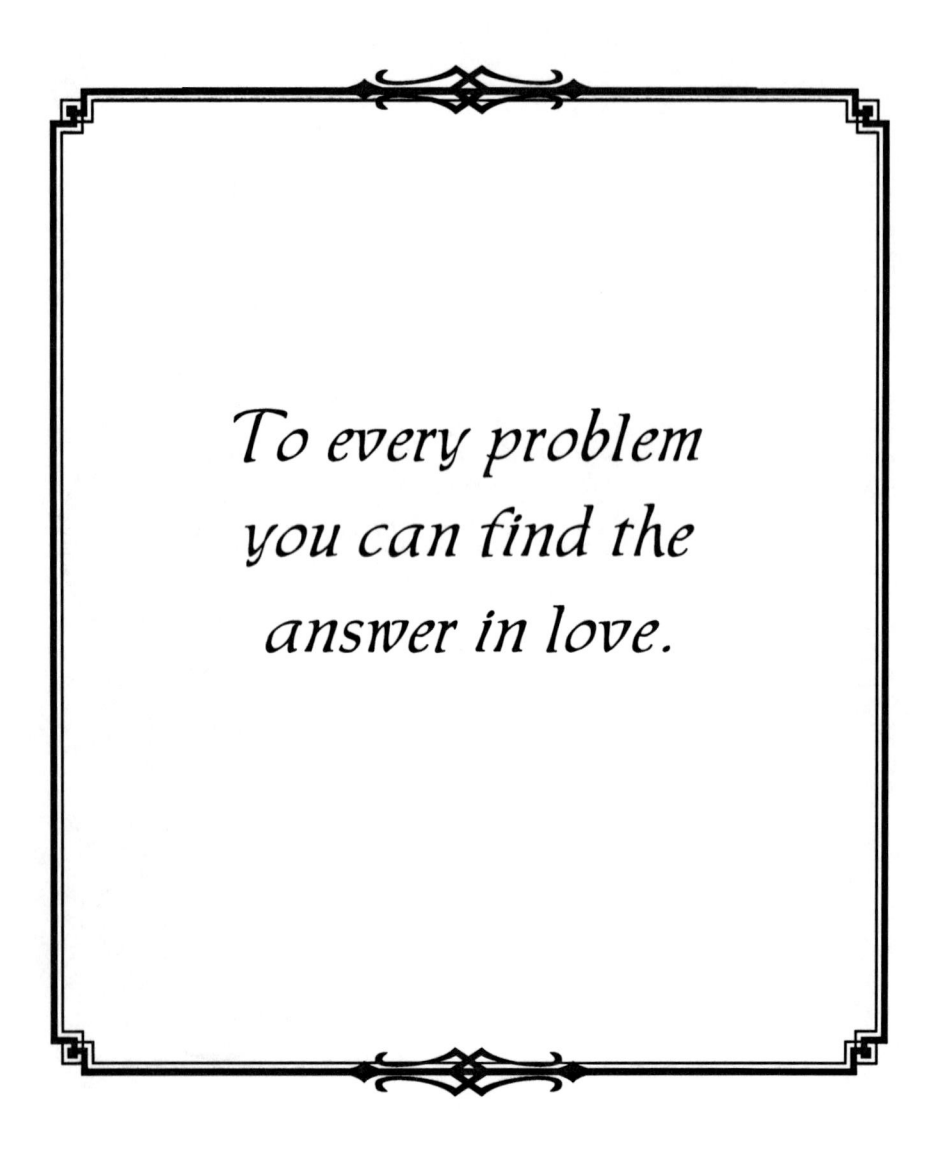

To every problem you can find the answer in love.

CLOCK

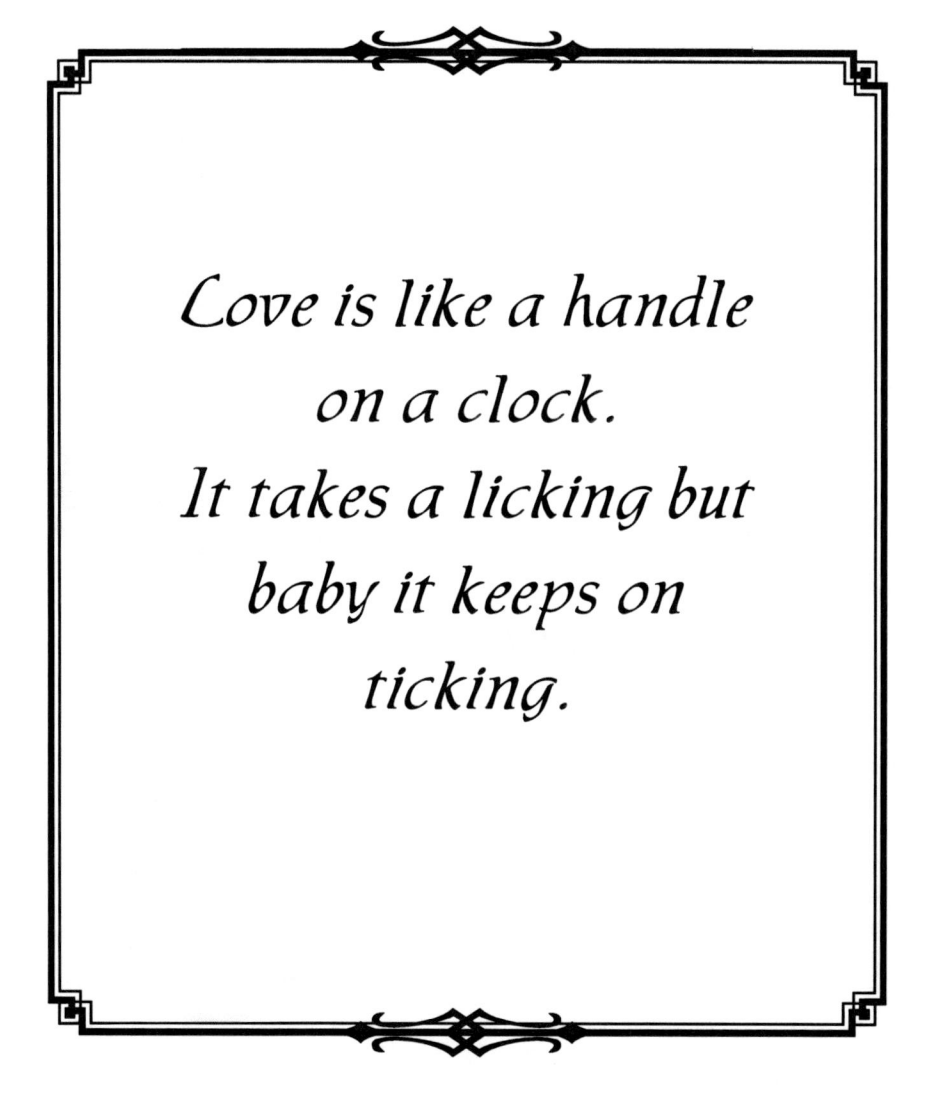

Love is like a handle on a clock. It takes a licking but baby it keeps on ticking.

EXPERIENCE THE MOMENT

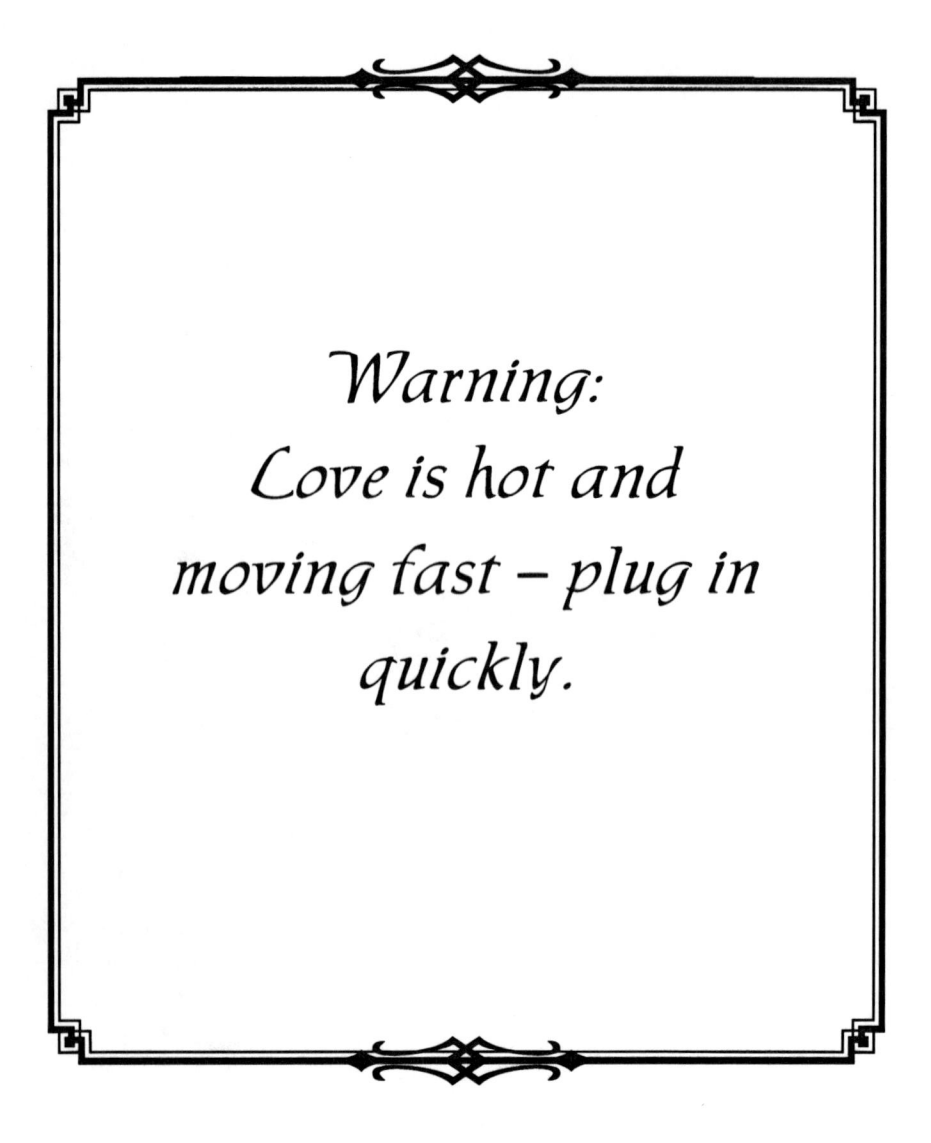

Warning: Love is hot and moving fast – plug in quickly.

FRIENDSHIP

You've shown me a love I never knew. I hope you feel the same way too.

SPEAK LOVE

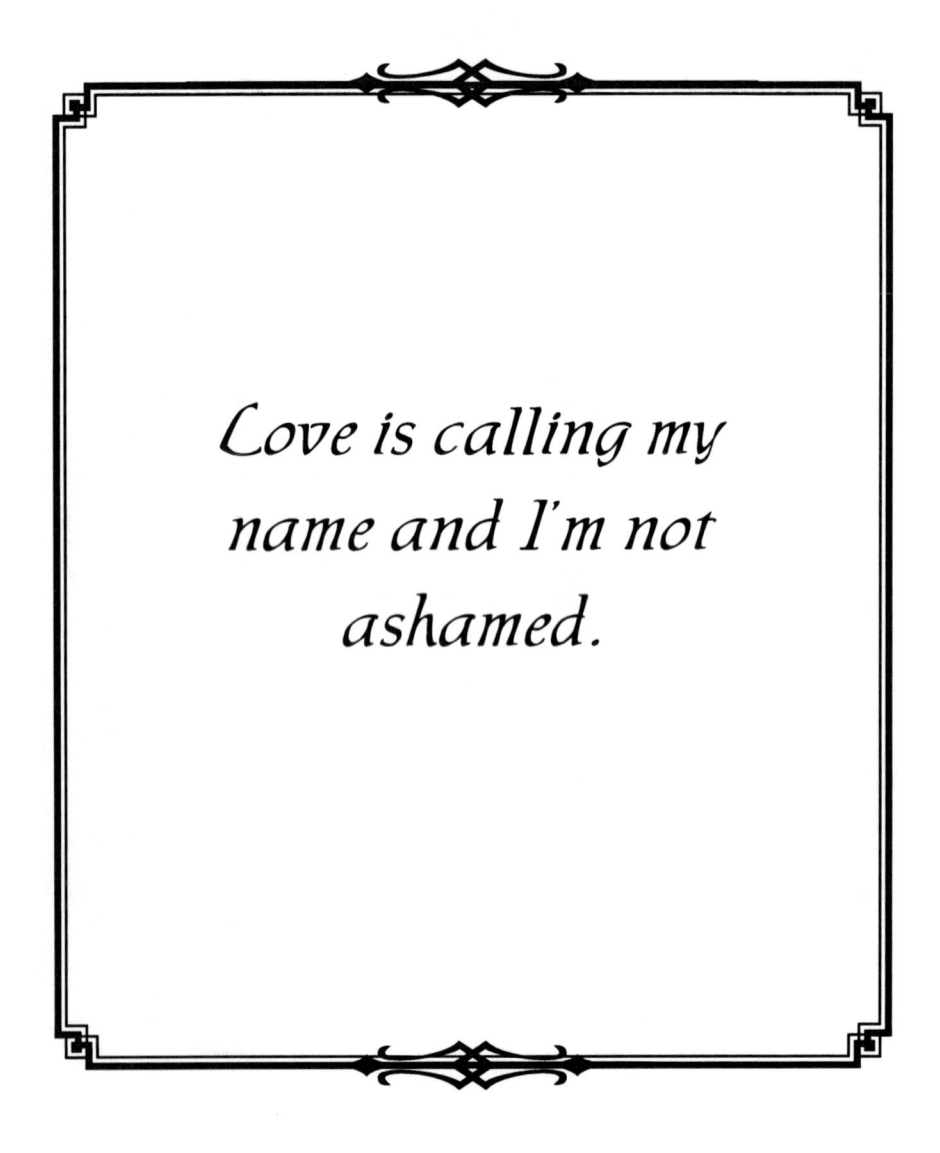

Love is calling my name and I'm not ashamed.

BABY IT IS GOOD

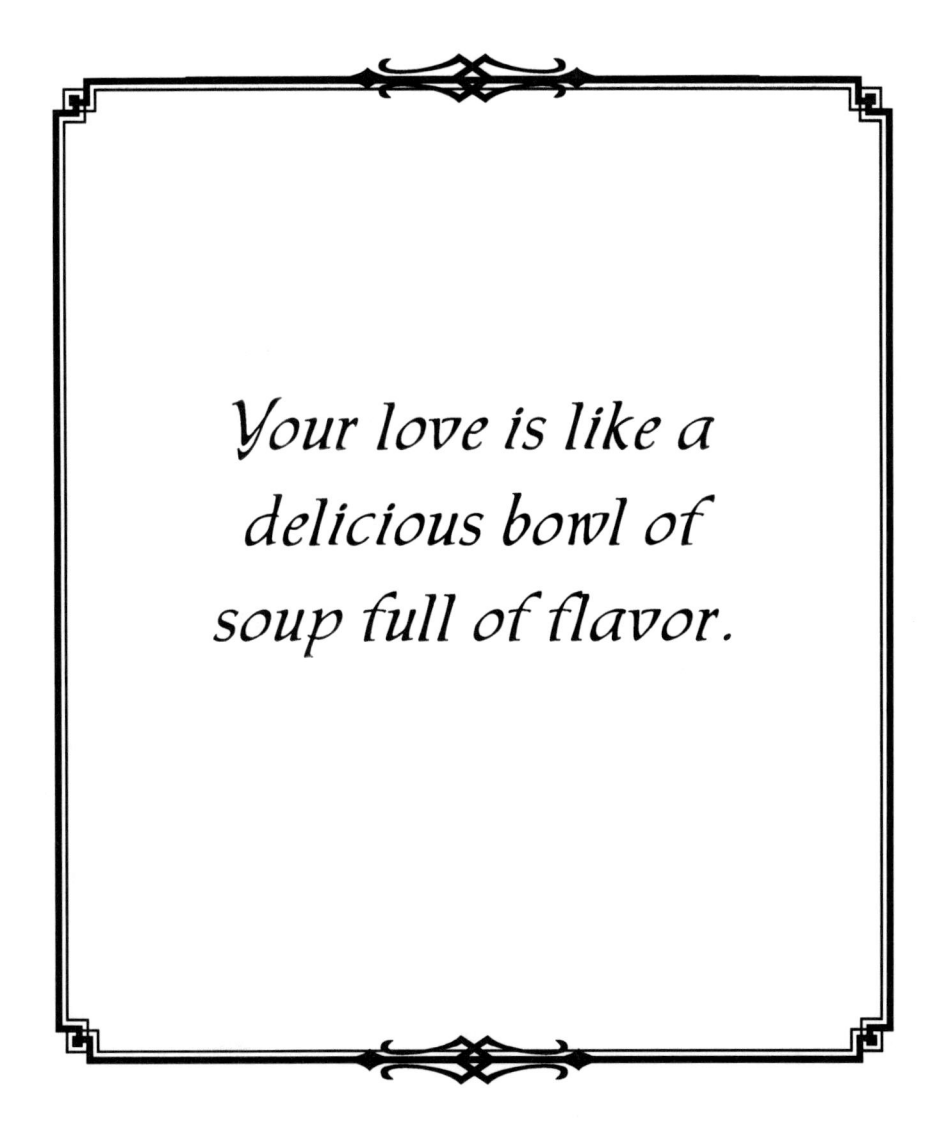

Your love is like a delicious bowl of soup full of flavor.

MAKING A WISH

I want my cake and ice cream too because it was prepared by the loving heart like you.

FACE IT

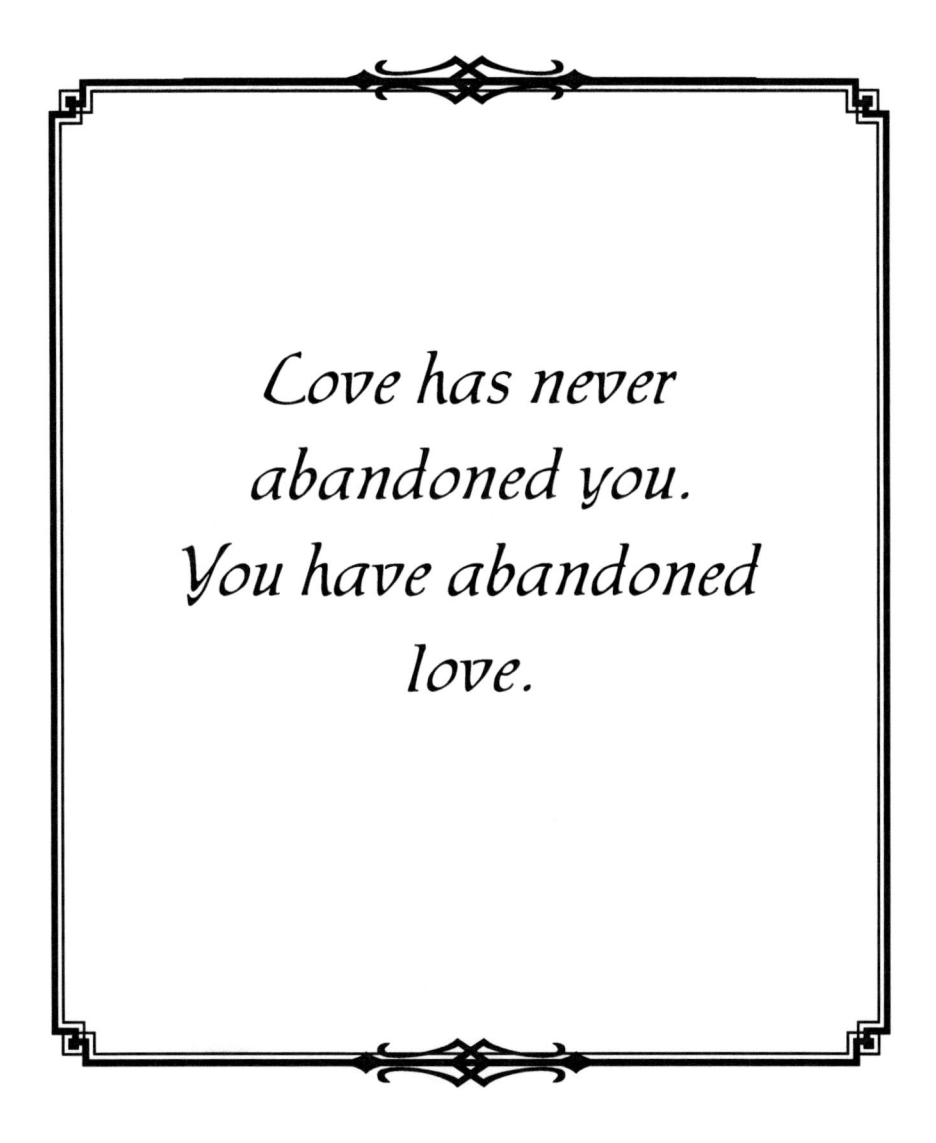

Love has never abandoned you. You have abandoned love.

A PIECE OF MY HEART

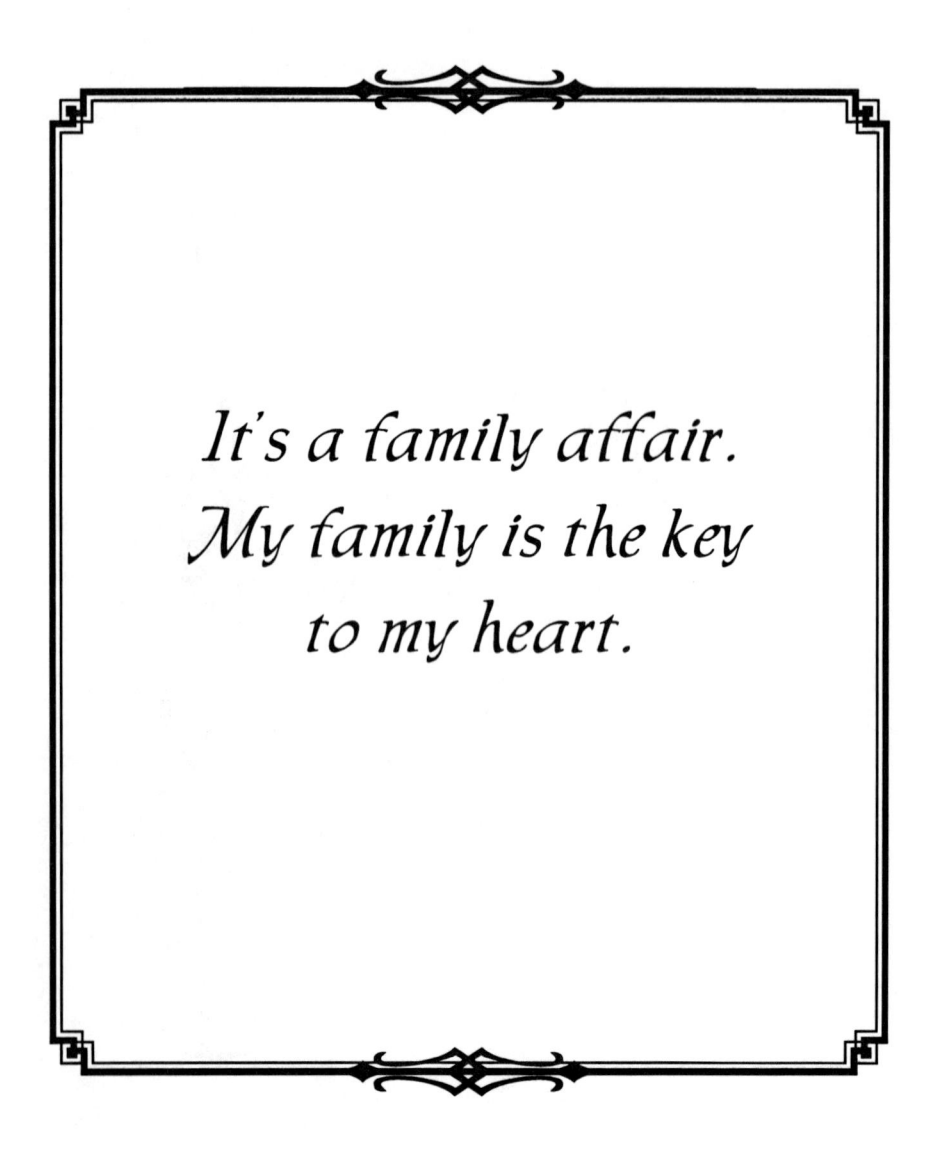

*It's a family affair.
My family is the key
to my heart.*

THE LAW OF MARRIAGE

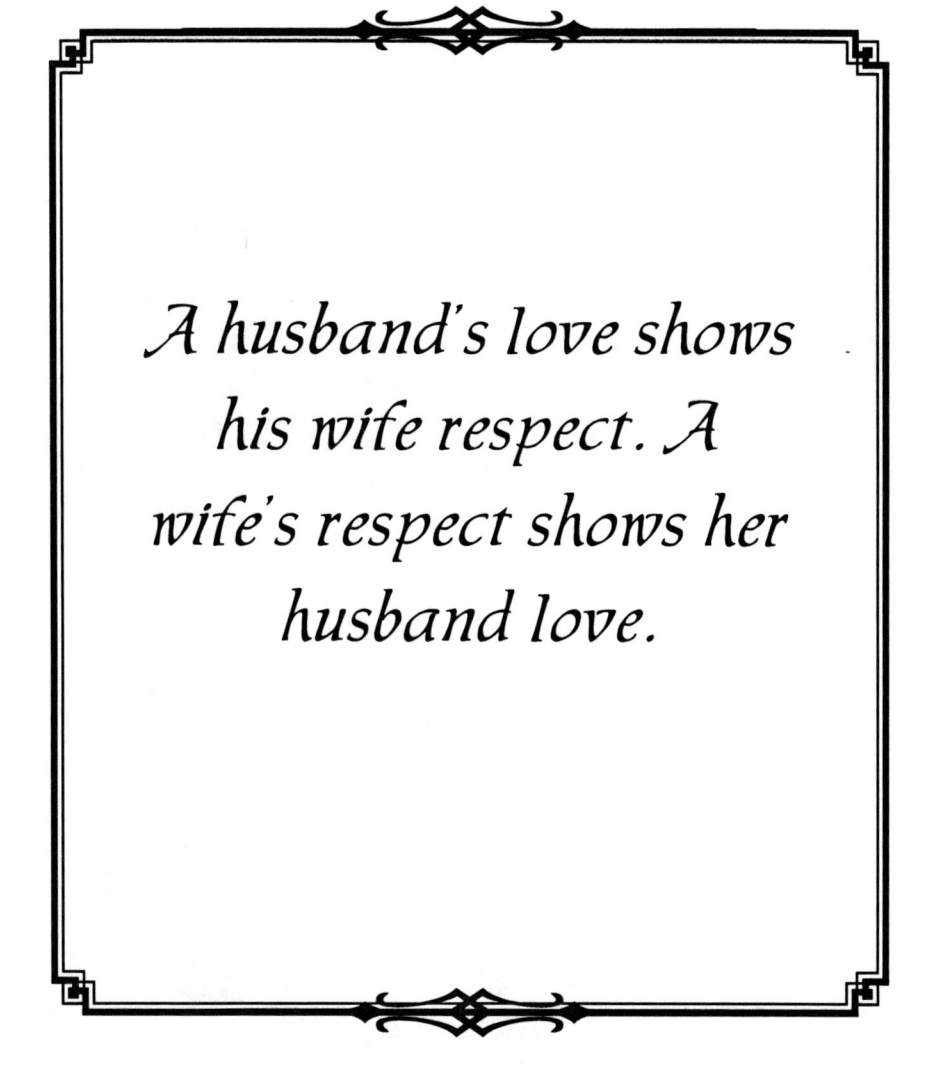

A husband's love shows his wife respect. A wife's respect shows her husband love.

TO MY WIFE, RAMONA

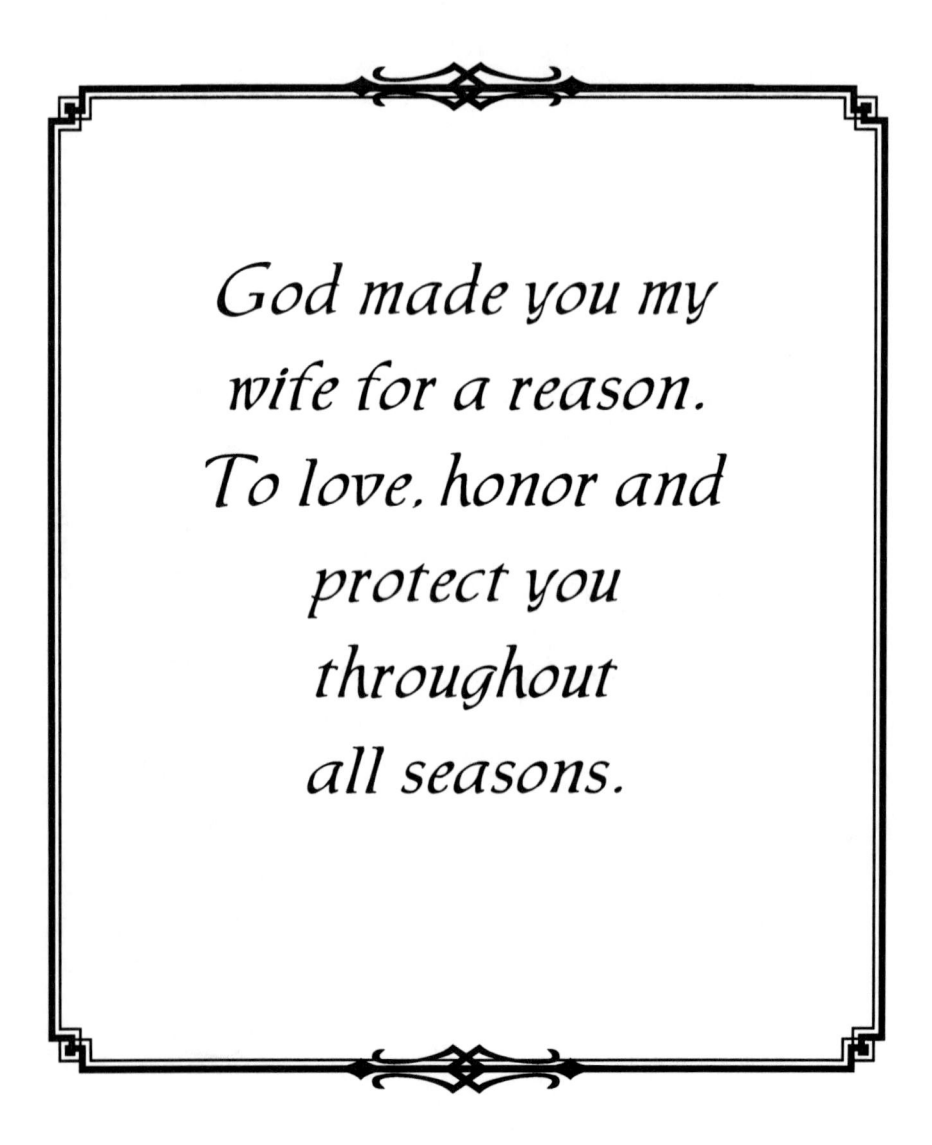

God made you my wife for a reason. To love, honor and protect you throughout all seasons.

A MOTHER'S LOVE

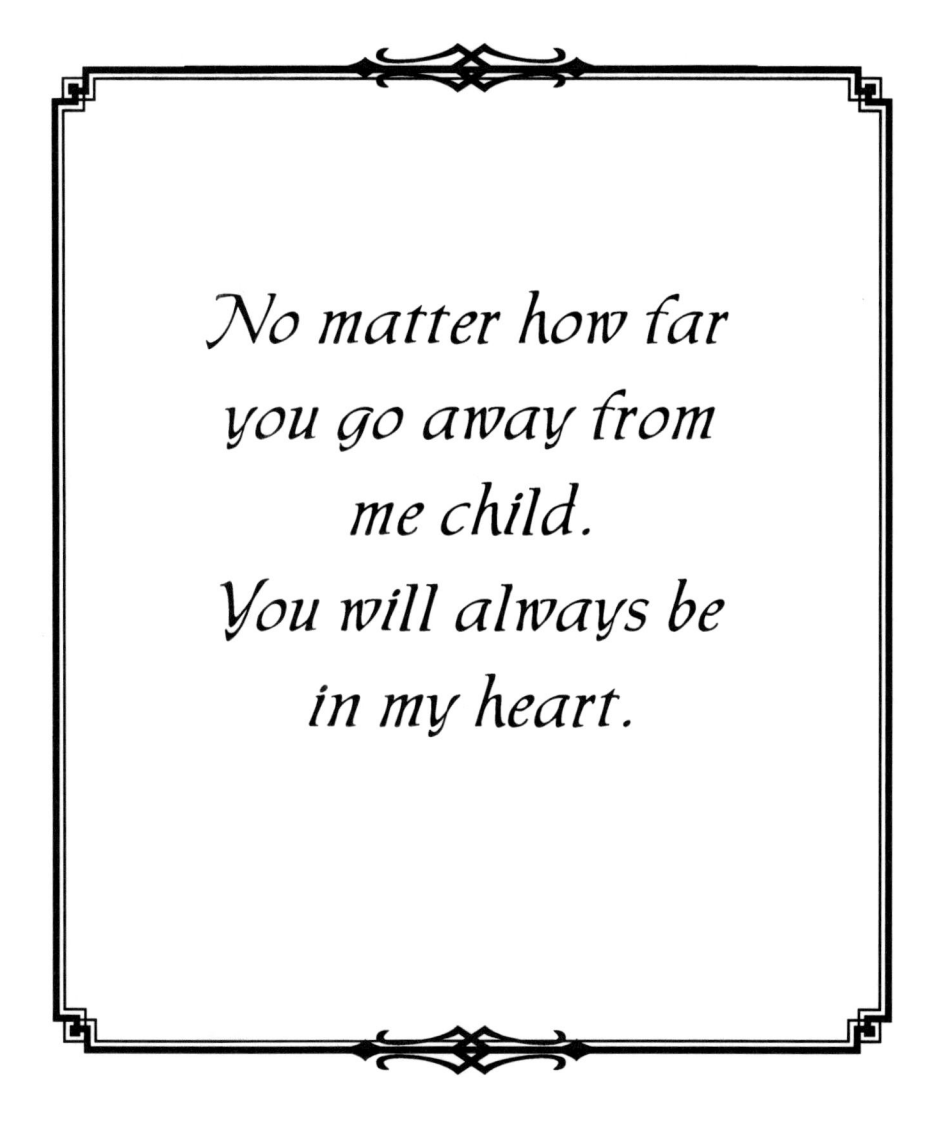

No matter how far you go away from me child. You will always be in my heart.

MOTHERS AND DAUGHTERS

Mothers and daughters are so much like the same, but neither wants to take the blame.

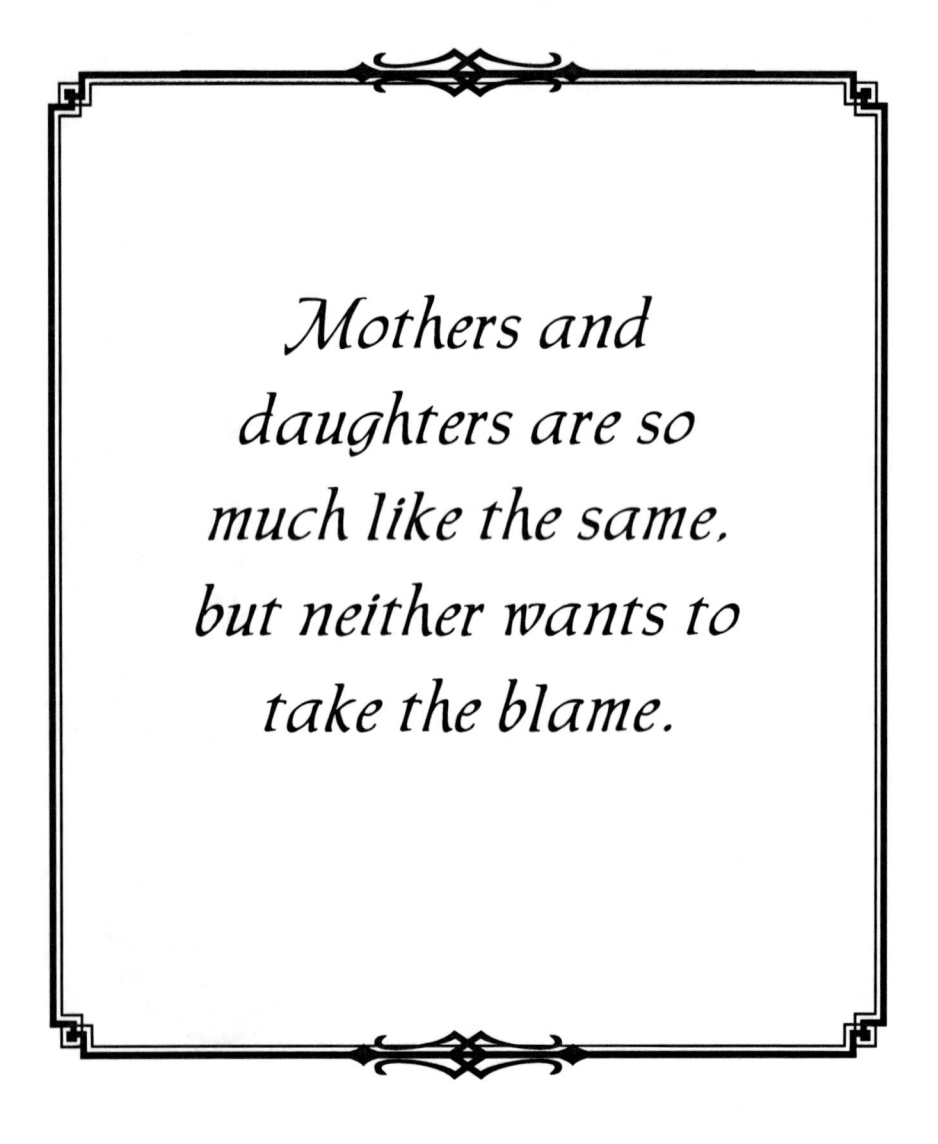

FATHER & SON

Fathers and sons think they are one, but when it's time to do the house chores no one wants to get it done.

RELATIVES

Relatives are cool, but some of them love to act a fool.

IN-LAWS

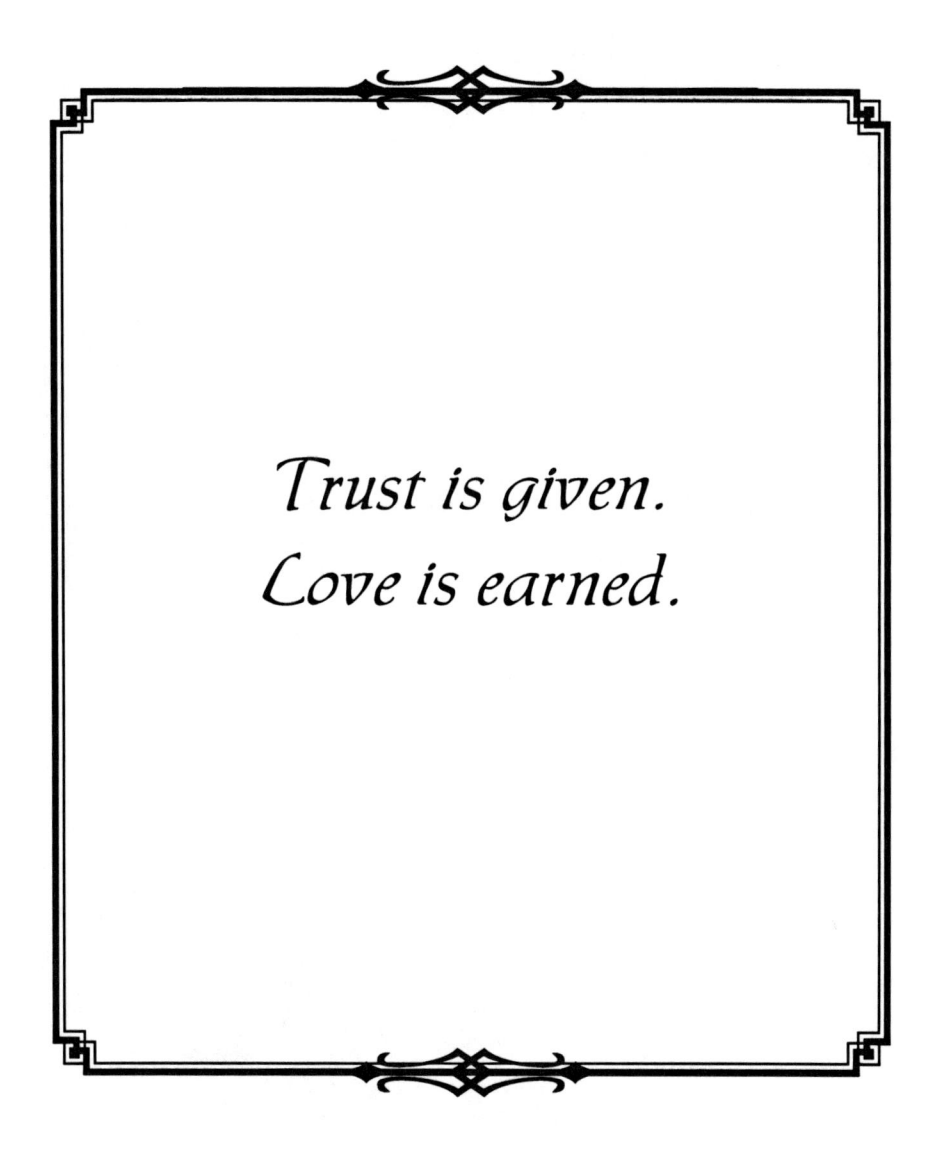

*Trust is given.
Love is earned.*

PEOPLE COME TOGETHER

Death radiates love when one has lived.

RITES OF PASSAGE

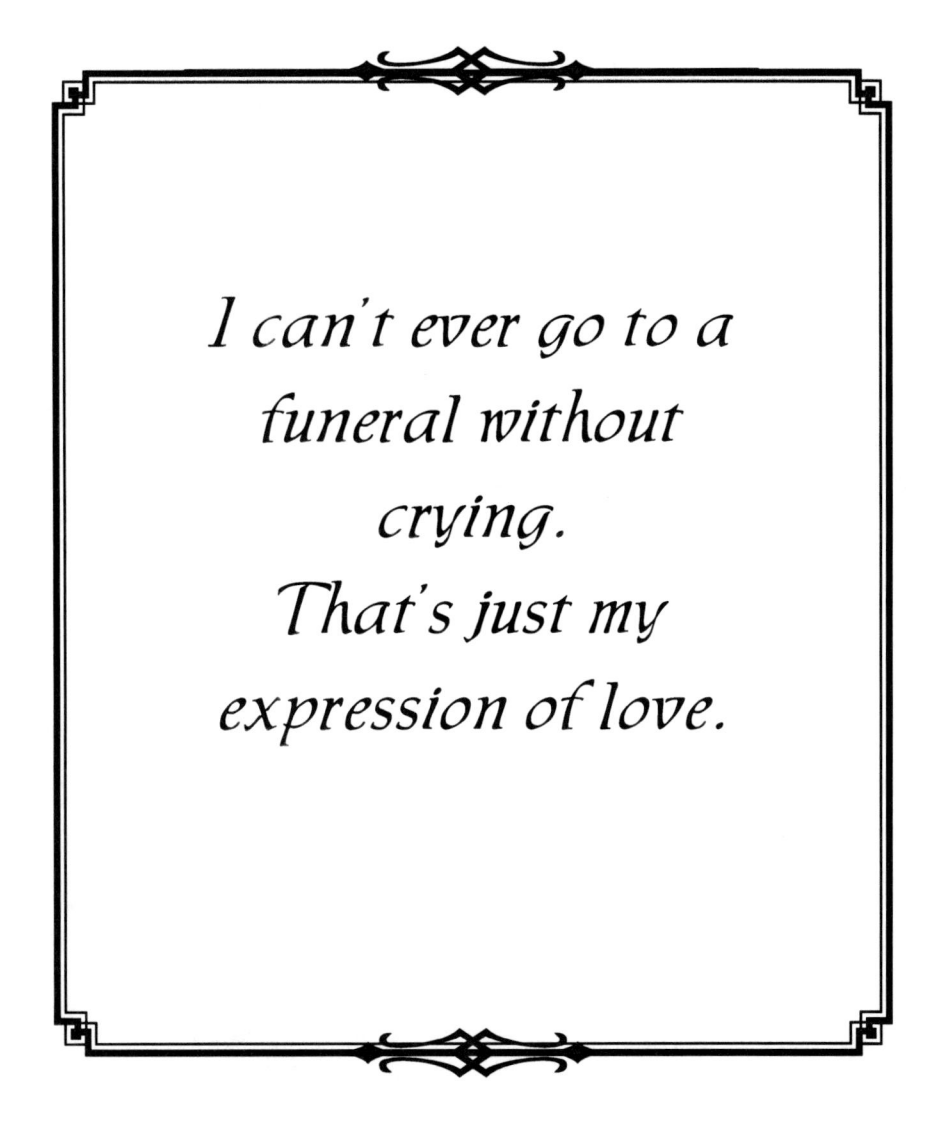

I can't ever go to a funeral without crying. That's just my expression of love.

CRY

When you cry, love cries along with you.

DIG IT

*Enter if you suffer
from despair.
Love is in here.*

GIVE MORE

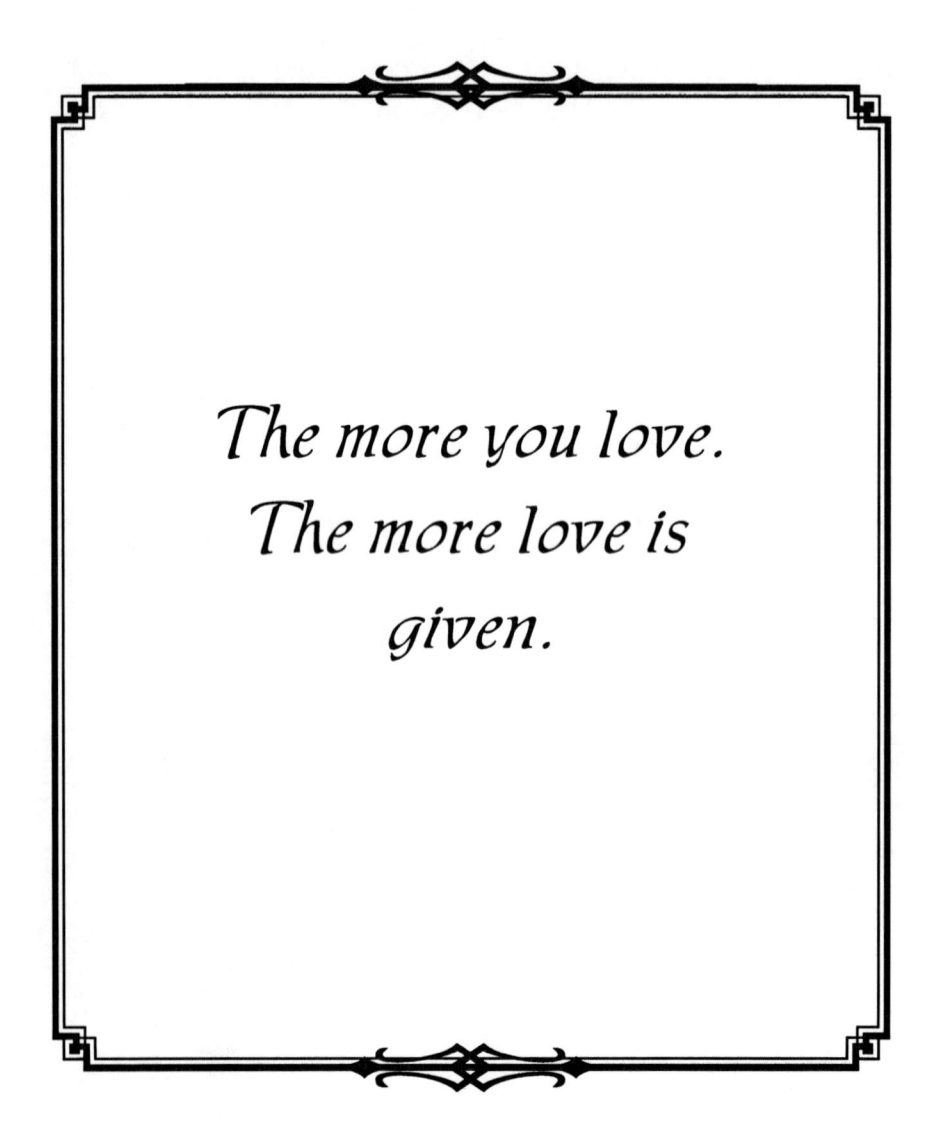

*The more you love.
The more love is given.*

BE THE FIRST

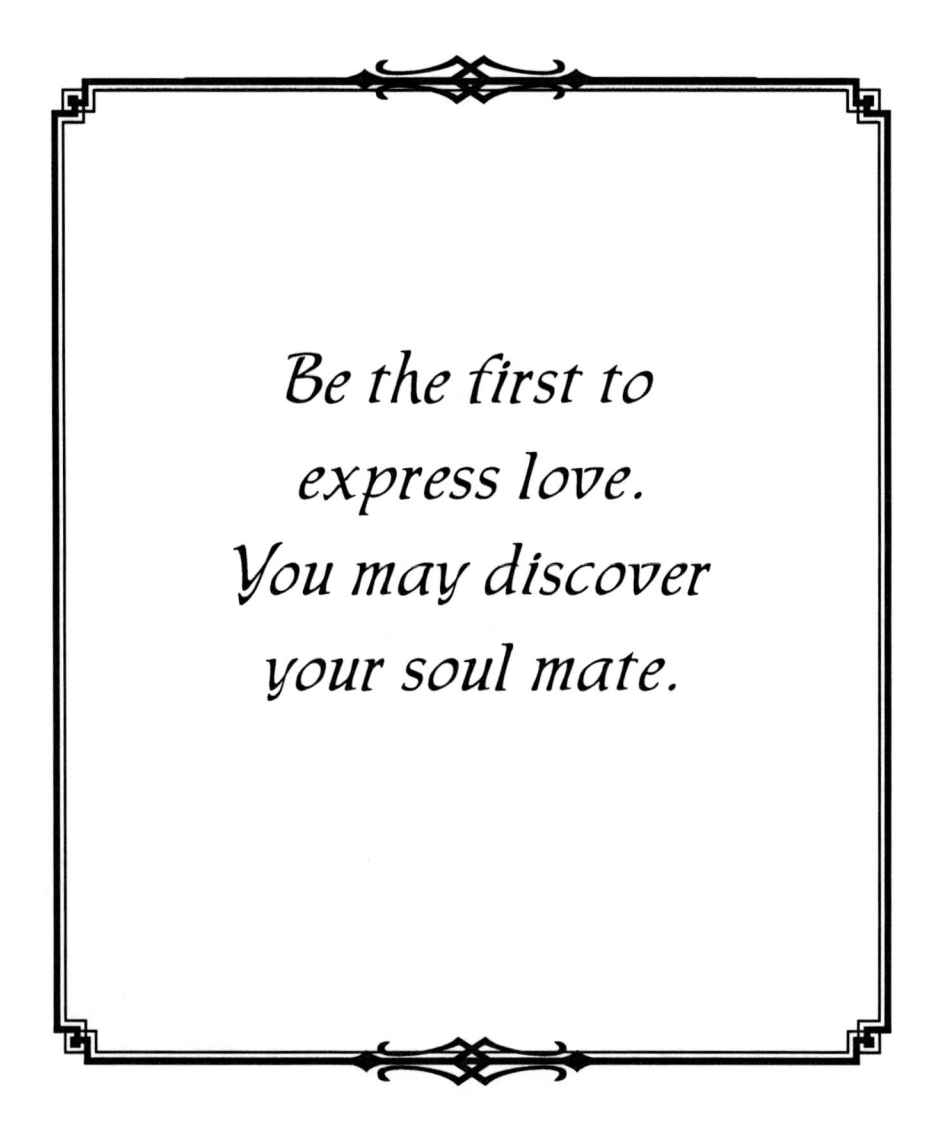

Be the first to express love. You may discover your soul mate.

A WASTE OF TIME

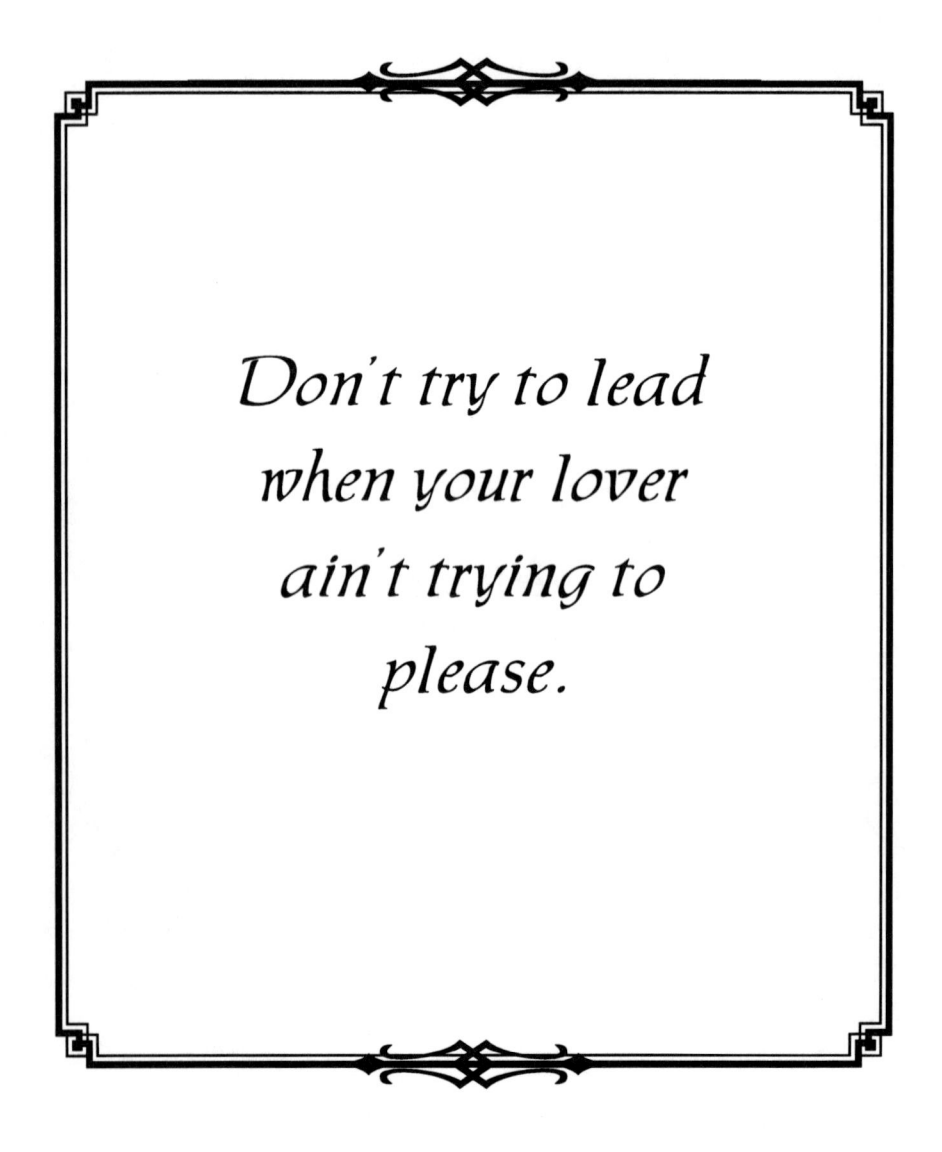

Don't try to lead when your lover ain't trying to please.

PEOPLE WATCHING

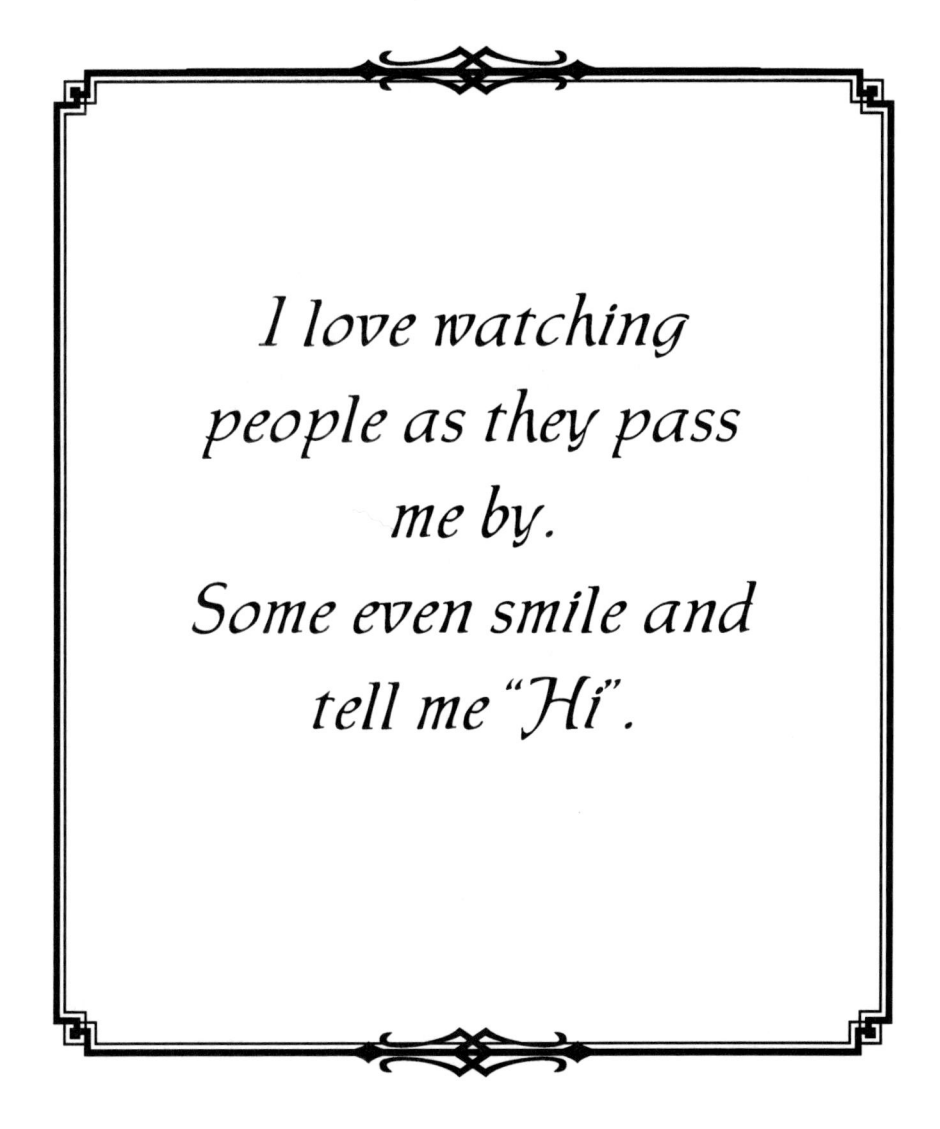

*I love watching people as they pass me by.
Some even smile and tell me "Hi".*

ARE YOU REALLY SURE?

*I fell in love with you the day you walked through my door.
Oh how much did I adore.*

PRACTITIONER LOVER

Please give your love to me girl that I may rock your world.

FIRST DATE

My very first date with you was cool. Thank you for not acting a fool.

I AM A GQ MAN

As a man, I love to smell good and the ladies say that's fine. Whenever one of them meet me they always want to buy me a glass of expensive wine.

PERFUME

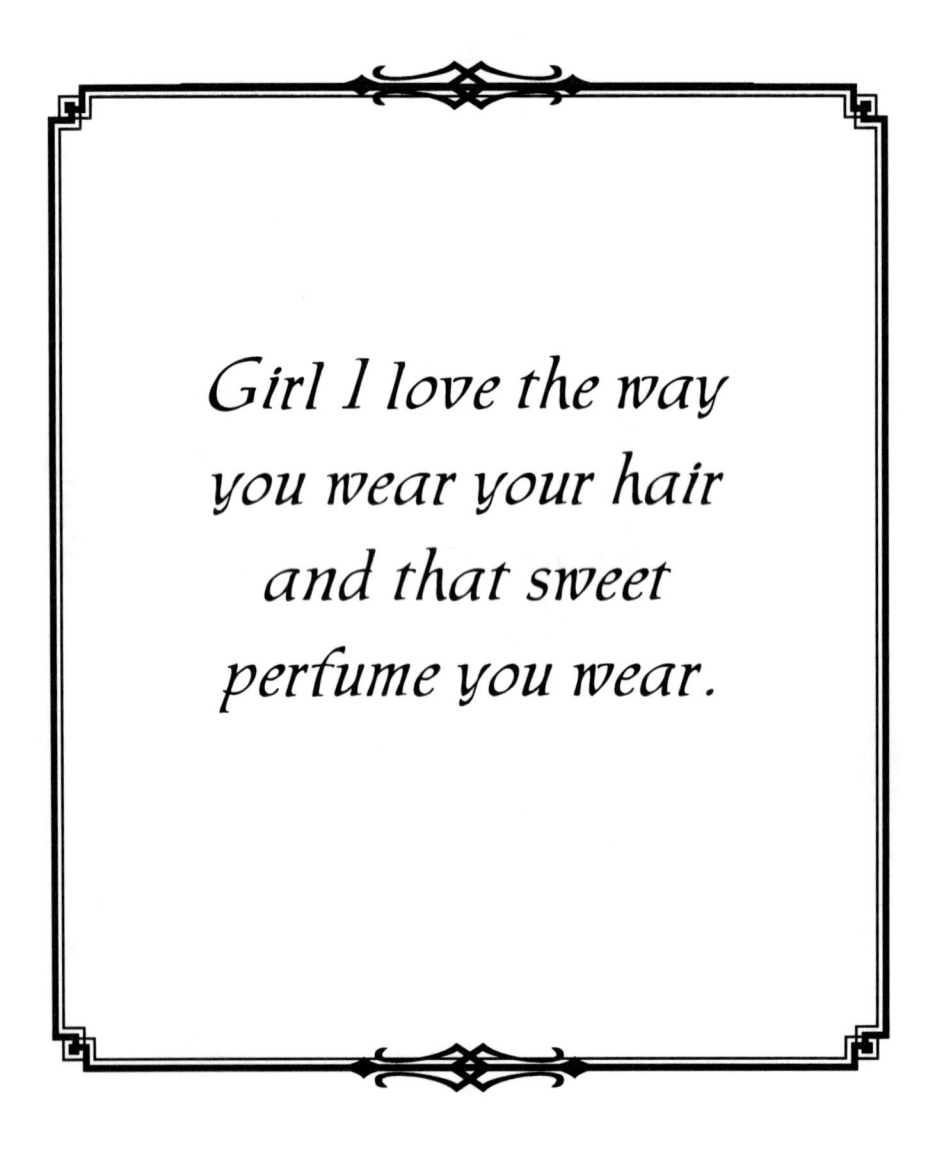

Girl I love the way you wear your hair and that sweet perfume you wear.

SENSUOUS

She said my love rained down on her and made her wet inside her womb.

SPICES

Love is the spice of the night when the loving is tight.

MUSIC TO MY EAR

I hear a symphony
of a wonderful sound
when your love
is around.

BLEND WITH ME

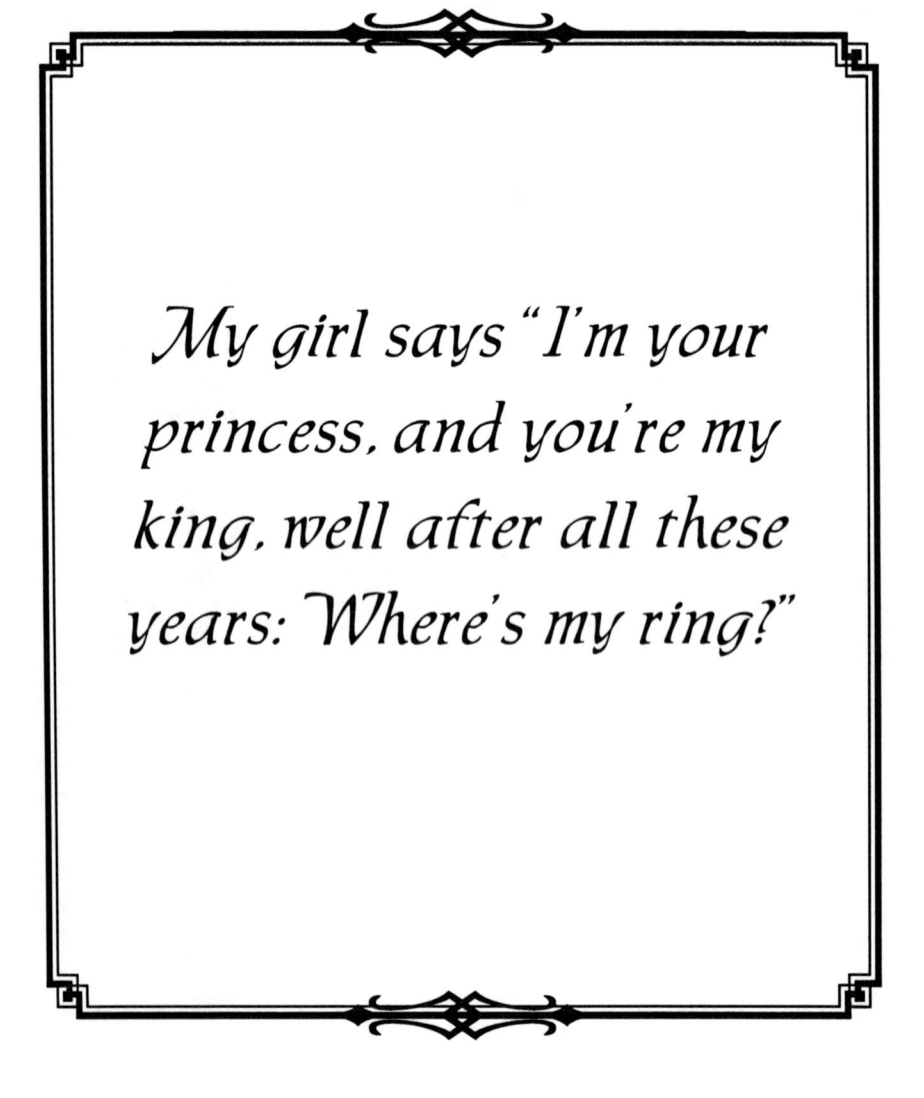

My girl says "I'm your princess, and you're my king, well after all these years: Where's my ring?"

MERRY CHRISTMAS

I wish you a Merry Christmas baby, and may our New Year be sweeter than the years gone by.

EMERALD

Rubies and gold she said is all wrapped up in my loving soul.

NO BULL

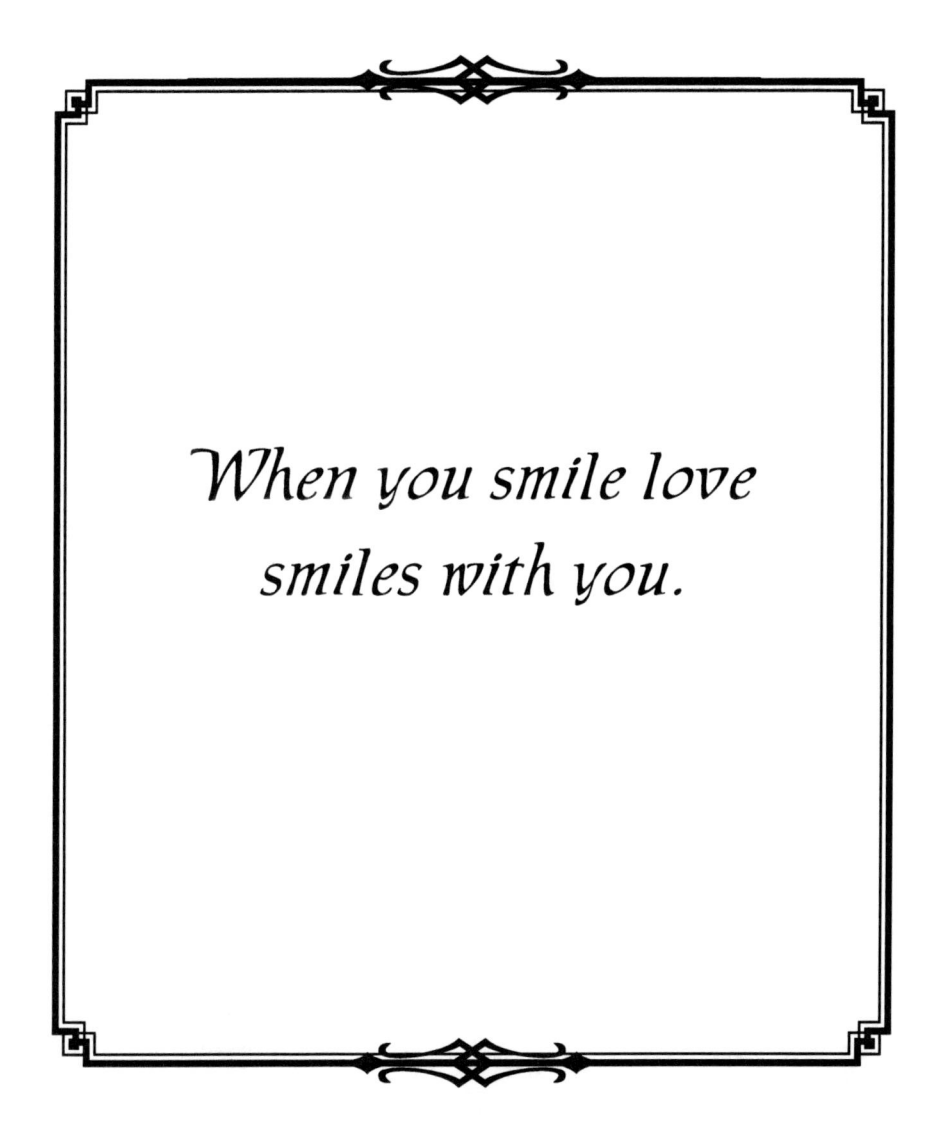

When you smile love smiles with you.

HUMAN RESOURCES

*Love surrounds me every day.
I have no complaints.*

SECRET LOVER

I'm single and I'm enjoying myself. When I'm in need of loving I know where to go and get some help.

RIDE BABY

Love feels good when it's inside.
A lady once told me
"Ride, baby ride".

THAT DAY

*In that moment I found love.
I gave you my biggest kiss and hug.*

STOP BY

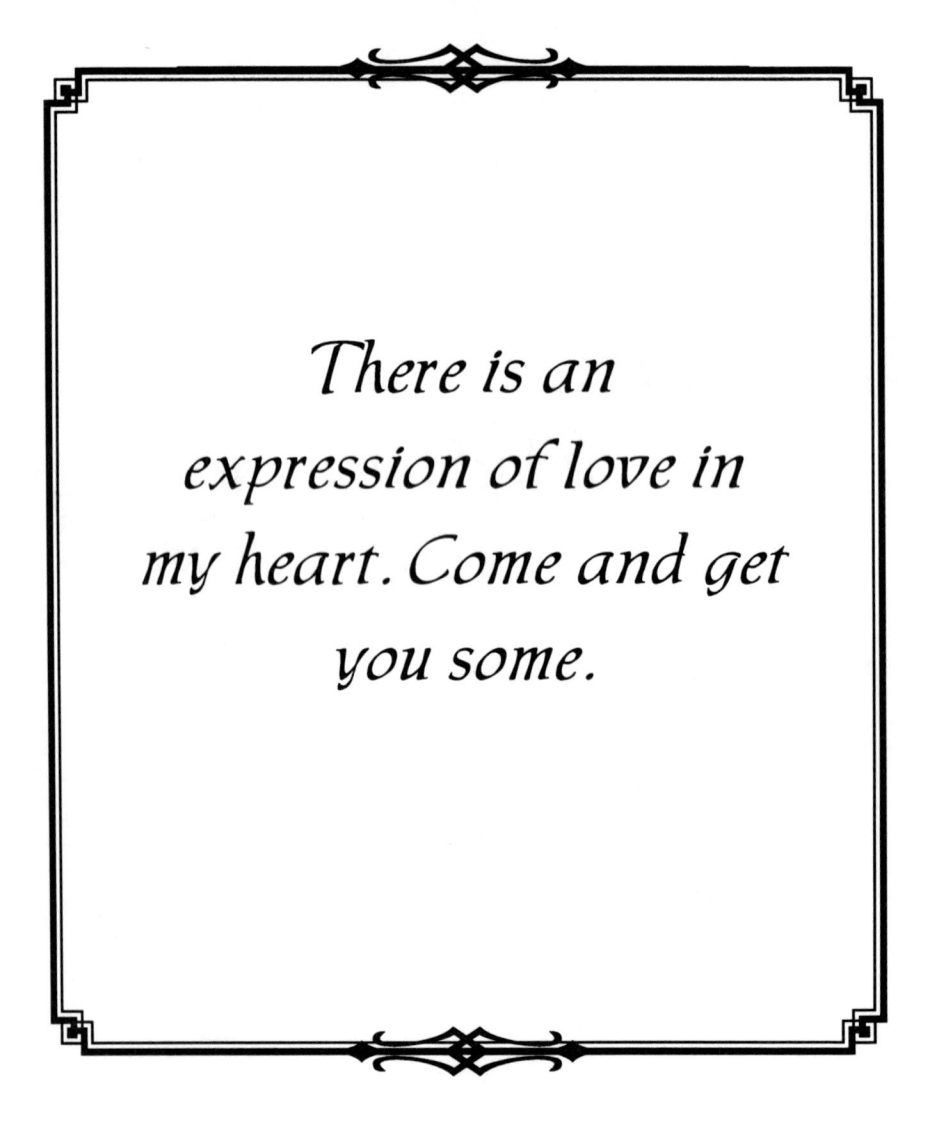

There is an expression of love in my heart. Come and get you some.

IT'S TRUE

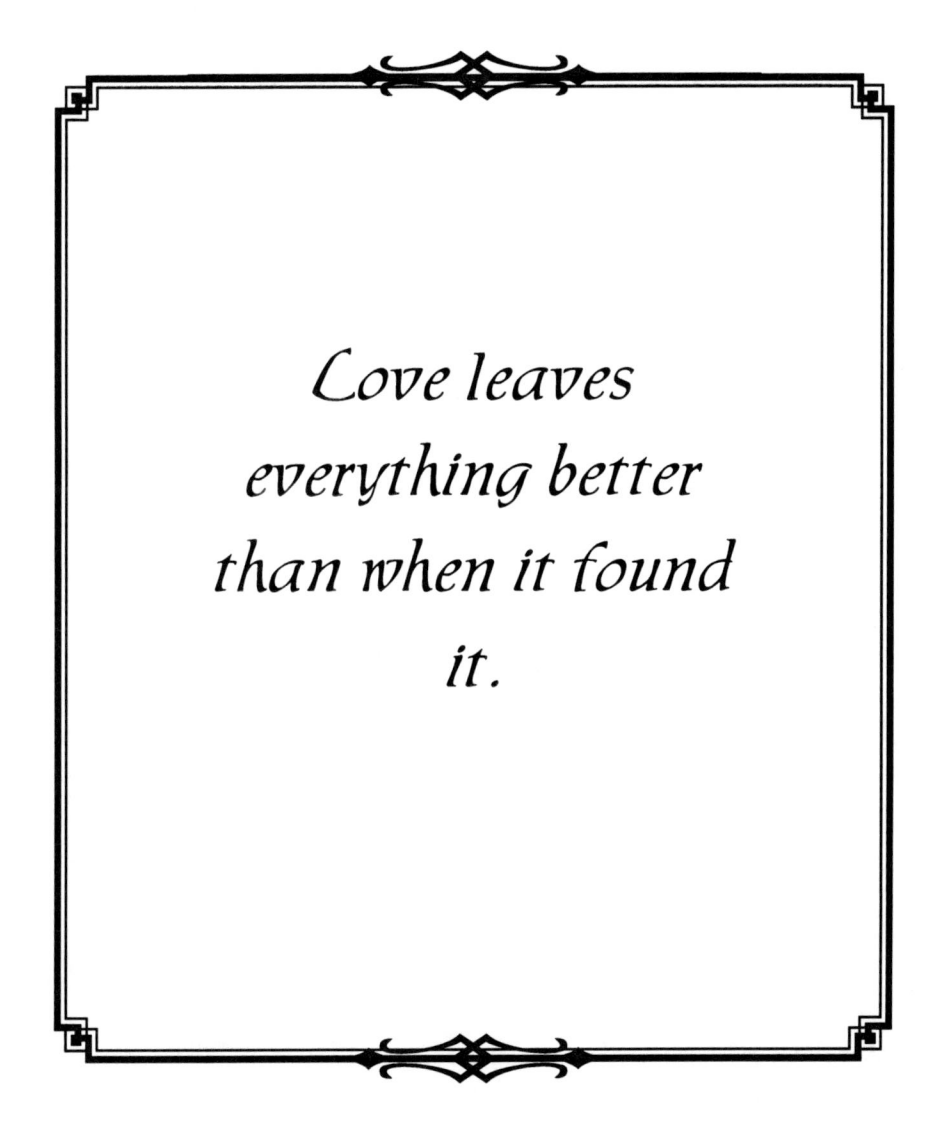

Love leaves everything better than when it found it.

ICE CREAM

Love is like ice cream each lick just gets sweeter and sweeter.

NOBODY TOLD ME

Love has its own power.

Dadisi Mwende Netifnet

SECURITY

*My heart is on lock down.
Why don't you come and unlock it.*

MY PRECIOUS BLOOD

Today I am going to give someone the gift of love.

MONEY

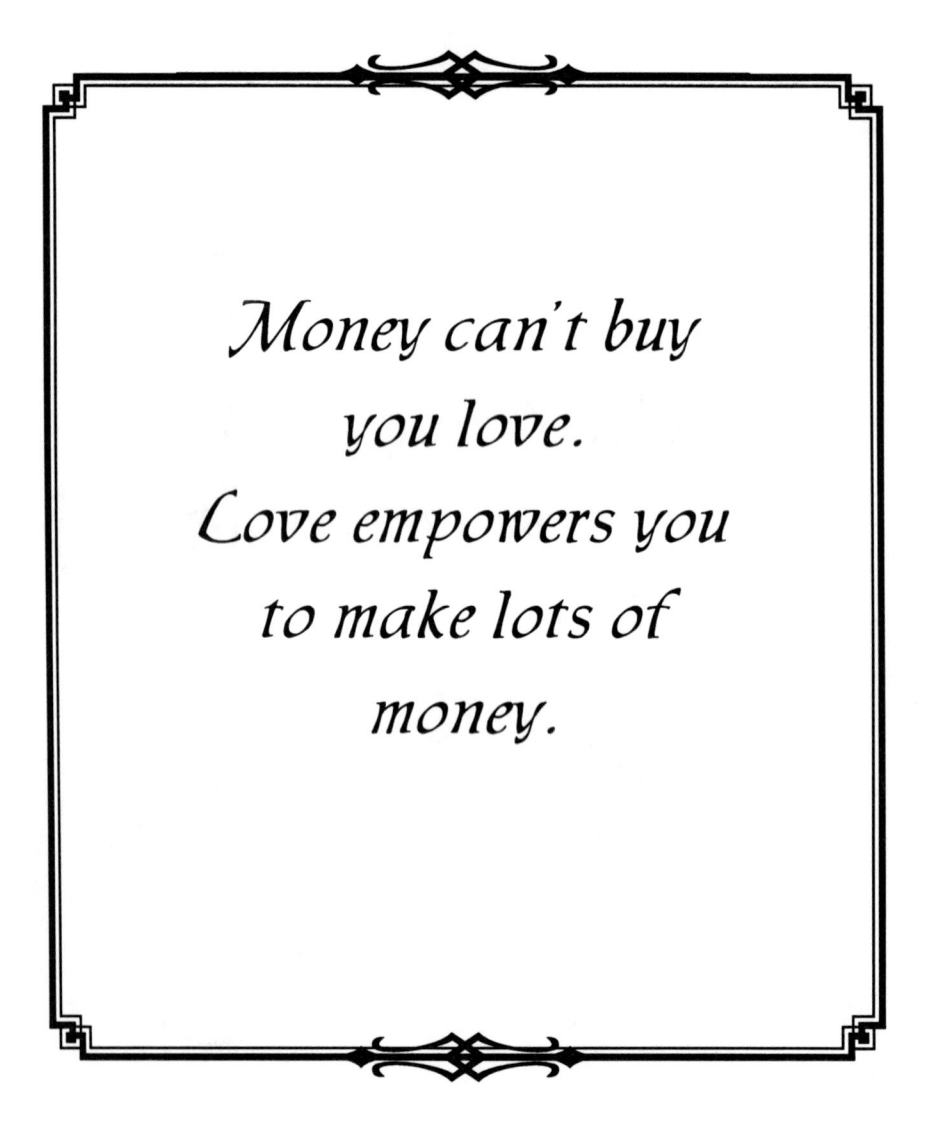

*Money can't buy you love.
Love empowers you to make lots of money.*

WOW

Honesty and love are two best friends.

TOP OF THE LIST

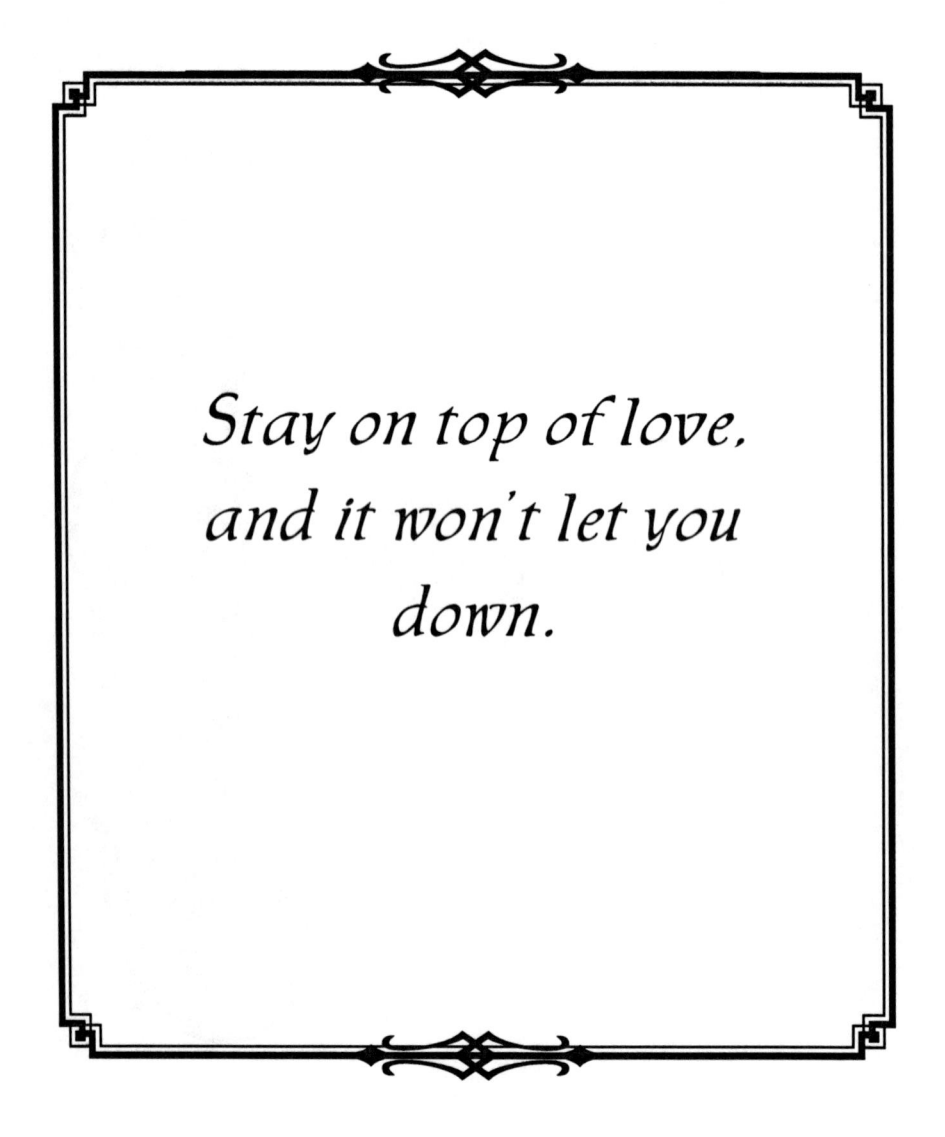

Stay on top of love, and it won't let you down.

BE THE LIGHT

Where there is light, there is love.

DO SOMETHING

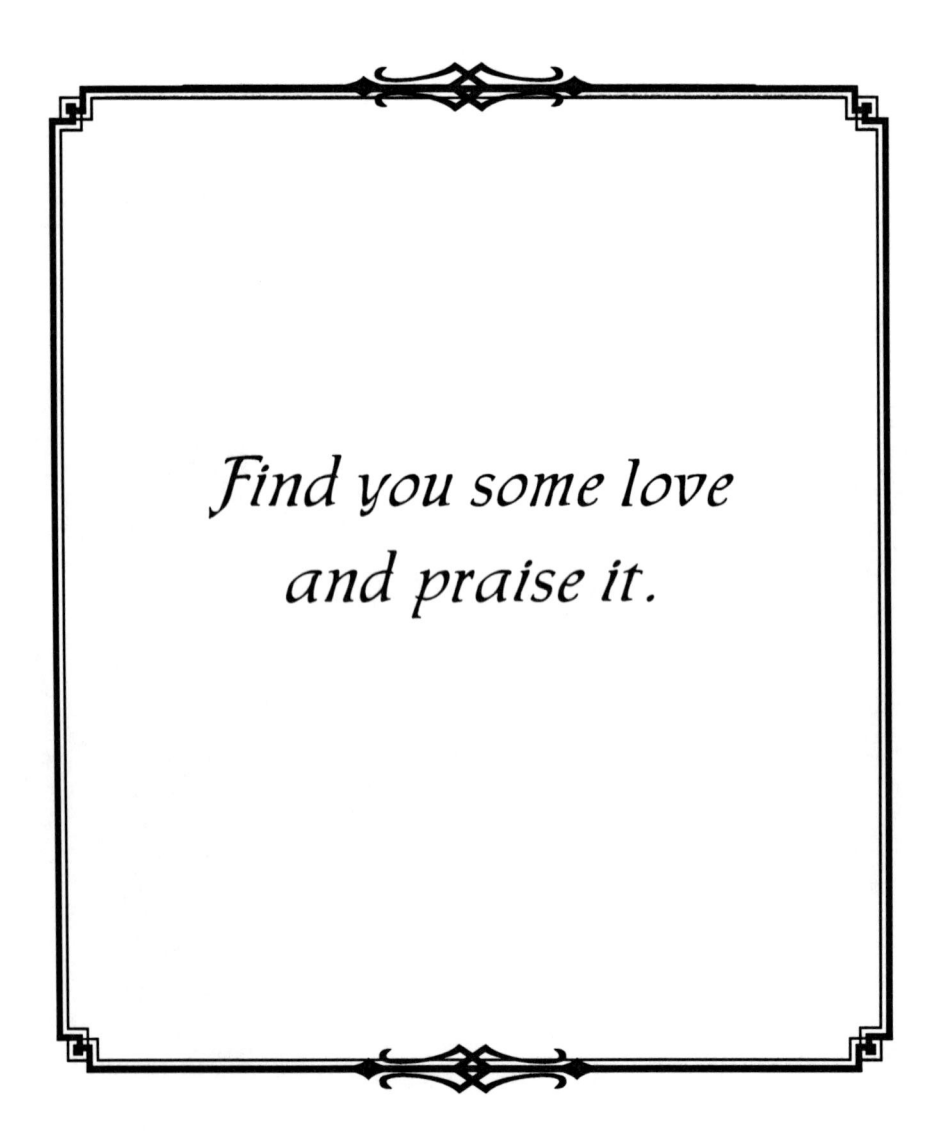

Find you some love and praise it.

PRAISE GOD

One person's love can inspire the hearts of a thousand souls.

TOUCH

Did love touch your lips today?

LOVE YOUR MIND

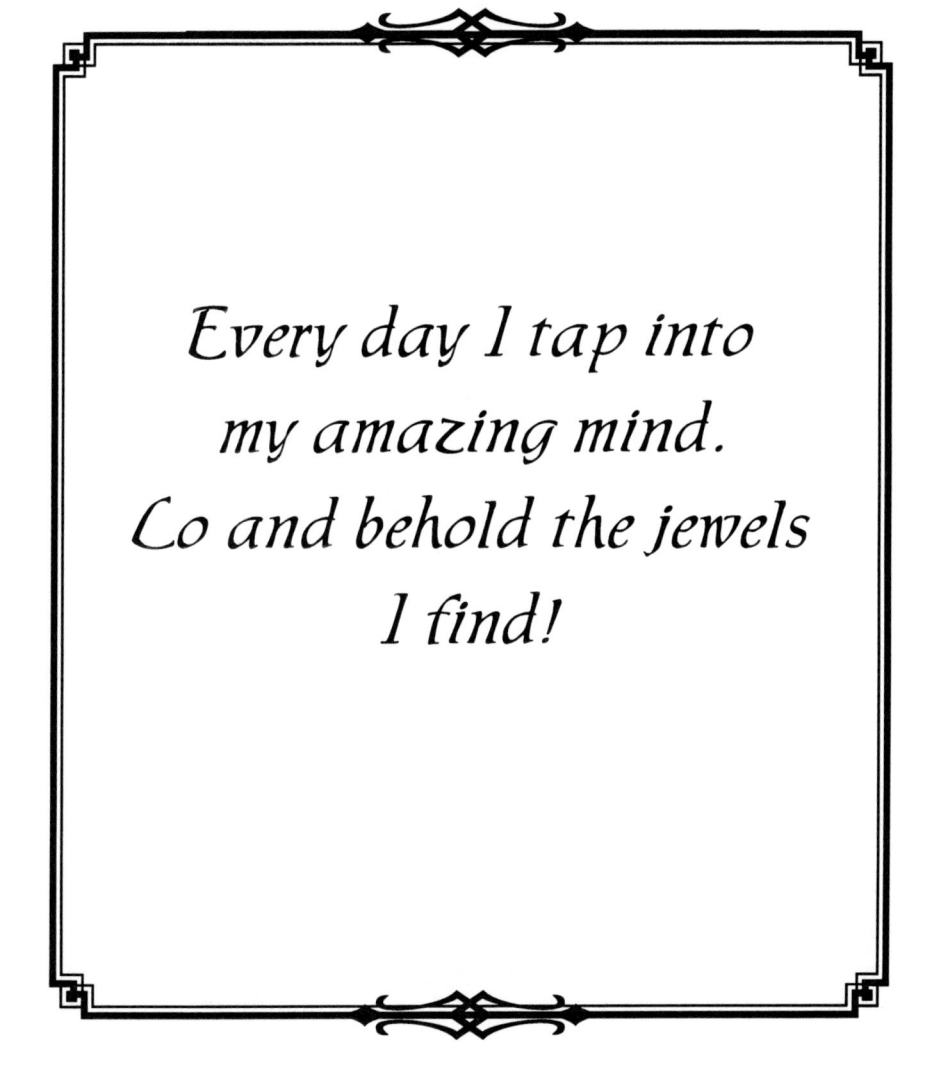

Every day I tap into my amazing mind. Go and behold the jewels I find!

Dadisi Mwende Netifnet

WHAT'S UP

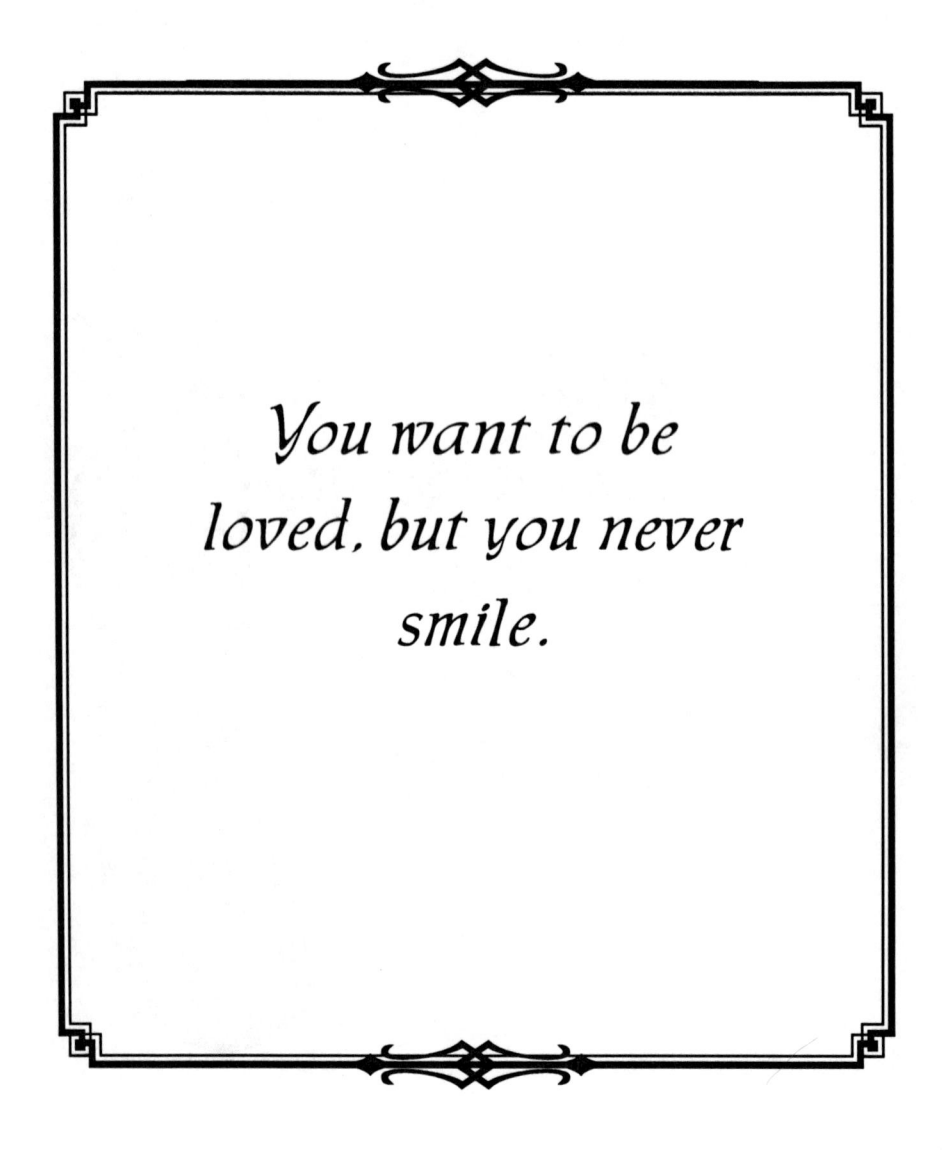

You want to be loved, but you never smile.

APPRECIATION

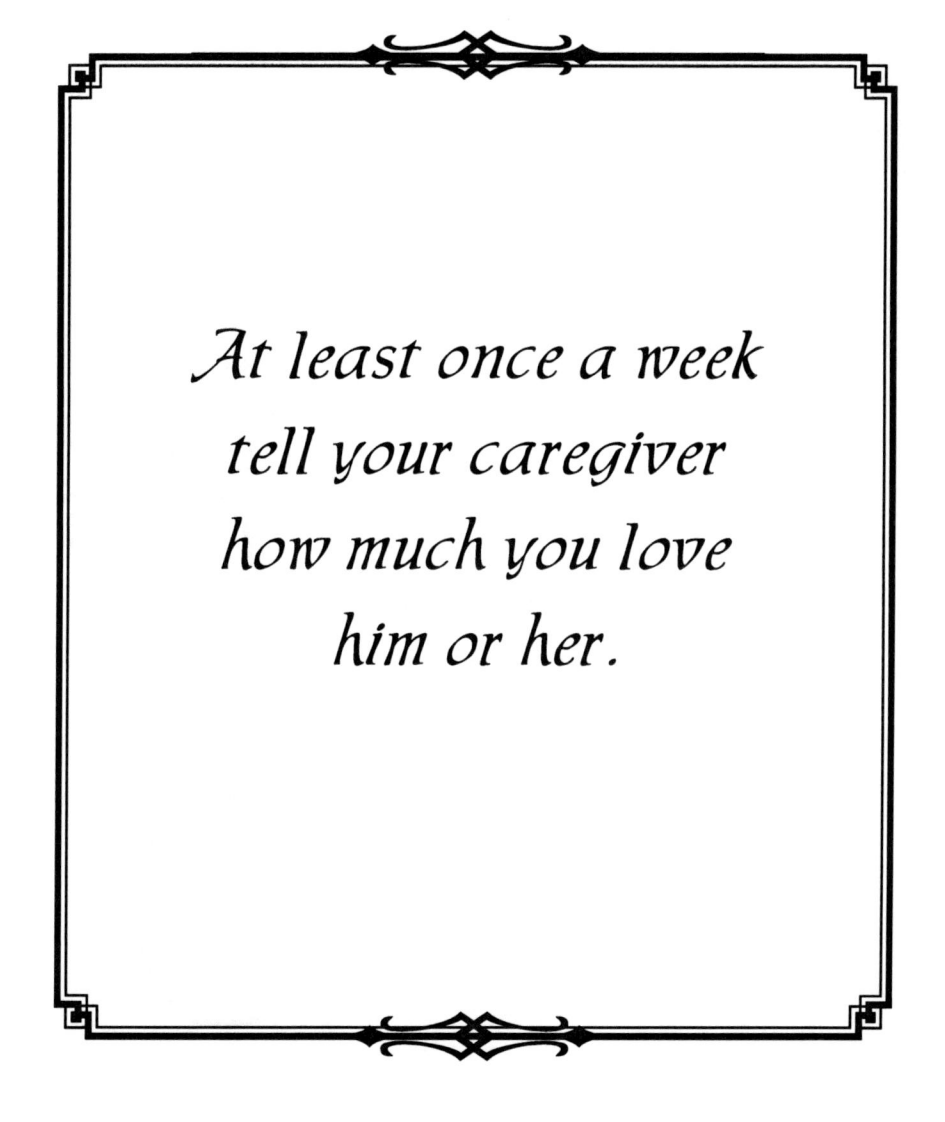

At least once a week tell your caregiver how much you love him or her.

Dadisi Mwende Netifnet

AGAINST EVIL

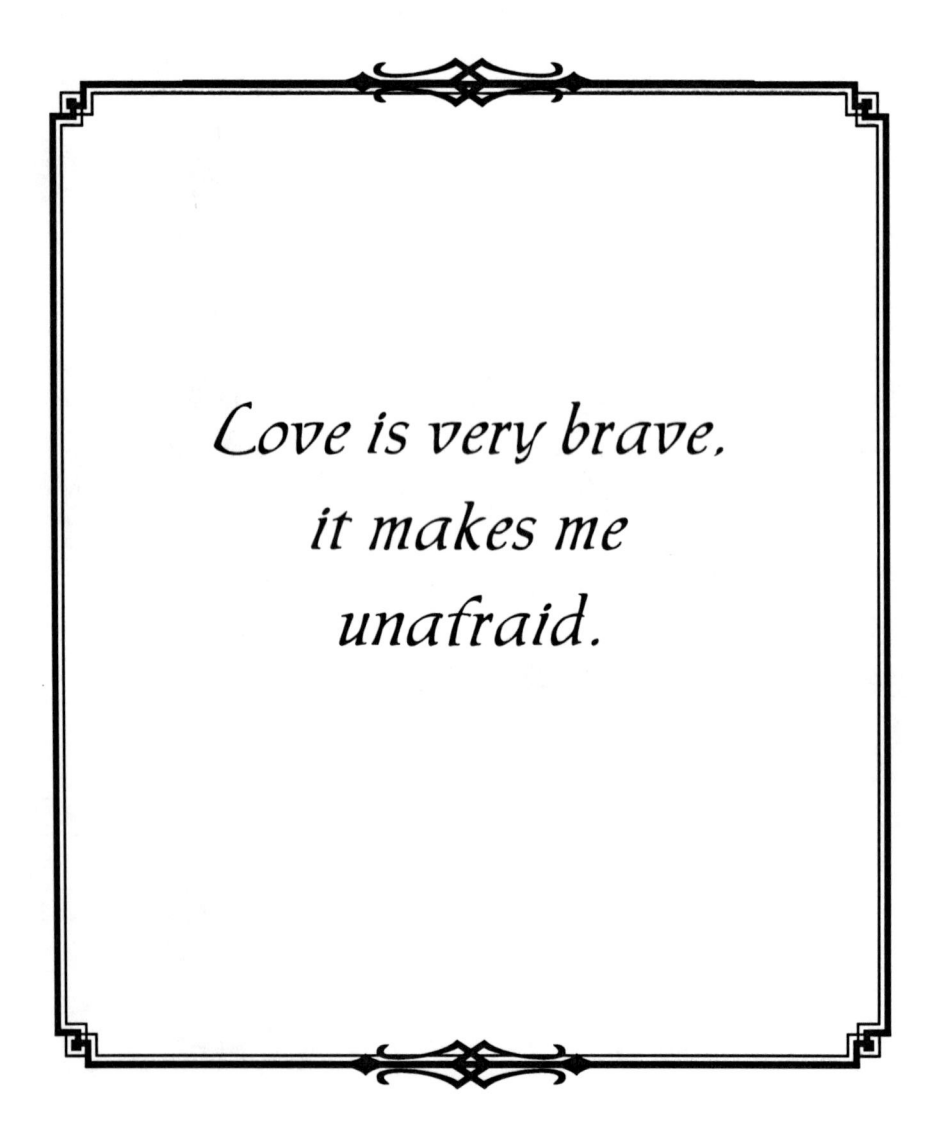

*Love is very brave,
it makes me
unafraid.*

TERRIFIC

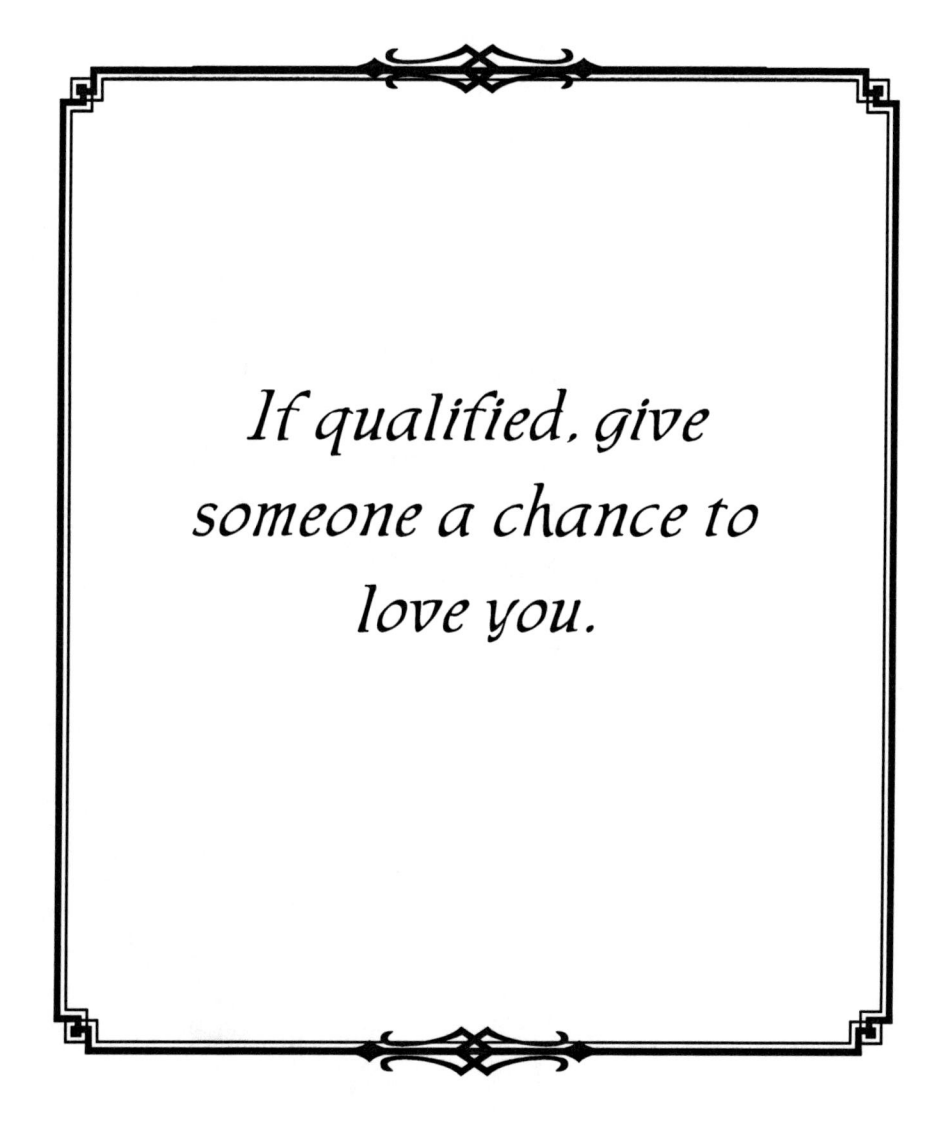

If qualified, give someone a chance to love you.

PASSION

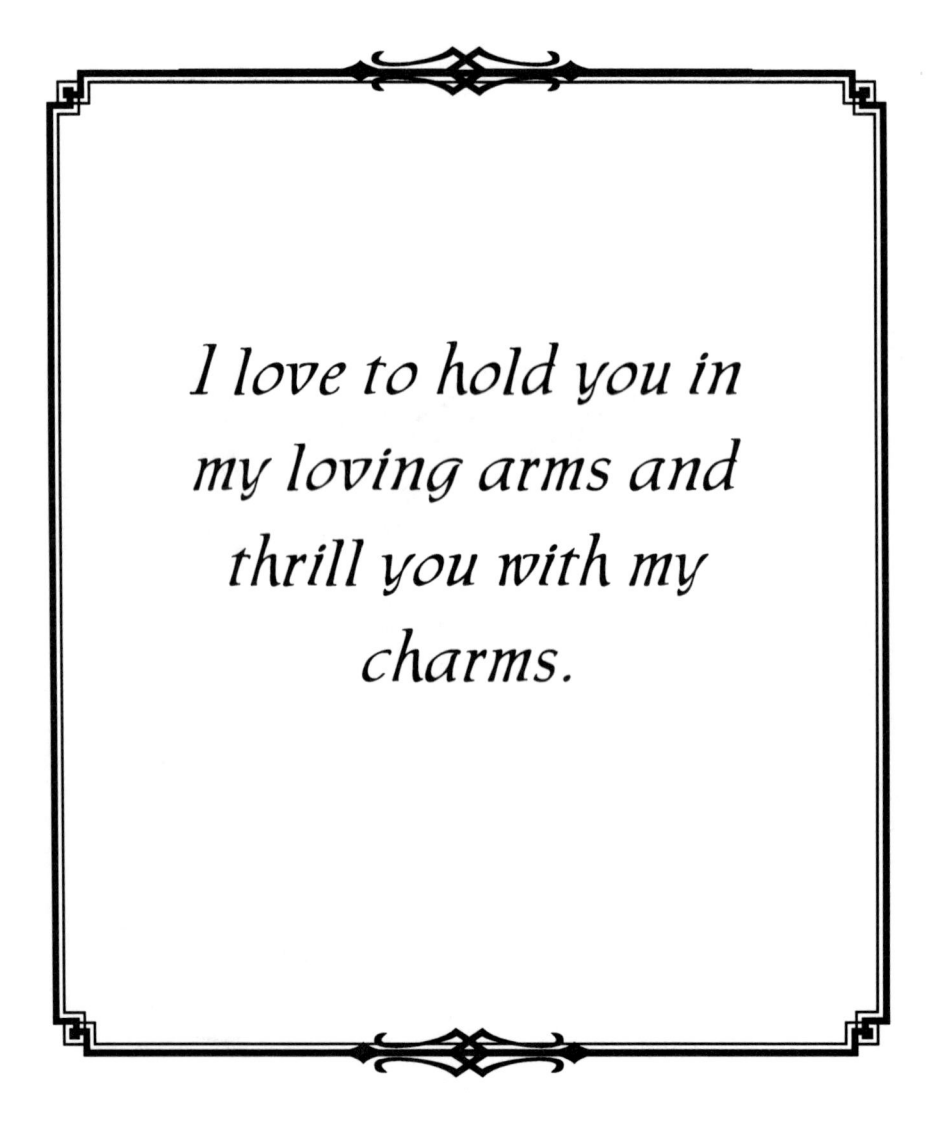

I love to hold you in my loving arms and thrill you with my charms.

GOODBYE MY SWEET ANGEL

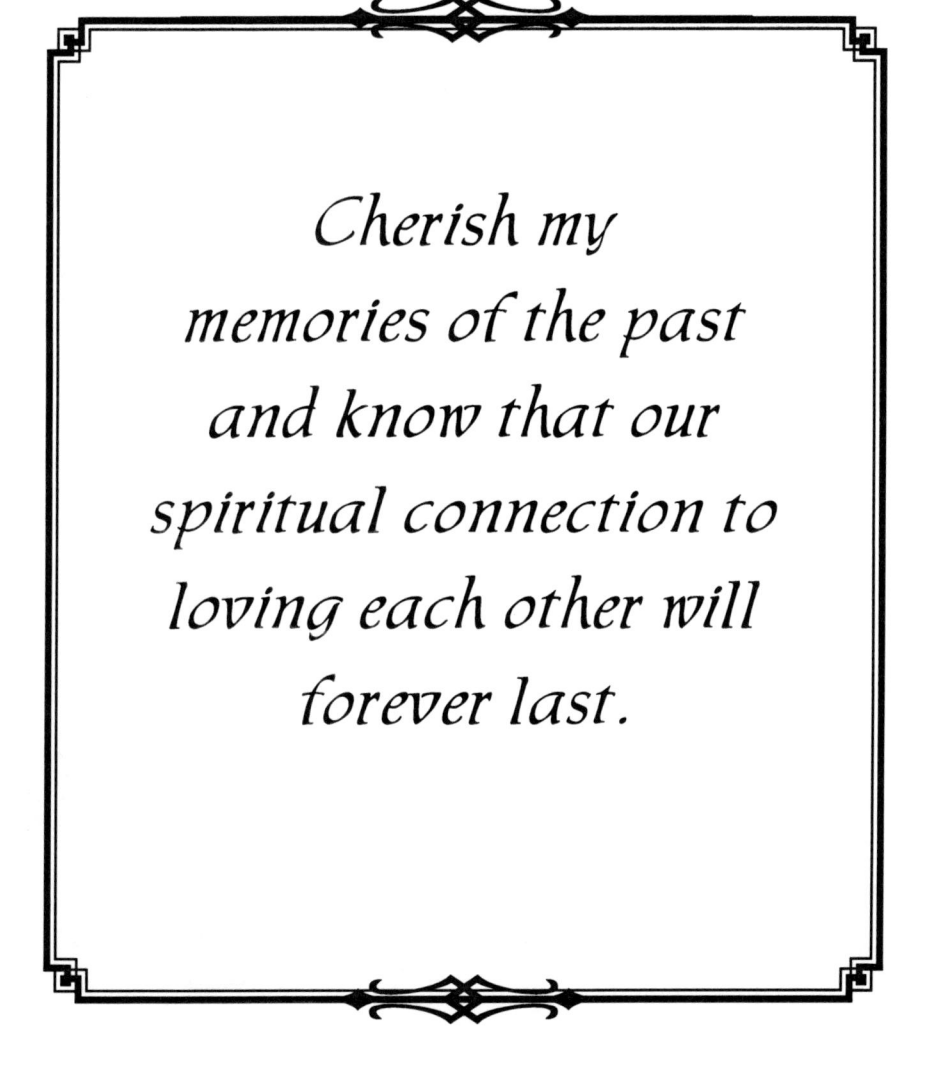

Cherish my memories of the past and know that our spiritual connection to loving each other will forever last.

ABOUT THE AUTHOR

Dadisi Mwende Netifnet, born Marvin Leroy Alston, in Charleston, South Carolina. Throughout the years, he has been in a relentless struggle to improve his art of writing. He has read his poetry in many cities throughout the United States and Canada. He has also read his poetry in many different countries throughout the world, such as: Egypt, Senegal, Gambia and Freeport, Grand Bahamas. In 2002, Dadisi was awarded the Shakespeare Trophy of Excellence and the 2002 Poet of the Year Gold Medallion by the Famous Poets Society. Dadisi resides in Houston, Texas with his wife. Look for him at area poetry readings, arrange for him to read to your group, or get his publications for your library. You will be uplifted and delighted.

To learn more about Poet Dadisi Netifnet please go to dcmoreproductions.com

CPSIA information can be obtained
at www.ICGtesting.com
Printed in the USA
LVOW07s1550270117
522426LV00001B/136/P

9 781463 416522